AF522397

Principles of Educational and Vocational Guidance

Principles of Educational and Vocational Guidance

Navendu Pratap

RANDOM PUBLICATIONS

NEW DELHI - 110 002 (INDIA)

Principles of Educational and Vocational Guidance

ISBN 978-93-51112-94-5

Published in 2014 in India by
Reprint 2020

RANDOM PUBLICATIONS
4376-A/4B, Gali Murari Lal, Ansari Road
New Delhi-110 002
Phone: +9111-43580356, 23289044
E-mail: randomexports@gmail.com; sales@randompublications.com; info@randompublications.com

Type Setting by: Friends Media, Delhi-110089
Printed at : Mehra Printers, Delhi-110092

Preface

We are social beings and, so in some way or other we need help and guidance of others. Mother, father, grand parents, teachers and other elders, home, school and society guide youngsters for successful living. Due to explosion of knowledge, industrialization and changes in socio-economic set up the need of professional guidance is felt in the present day society. Literally guidance means to direct', to point out', to show the path'. It is the assistance or help rendered by a more experienced person to a less experiences person to solve certain major problems of the individual i.e. educational, vocational, personal etc. Guidance is a concept as well as a process. As a concept guidance is concerned with the optimal development of the individual. As a process guidance helps the individual in self understanding and in self-direction. The terms guidance' and counselling' have been loosely or interchangeably used. Guidance is a term which is broader than counselling and it includes counselling as one of its services. Butter makes a logical separation of the counselling process i.e. Adjustive and distibutive phase. In the adjustive phase, the emphasis is on social, personal and emotional problems of the individual, in the distributive phase the focus is upon educational, vocational and occupational problems. The distributive phase' can be most aptly described as guidance' while the adjustive' phase can be considered as description of counselling'. The school is expected to provide more than just teaching and instruction. A school guidance programme includes all those activities other than instructional which are carried out to render assistance to pupils in their educational, vocational, personal development and adjustment. The fundamental aim of guidance programme being the maximum development of the child, all guidance programme must be geared toward attainment of the goal. Guidance services can assist the pupils in knowing themselves-their potentialities and limitations, making appropriate choices in educational, vocational and other fields.

Effective educational and vocational guidance and counselling can assist individuals to understand their talents and potential and enable them to plan the appropriate steps to develop essential skills that will lead to personal, educational, economic and social advancement for the individual, family, community and nation. Quality educational and vocational guidance, counselling and management is a regular and continuous process, it is not a single intervention. It accompanies and enhances life-long and life wide learning and helps individuals to avoid or shorten periods of unemployment. Educational and vocational guidance and counselling contributes to equality of opportunity. High quality educational and vocational counselling not only aids the personal development and career opportunities of every individual, but also contributes to wider social , economic and sustainable development as a whole.

The primary aim of this book is to present a succinct account of the essential features of this subject. It is being prepared by keeping in view the requirements of the students and academic professionals.

I thank all members of my team who have helped in the preparation of the book. My special thanks go to "Random Publications" who have published the book.

—Navendu Pratap

Contents

1. **Introduction** **1**
   - Principles of Guidance 1
   - Types and Agencies of Guidance 7
   - Education Retrospect 11
   - Homeschooling 15
   - Vocational Education 24
   - Vocationalisation of Education in India 25
2. **Educational and Other Forms of Guidance** **30**
   - Vocational Guidance in American Colleges 32
   - Career Counseling 33
   - Psychology and Vocational Guidance 38
   - Avocation 40
   - Volunteering 40
   - Counseling Psychology 48

3. Vocational Education 51

- VET Internationally 52
- Apprenticeship 66
- Educational Theory of Apprenticeship 67
- India 78
- School-to-work Transition 87
- Criticism of Educational Reforms Associated with OBE 97
- Standards-based Education Reform in the United States 101
- Internship 106
- Mentorship 115
- Mentorship in Education 121

4. State Interest in Vocational Education 122

- Paramedical Training Status for Rural India 126
- Smith–Hughes Act 135

5. Preparing Counsellors 141

- Challenges of the Twenty-first Century 142

- Innovations at the Turn of the Millennium 143
- Intelligence Quotient 150
- The War Years in the United States 153
- Cattell–Horn–Carroll Theory 154
- IQ and Brain Anatomy 163
- IQ and Crime 166
- Group Differences 169
- Criticism of g 171
- Dynamic Assessment 173
- Emotional Intelligence 174

6. Employment Testing **198**

- Legal Context (United States) 198
- Aptitude Testing 201
- Attitude Testing 202
- Elaboration Likelihood Model 212
- Elaboration Types 214
- Model Testing 214
- Expectancy-value Theory 216

7. Job Description and Specification Outlines 218

- Creating a Job Description 218
- Strategic Human Resource Planning 219
- Competency-based Management 222
- Talent Management 223
- Competency-based Recruitment 226
- International Standard Classification of Occupations 229

8. Guidance and Counselling for Learning, Career and Employment in Europe 230

- Defining guidance in both the school and labour market sector in Greece and in French-speaking Belgium 232
- Government Regulations 238
- Mechanism for Coordination 240
- Role of Trade Unions 243
- Different Methods for Different Groups 253
- Work-place Experience 267

- Guidance at Tertiary Level 273
- Differential Access to ICTs Across Europe 284
- Organisation of a Guidance Programme 293
- Guidance and Counselling Programme 302

Bibliography 317

Index 319

1

Introduction

We are social beings and, so in some way or other we need help and guidance of others. Mother, father, grandparents, teachers and other elders, home, school and society guide youngsters for successful living. Due to explosion of knowledge, industrialization and changes in socio-economic set up the need of professional guidance is felt in the present day society.

Literally guidance means 3to direct', 3to point out', to show the path'. It is the assistance or help rendered by a more experienced person to a less experiences person to solve certain major problems of the individual (less experienced) i.e. educational, vocational, personal etc.

Guidance is a concept as well as a process. As a concept guidance is concerned with the optimal development of the individual. As a process guidance helps the individual in self understanding (understanding one's strengths, limitations, and other resources) and in self-direction (ability to solve problems, make choices and decision on one's own).

The aim of education is to achieve the fullest possible realization of possibilities inherent in the individual. Education fosters all aspects of an individual's personality. Guidance is an integral part of education and helps in achieving the goals of education. Guidance is quite essential for the development of individual which is the main objective of education.

Principles of Guidance

Guidance is based upon the following principles.

(i) *Holistic development of individual:* Guidance needs to be provided in the context of total development of personality.

(ii) Recognition of individual differences and dignity: Each individual is different from every other individual. Each individual is the combination of characteristics which provides uniqueness to each person. Similarly human beings have an immense potential. The dignity of the individual is supreme.

(iii) Acceptance of individual needs: Guidance is based upon individual needs i.e. freedom, respect, dignity.

(iv) The individual needs a continuous guidance process from early childhood throughout adulthood.

(v) Guidance involves using skills to communicate love, regard, respect for others.

Need and Importance of Guidance

Guidance is needed wherever there are problems. The need and importance of guidance are as follows:

- Self understanding and self direction: Guidance helps in understanding one's strength, limitations and other resources. Guidance helps individual to develop ability to solve problems and take decisions.
- Optimum development of individual
- Solving different problem of the individual
- Academic growth and development
- Vocational maturity, vocational choices and vocational adjustments
- Social personal adjustment
- Better family life
- Good citizenship
- For conservation and proper utilization of human resources
- For national development
- Guidance is helpful not only for student and teacher in an educational institution but also to the parents, administrators, planners and community members

Different School Guidance Services

The school is expected to provide more than just teaching and instruction. A school guidance programme includes all those activities other than instructional which are carried out to render assistance to pupils in their educational, vocational, personal development and adjustment. The fundamental aim of guidance programme being the maximum evelopment of the child, all guidance programme must be geared towards attainment of the goal. Guidance services can assist the pupils in knowing themselves-their potentialities and limitations, making appropriate choices in educational, vocational and other fields. Some of the important guidance services are;

- The orientation services
- Student inventory services
- Career Information services
- Counseling services
- Group guidance services
- Placement services
- Research and evaluation service

Implications of Areas of Guidance in Global Context

The students life is getting complex day by day. Students in the twenty-first century have facing many perplex and difficult situations i.e. to make wise curricular and other curricular choices, to acquire basic study skills for optimum achievement, adjustment with peers etc. In its beginning guidance was concentrated on problems relating to vocations. It was largely concerned with getting jobs for young people. Now guidance has gone for beyond this. It is now concerned with the entire individual in all aspects.

The areas of guidance are very vast. The following are some of the important areas of guidance.

Personal: Students face many personal problems related to themselves, their parents and family, friends and teachers, etc. They often have memories related to home or family which creates feeling of disappointment in them. If their parents are expecting too much of them it leaves them with a feeling of incompetence and insecurity leading poor self-concept and self esteem. The objectives of personal guidance are to help the individual in his/her physical, emotional, social, rural and spiritual development.

The aims and objectives of personal guidance are :

- To assist the individual in understanding himself/herself.
- To assist the individual involving the personal problems.
- To assist the individual in taking independent decisions and judgement.
- To assist the individual to view the world and the social environment in right perspective.

- To assist the individual in making sound adjustments to different problems confronted in life.

Personal guidance is necessary at all stages of life. At the elementary school stage opportunities should be given to students for their self expression. Personal guidance at this stage deals with the problems related to feeling of insecurity, social acceptance, discipline etc.

At the secondary stage, the students have more intricate personal problems. During the secondary stage adolescent students due to peculiar physical, emotional and social developments undergo noticeable changes in their attitude and behaviour. Personal guidance at this stage should therefore focus on personal and social adjustment.

Personal guidance at the tertiary stage aims at helping them view life in relation to reality. The scope of personal guidance at this stage is very wider.

Educational Guidance: If one closely examines the problems of young pupils in schools and colleges, one would

Exactly realize the need of educational guidance.

Educational problems head the needs of students' problems. So education is an important guidance area.

Educational guidance is related to every aspect of education school / colleges, the curriculum, the methods of instruction, other curricular activities, disciplines etc. Educational guidance is the assistance given to the individual (i) to understand his/her potentialities (ii) have a clear cut idea of the different educational opportunities and their requirements (iii) to make wise choices as regards to school, colleges, the course : curricular and extra curricular.

Some of the aims and objectives of educational guidance are:

- To assist the pupil to understand him/herself i.e. to understand his/her potentialities, strength and limitations.
- To help the child make educational plans consist with his/her abilities, interests and goals.
- To enable the student to know detail about the subject and courses offered.
- To assist the student in making satisfactory progress in various school/ college subjects.
- To help the child to adjust with the schools, its rules, regulations, social life connected with it.
- To help the child in developing good study habits.

- To help the child to participate in out of class educational activities in which he can develop leadership and other social qualities.

At the elementary stage guidance programme must help the children to make good beginning, to plan intelligently, to get the best out of their education and prepare them for secondary schools.

Educational guidance needs to be used in diagnosing difficulties, in identifying the special needs of children.

At the secondary stage educational guidance should help the pupils to understand themselves better, to understand different aspects of the school, to select appropriate courses to get information about different educational opportunities, to develop good study habits. The students should be helped to be acquainted with the vocational implications of various school subjects.

Educational guidance at the tertiary stages must oriented students about purpose and scope of higher studies and helps them to stimulate their studies. Each college/ university must have a guidance unit with due provision of guidance services.

Vocational Guidance: You know that bread and butter aims is one of the main aims of education. Due to advancement in science and technology and consequent charges in industry and occupations have been emerged. There are thousands of specialized jobs/ occupations. In this context, there is a great need for vocational guidance.

Vocational guidance is a process of assisting the individual to choose an occupation, prepare for it, enter upon it and progress in it. It is concerned primarily with helping individuals make decisions and choices involved in planning a future and building a career. The purpose behind assisting the youth to choose, prepare, enter and progress in a vocation is the optimum growth of the individual.

Some of the aims and objectives of vocational guidance are: Assisting pupil to discover his/her own abilities and skills to feet them into general requirements of the occupation under consideration.

Helping the individual to develop an attitude towards work that will dignify whatever type of occupation s/he may wish to enter.

Assisting the individual to think critically about various types of occupations and to learn A technique for analysing information about vocations. Assisting pupils to secure relevant information about the facilities offered by various educational institutions engaging in vocational training.

At the elementary stage, although no formal guidance programmes are needed, the orientation to vocation can be initiated at this stage. At this stage some qualities and skills which have grater vocational significance viz. love and respect for manual work (ii) training in use of hands (iii) spirit of cooperative work (iii) sharing (vi) appreciation for all works (vii) good interpersonal relationship are to be developed.

At the secondary stage vocational guidance should help the students to know themselves, to know the world of work, to develop employment readiness to develop decision making rules.

At the higher education stages it should be more formal one. The objectives of guidance at this stage are to help the students to get information about different career, training facilities, apprenticeship etc.

A vocational Guidance: The individual student spends only a small portion of his time i.e. 4 to 6 hours per day in school.

The rest of the time needs to be effectively managed and utilized by the child for his/her progress and development. A vocational guidance helps the child to judiciously utilize the leisure time. The other co-curricular activities play an important role in all-round development of the child. But many parents, teachers and children put secondary importance to these activities. The students need to be properly guided for effective participation in varied types of a vocational pursuits so that they are able to shape their interpersonal behaviour in desirable direction and widen their outlook.

Social Guidance: We are social animals. But social relationships constitute a problem area for most of the students. School/educational institution is a miniature society and pupil from different socio-economic status, linguistic and socio-cultural background read there.

Students some time may face problems in adjustment and social relationship. It is very important that the students to be helped in acquiring in feeling of security and being accepted by the group; in developing social relationship and in becoming tolerant towards others. This is the task of social guidance. Formally social guidance can be given by educational institutions whereas informal guidance may be provided by Family, religious institutions, Media etc.

Moral Guidance: Moral values occupy an important place in our life. Some times due to influence of diverse factors students tell lies and indulge in undesirable practices. Moral guidance helps in bringing these students in to proper track and help in their all round development.

Health Guidance: Health is regarded as the wealth. Total health i.e. preventive and curative is the goal of health guidance. The health guidance may be a cooperative effort of Principal, Doctors, Counsellor/ psychologist, Teachers, Students and parents. For promoting preventive care the conditions of school hostel, canteen needs to be checked. Similarly health education through formal classes and information is essential in school education stages. In the present day the concern of health guidance also pertains to guidance in HIV/AIDs.

Leisure –time guidance: Guidance for leisure is basically a part of personal guidance.

The individual should know how to utilize his/her leisure time fruitfully. Leisure generally refers to free time a person at his disposal. Leisure in modern time is available to those who are technically trained and efficient. But, unfortunately most of us do not know how to utilize the leisure time. That is why guidance for leisure is necessary.

Leisure can be fruitfully utilized for two purposes. First of all Leisure provides us time for personal development. One can increase his efficiency by utilizing his leisure time.

The second use of leisure is that it helps the individual to be more productive by getting the necessary rest and recreation.

Jones divides leisure time activities into four groups.

1. Escape activities
2. General culture or appreciation activities.
3. Creative activities and
4. Service activities

It has also been suggested that individuals should spend their leisure time in social welfare activities. For professional growth are must take active interest in the professional society of his profession.

Thus it is quite evident that guidance for leisure is extremely important in modern society because it helps the individual to attain efficiency and become a useful member of the society. Therefore, it has been suggested that in the school curriculum there should be provision for teaching about various leisure time activities so that children will able to know about them.

Types and Agencies of Guidance

Individual guidance: Individual guidance is tailored to an individual. It is advice, strategy or planning designed for a singular person or thing and their unique situation. This is in contrast to general guidance which is frequently based on demographic information such as age or income or meant for the general population. The most common reference to individual guidance is in reference to children or students. This is ideally the role of guidance, educational or career counsellors.

Individual guidance can be used to refer to any advice, usually professional advice, given to a person based on their unique circumstances. This could include legal services, career counseling, financial planning, medical or psychological advice or a number of other areas where a trained professional is looked to for direction in a given area.

Group Guidance: Concept, Need and Significance: Group refers to collection of people, interaction between individuals, development of shared perceptions, the development of affective ties and the development of interdependence of roles. For example many students and teacher/teachers at one school may gather together to form a group.

Group guidance encompasses those activities of guidance which are carried on in a group situation to assist its members to have experiences desirable or even necessary for making -appropriate decisions in the prevailing contexts.

In a more specific term, it is guiding the individual in a group situation. Group could be of any type, but for guidance purposes a group should have a common goal. Just collection of individual may not be called a group for organizing guidance activities. Selection of group members will have to depend on sharing a common problem, volunteering to be members and willingness to group activities.

Group guidance is used to address the developmental needs of a functional group consisting of a number of students to implement programme that would benefit them at all time. Students in group with common problems and concerns are helped in groups i.e. small or large. In other words, if guidance is to be available to all, it should be planned in groups.

Some of the objectives of group guidance are:

1. To help people in identifying common problems, analyse them and find relevant solutions
2. To place a wide range of information before people with common problems which could be useful for them for finding solutions?

3. To provide a platform where people with common problems could interact with each other and could be benefited by each other's perspectives, ideas and experiences
4. To help in creating an atmosphere where people could get an opportunity to express themselves and in the process analyse themselves.

Organization of Group Guidance Activities: Planning of group guidance activity may focus the following points.

1. Need Assessment : The need assessment must be done to find out the common problems of individuals in the group.

This can be done by administering questionnaire, checklists and interview.

2. Determining size of the group and time, venue for group activities: Depending upon the group activity the size of the group should be fixed. The size should be approachable and manageable. The venue should be selected taking in to account the group selected for activity.
3. Selection of members and role specifications: The participants selection for group guidance activity is also very important. The students for example should be communicated about their roles in group activities.
4. Orientation of Members: The group goals should be clarified. It should be stated in clear, objective and measurable terms.
5. Monitoring of activities and evaluation of outcomes: If we want to conduct the activities purposefully, it should be properly monitored taking into account the goal/s. Feedback about activity needs to be collected from participants.

Some of the common group guidance activities are: Class talk, career talk, displays and exhibitions.

Techniques of Group Guidance : A Number of Techniques are used in Organizing Group Guidance

Group Discussion: For example at senior secondary stage students should have knowledge about different career. A group discussion may be organized in the school. For organization of the group discussion proper room/hall, group and relevant topic and expert/ resource person should be selected. The group discussion will be useful only if the members participate effectively without the fear and all the members have the opportunity to participate. But the effectiveness of the group discussion depends upon the facilitator and the group selected.

Problem-solving: For solving individual as well as common problems, problem solving can be applied as a technique. It comprises of the following steps;

- Existence of common problem
- Focused description of the problem
- Initiation of action for solving problem based on relevant facts
- Analysis of problem in the light of data collected
- Listing of possible solutions and Evaluation of them
- Acceptance of degree of acceptance of solution in the group

Role play: In small group role playing can be adopted as a technique of guidance. Role playing is a method where real life situations are simulated by group members/participants. This provide new insight, intuitions, skills and understanding of opposing viewpoints. The role playing may comprise of the following steps;

- Existence of common problem
- Orientation of group to role playing and the problem
- Assigning of roles
- Preparation of other members/audience to observe intelligently
- Assessing the role play
- Concluding session and feedback
- Other methods like case study and socio-metric technique can be used as group guidance technique.

***Advantages of Group guidance*:** Some of the advantages of group guidance are as follows:

- Inspires learning and understanding: Interaction in group setting inspires learning and understanding of students. The student learns from other member of group.
- Saves time and effort: Group guidance technique can save time and effort of both the counselor and students. The time saved can be used for the more difficult and complex problems of students.
- Improvement of student's attitude and behaviour
- Development of wholesome and helpful awareness of unrecognized needs and problems of student/s

Limitations of Group Guidance: Group guidance though serves a useful purpose, but they cannot be taken as a substitute for in dividual counseling. Group activities serve many of the objectives of the school guidance programme, but not all of these. Further students may feel hesitant to come out with their personal problems in the group. So, in these cases group guidance cannot be of help.

Group guidance activities serve useful purposes specially saving in time and effort. While organizing these activities, some problems that a counsellor may face are mentioned below:

A rigid type of administration is often a major cause of trouble. Generally, when the counselor asks for time in the time table for conducting these guidance activities, he/she may get a discouraging reply, the time table is already full. No periods are free. So the counsellor is left with no other choice than to take the substitute management period.

Lack of cooperation on part of the administration as well as the staff members may also create problems in organizing such activities. Teacher may feel this as an addition burden. Lack of adequate funds is another problem.

Education Retrospect

India's education system is divided into different levels such as pre-primary level, primary level, elementary education, secondary education, undergraduate level and postgraduate level. The National Council of Educational Research and Training (NCERT) is the apex body for curriculum related matters for school education in India. The NCERT provides support and technical assistance to a number of schools in India and oversees many aspects of enforcement of education policies. In India, the various curriculum bodies governing school education system are:

- The state government boards, in which the majority of Indian children are enrolled.
- The Central Board of Secondary Education (CBSE). CBSE conducts two examinations, namely, the All India Secondary School Examination, AISSE (Class/Grade 10) and the All India Senior School Certificate Examination, AISSCE (Class/Grade 12).
- The Council for the Indian School Certificate Examinations (CISCE). CISCE conducts three examinations, namely, the Indian Certificate of Secondary Education (ICSE - Class/ Grade 10); The Indian School Certificate (ISC - Class/ Grade 12) and

the Certificate in Vocational Education (CVE - Class/Grade 12).

- The National Institute of Open Schooling (NIOS) conducts two examinations, namely, Secondary Examination and Senior Secondary Examination (All India) and also some courses in Vocational Education.
- International schools affiliated to the International Baccalaureate Programme and/or the Cambridge International Examinations.
- Islamic Madrasah schools, whose boards are controlled by local state governments, or autonomous, or affiliated with Darul Uloom Deoband.
- Autonomous schools like Woodstock School, The Sri Aurobindo International Centre of Education Puducherry, Auroville, Patha Bhavan and Ananda Marga Gurukula.

In addition, NUEPA (National University of Educational Planning and Administration) and NCTE (National Council for Teacher Education) are responsible for the management of the education system and teacher accreditation.

10+2+3 Pattern

The central and most state boards uniformly follows the "10+2+3" pattern of education. In this pattern, 10 years of primary and secondary education is followed by 2 years of higher secondary (usually in schools having the higher secondary facility, or in colleges), and then 3 years of college education for bachelor's degree.

The 10 years is further divided into 5 years of primary education and 3 years of upper primary, followed by 2 years of high school. This pattern originated from the recommendation the Education Commission of 1964–66.

Primary education system in India

The Indian government lays emphasis on primary education up to the age of fourteen years, referred to as elementary education in India. The Indian government has also banned child labour in order to ensure that the children do not enter unsafe working conditions.

However, both free education and the ban on child labour are difficult to enforce due to economic disparity and social conditions. 80% of all recognized schools at the elementary stage are government run or supported, making it the largest provider of education in the country.

Figure: *School children, Mumbai*

However, due to a shortage of resources and lack of political will, this system suffers from massive gaps including high pupil to teacher ratios, shortage of infrastructure and poor levels of teacher training. Figures released by the Indian government in 2011 show that there were 5,816,673 elementary school teachers in India. As of March 2012 there were 2,127,000 secondary school teachers in India. Education has also been made free for children for 6 to 14 years of age or up to class VIII under the Right of Children to Free and Compulsory Education Act 2009.

There have been several efforts to enhance quality made by the government. The District Education Revitalization Programme (DERP) was launched in 1994 with an aim to universalize primary education in India by reforming and vitalizing the existing primary education system. 85% of the DERP was funded by the central government and the remaining 15 percent was funded by the states. The DERP, which had opened 160000 new schools including 84000 alternative education schools delivering alternative education to approximately 3.5 million children, was also supported by UNICEF and other international programmes.

This primary education scheme has also shown a high Gross Enrollment Ratio of 93–95% for the last three years in some states. Significant improvement in staffing and enrollment of girls has also been made as a part of this scheme. The current scheme for universalization of Education for All is the Sarva Shiksha Abhiyan which is one of the largest education initiatives in the world. Enrollment has been enhanced, but the levels of quality remain low.

Private Education

Figure: *Dhirubhai Ambani School, Mumbai*

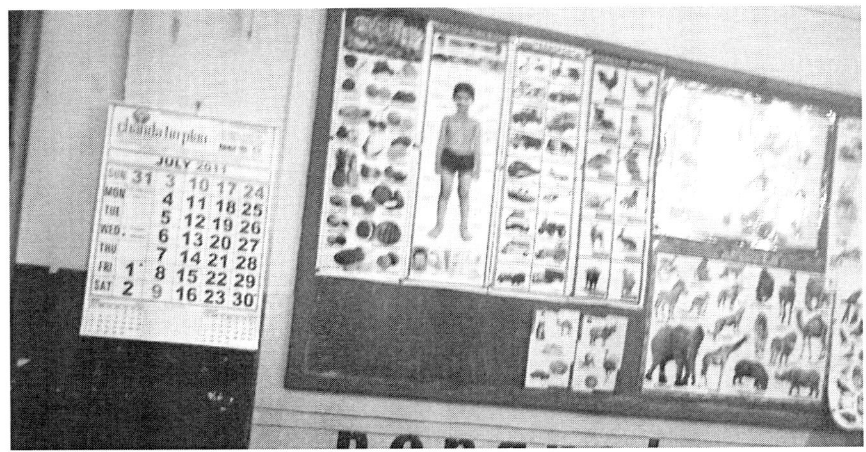

Figure: *School wall of a Private School in India.*

In India, due to the British influence, a *public school* implies a non-governmental, historically elite educational institution, often modelled on British public schools which are in certain cases governmental. There are privately owned and managed schools, many of whom have the appellation "Public" attached to them, e.g. the Delhi

Public Schools, or Frank Anthony Public Schools. Most middle-class families send their children to such schools, which might be in their own city or distant boarding school such as Rajkumar College, Rajkot, the oldest public school in India. The medium of education is English, but Hindi and/or the state's official language is also taught as a compulsory subject. Preschool education is mostly limited to organised neighbourhood nursery schools with some organised chains.

According to current estimates, 80% of all schools are government schools making the government the major provider of education. However, because of poor quality of public education, 27% of Indian children are privately educated. With more than 50% children enrolling in private schools in urban areas, the balance has already tilted towards private schooling in cities; even in rural areas, nearly 20% of the children in 2004-5 were enrolled in private schools. According to some research, private schools often provide superior results at a multiple of the unit cost of government schools. However, others have suggested that private schools fail to provide education to the poorest families, a selective being only a fifth of the schools and have in the past ignored Court orders for their regulation.

In their favour, it has been pointed out that private schools cover the entire curriculum and offer extra-curricular activities such as science fairs, general knowledge, sports, music and drama. The pupil teacher ratios are much better in private schools (1:31 to 1:37 for government schools and more teachers in private schools are female. There is some disgreement over which system has better educated teachers. According to the latest DISE survey, the percentage of untrained teachers (paratechers) is 54.91% in private, compared to 44.88% in government schools and only 2.32% teachers in unaided schools receive inservice training compared to 43.44% for government schools. The competition in the school market is intense, yet most schools make profit. However, the number of private schools in India is still low - the share of private institutions is 7% (with upper primary being 21% and secondary 32% - *source : fortress team research*).

Even the poorest often go to private schools despite the fact that government schools are free. A study found that 65% of schoolchildren in Hyderabad's slums attend private schools.

Homeschooling

Homeschooling is legal in India, though it is the less explored option. The Indian Government's stance on the issue is that parents are free to teach their children at home, if they wish to and have the means. HRD Minister Kapil Sibal has stated that despite the RTE Act of 2009, if someone decides not to send his/her children to school, the government would not interfere.

Secondary Education

The National Policy on Education (NPE), 1986, has provided for environment awareness, science and technology education, and introduction of traditional elements such as Yoga into the Indian secondary school system. Secondary education covers children 14–18 which covers 88.5 million children according to the Census, 2001.

A significant feature of India's secondary school system is the emphasis on inclusion of the disadvantaged sections of the society. Professionals from established institutes are often called to support in vocational training. Another feature of India's secondary school system is its emphasis on profession based vocational training to help students attain skills for finding a vocation of his/her choosing. A significant new feature has been the extension of SSA to secondary education in the form of the Madhyamik Shiksha Abhiyan

A special Integrated Education for Disabled Children (IEDC) programme was started in 1974 with a focus on primary education. But which was converted into Inclusive Education at Secondary Stage Another notable special programme, the *Kendriya Vidyalaya* project, was started for the employees of the central government of India, who are distributed throughout the country.

The government started the *Kendriya Vidyalaya* project in 1965 to provide uniform education in institutions following the same syllabus at the same pace regardless of the location to which the employee's family has been transferred.

Higher Education

> *Our university system is, in many parts, in a state of disrepair...In almost half the districts in the country, higher education enrollments are abysmally low, almost two-third of our universities and 90 per cent of our colleges are rated as below average on quality parametres... I am concerned that in many states university appointments, including that of vice-chancellors, have been politicised and have become subject to caste and communal considerations, there are complaints of favouritism and corruption.*
>
> — Prime Minister Manmohan Singh in 2007

Figure: *The Auditorium at Indian Institute of Management Calcutta, Kolkata.*

Figure: *The social sciences and business management departments are housed at the Alipore campus, University of Calcutta in Kolkata*

After passing the Higher Secondary Examination (the grade 12 examination), students may enroll in general degree programmes such as bachelor's degree in arts, commerce or science, or professional degree programmes such as engineering, law or medicine. India's higher education system is the third largest in the world, after China and the United States. The main governing body at the tertiary level is the University Grants Commission (India), which enforces its standards, advises the government, and helps coordinate between the centre and the state. Accreditation for higher learning is overseen by 12 autonomous institutions established by the University Grants Commission. In India, education system is reformed. In future, India will be one of the largest education hub.

As of 2009, India has 20 central universities, 215 state universities, 100 deemed universities, 5 institutions established and functioning under the State Act, and 33 institutes which are of national importance. Other institutions include 16,000 colleges, including 1,800 exclusive women's colleges, functioning under these universities and institutions. The emphasis in the tertiary level of education lies on science and technology. Indian educational institutions by 2004 consisted of a large number of technology institutes. Distance learning is also a feature of the Indian higher education system.

Some institutions of India, such as the Indian Institutes of Technology (IITs), have been globally acclaimed for their standard of undergraduate education in engineering. The IITs enroll about 10,000 students annually and the alumni have contributed to both the growth of the private sector and the public sectors of India. However the IIT's have not had significant impact on fundamental scientific research and innovation. Several other institutes of fundamental research such as the Indian Association for the Cultivation of Science (IACS), Indian Institute of Science IISC), Tata Institute of Fundamental Research (TIFR), Harishchandra Research Institute (HRI), are acclaimed for their standard of research in basic sciences and mathematics. However, India has failed to produce world class universities both in the private sector or the public sector.

Besides top rated universities which provide highly competitive world class education to their pupils, India is also home to many universities which have been founded with the sole objective of making easy money. Regulatory authorities like UGC and AICTE have been trying very hard to extirpate the menace of private universities which are running courses without any affiliation or recognition. Indian Government has failed to check on these education shops, which are run by big businessmen & politicians. Many private colleges and universities do not fulfill the required criterion by the Government and central bodies (UGC, AICTE, MCI, BCI etc.) and take students for a ride. For example, many institutions in India continue to run unaccredited courses as there is no legislation strong enough to ensure legal action against them. Quality assurance mechanism has failed to stop misrepresentations and malpractices in higher education. At the same time regulatory bodies have been accused of corruption, specifically in the case of deemed-universities. In this context of lack of solid quality assurance mechanism, institutions need to step-up and set higher standards of self-regulation.

The Government of India is aware of the plight of higher education sector and has been trying to bring reforms, however, 15 bills are still awaiting discussion and approval in the Parliament. One of the most talked about bill is Foreign Universities Bill, which is supposed to facilitate entry of foreign universities to establish campuses in India. The bill is still under discussion and even if it gets passed, its feasibility and effectiveness is questionable as it misses the context, diversity and segment of international foreign institutions interested in India. One of the approaches to make internationalization of Indian higher education effective is to develop a coherent and comprehensive policy which aims at infusing excellence, bringing institutional diversity and aids in capacity building.

Three Indian universities were listed in the Times Higher Education list of the world's top 200 universities — Indian Institutes of Technology, Indian Institutes of Management, and Jawaharlal Nehru University in 2005 and 2006. Six Indian Institutes of Technology and the Birla Institute of Technology and Science – Pilani were listed among the top 20 science and technology schools in Asia by *Asiaweek*. The Indian School of Business situated in Hyderabad was ranked number 12 in global MBA rankings by the *Financial Times* of London in 2010 while the All India Institute of Medical Sciences has been recognized as a global leader in medical research and treatment.

Technical Education

The number of graduates coming out of technical colleges increased to over 700,000 in 2011 from 550,000 in FY 2010. However, according to one study, 75% of technical graduates and more than 85% of general graduates are unemployable by India's most demanding and high-growth global industries, including information technology. Nevertheless, that still means that India offers the largest pool of technically skilled graduates in the world.

Figure: *Institute Main Building, IIT Kharagpur*

From the first Five Year Plan onwards India's emphasis was to develop a pool of scientifically inclined manpower. India's National Policy on Education (NPE) provisioned for an apex body for regulation and development of higher technical education, which came into being as the All India Council for Technical Education (AICTE) in 1987 through an act of the Indian parliament. At the federal level, the Indian Institutes of Technology, the Indian Institute of Space Science and Technology, the National Institutes of Technology and the Indian Institutes of Information Technology, Rajiv Gandhi Institute of Petroleum Technology are deemed of national importance.

The Indian Institutes of Technology are among the nation's premier education facilities. Since 2002, Several Regional Engineering Colleges(RECs) have been converted into National Institutes of Technology giving them Institutes of National Importance status.

The Rajiv Gandhi Institute of Petroleum Technology : The Ministry of Petroleum and Natural Gas (MOP&NG), Government of India set up the institute at Jais, Rae Bareli district, Uttar Pradesh through an Act of Parliament. RGIPT has been accorded "Institute of National Importance" along the lines of the Indian Institute of Technology (IIT), Indian Institute of Management (IIM) and National Institute Of Technology(NIT). With the status of a Deemed University, the institute awards degrees in its own right.

The UGC has inter-university centres at a number of locations throughout India to promote common research, e.g. the Nuclear Science Centre at the Jawaharlal Nehru University, New Delhi. Besides there are some British established colleges such as Harcourt Butler Technological Institute situated in Kanpur and King George Medical University situated in Lucknow which are important centre of higher education. Central Universities such as Banaras Hindu University, Jamia Millia Islamia University, Delhi University, Mumbai University, University of Calcutta, etc. are too pioneers of technical education in the country.

In addition to above institutes, efforts towards the enhancement of technical education are supplemented by a number of recognized Professional Engineering Societies such as

1. Institution of Mechanical Engineers (India)
2. Institution of Engineers (India)
3. Institution of Chemical Engineering (India)
4. Institution of Electronics and Tele-Communication Engineers (India)
5. Indian Institute of Metals
6. Institution of Industrial Engineers (India)
7. Institute of Town Planners (India)
8. Indian Institute of Architects
9. Birla Institute of Technology and Science, Pilani

that conduct Engineering/Technical Examinations at different levels(Degree and diploma) for working professionals desirous of improving their technical qualifications.

In addition to recognized institutes for technical education there are many private technical institutes such as

1. NIIT
2. The Tourism School

Open and Distance Learning

At school level, National Institute of Open Schooling (NIOS) provides opportunities for continuing education to those who missed completing school education. 14 lakh students are enrolled at the secondary and higher secondary level through open and distance learning.. In 2012 Various state government also introduce “STATE OPEN SCHOOL” to provide distance education.

At higher education level, Indira Gandhi National Open University (IGNOU) co-ordinates distance learning. It has a cumulative enrolment of about 15 lakhs, serviced through 53 regional centres and 1,400 study centres with 25,000 counsellors. The Distance Education Council (DEC), an authority of IGNOU is co-coordinating 13 State Open Universities and 119 institutions of correspondence courses in conventional universities. While distance education institutions have expanded at a very rapid rate, but most of these institutions need an up gradation in their standards and performance. There is a large proliferation of courses covered by distance mode without adequate infrastructure, both human and physical. There is a strong need to correct these imbalances.

Arjun Singh Centre for Distance and Open Learning, Jamia Millia Islamia University was established with the assistance of Distance Education Council in September 2002. Major objectives of the Centre is to provide opportunities for higher education to those who are not able to draw benefits from formal system of education. The Open Learning System allows a learner to determine his pace of learning and provides education at the doorstep of the learner. The mode of transaction is through self-learning print material, supplemented by audio and video programmes. It has further scope of students accessing material through internet and various other media.

Literacy

According to the Census of 2011, "every person above the age of 7 years who can read and write in any language is said to be literate". According to this criterion, the 2011 survey holds the National Literacy Rate to be around 74.07%. Government statistics of 2001 also hold that the rate of increase in literacy is more in rural areas than in urban areas. Female literacy was at a national average of 65% whereas the male literacy was 82%. Within the Indian states, Kerala has shown the highest literacy rates of 93% whereas Bihar averaged 63.8% literacy. The 2001 statistics also indicated that the total number of 'absolute non-literates' in the country was 304 million.

Attainment

The Economist reports that half of 10-year-old rural children could not read at a basic level, over 60% were unable to do division, and half dropped out by the age 14.

An optimistic estimate is that only one in five job-seekers in India has ever had any sort of vocational training. However, this figure is likely to be much higher in 2013.

Higher Education

As per Report of the Higher education in India, Issues Related to Expansion, Inclusiveness, Quality and Finance, the access to higher education measured in term of gross enrolment ratio increased from 0.7% in 1950/51 to 1.4% in 1960–61. By 2006/7 the GER increased to about 11 percent. Notably, by 2012, it had crossed 20% (as mentioned in an earlier section).

Women's Education

Women have a much lower literacy rate than men. Far fewer girls are enrolled in the schools, and many of them drop out. In the patriarchal setting of the Indian family, girls have lower status and fewer privileges than boy children. Conservative cultural attitudes prevents some girls from attending school.

The number of literate women among the female population of India was between 2–6% from the British Raj onwards to the formation of the Republic of India in 1947. Concerted efforts led to improvement from 15.3% in 1961 to 28.5% in 1981. By 2001 literacy for women had exceeded 50% of the overall female population, though these statistics were still very low compared to world standards and even male literacy within India. Recently the Indian government has launched Saakshar Bharat Mission for Female Literacy. This mission aims to bring down female illiteracy by half of its present level.

Sita Anantha Raman outlines the progress of women's education in India: Since 1947 the Indian government has tried to provide incentives for girls' school attendance through programmes for midday meals, free books, and uniforms. This welfare thrust raised primary enrollment between 1951 and 1981. In 1986 the National Policy on Education decided to restructure education in tune with the social framework of each state, and with larger national goals. It emphasized that education was necessary for democracy, and central to the improvement of women's condition. The new policy aimed at social change through revised texts, curricula, increased funding for schools, expansion in the numbers of schools, and policy improvements. Emphasis was placed on expanding girls' occupational centres and primary education; secondary and higher education; and rural and urban institutions. The report tried to connect problems like low school attendance with poverty, and the dependence on girls for housework and sibling day care. The National Literacy Mission also worked through female tutors in villages. Although the minimum marriage age is now eighteen for girls, many continue to be married much earlier. Therefore, at the secondary level, female dropout rates are high.

The education of women in India plays a significant role in improving livings standards in the country. A higher women literacy rate improves the quality of life both at home and outside of home, by encouraging and promoting education of children, especially female children, and in reducing the infant mortality rate. Several studies have shown that a lower level of women literacy rates results in higher levels of fertility and infant mortality, poorer nutrition, lower earning potential and the lack of an ability to make decisions within a household. Women's lower educational levels is also shown to adversely affect the health and living conditions of children. A survey that was conducted in India showed results which support the fact that infant mortality rate was inversely related to female literacy rate and educational level. The survey also suggests a correlation between education and economic growth.

In India, it was found that there is a large disparity between female literacy rates in different states. For example, while Kerala actually has a female literacy rate of about 86 percent, Bihar and Uttar Pradesh have female literacy rates around 55-60 percent. These values are further correlated with health levels of the Indians, where it was found that Kerala was the state with the lowest infant mortality rate while Bihar and Uttar Pradesh are the states with the lowest life expectancies in India. Furthermore, the disparity of female literacy rates across rural and urban areas is also significant in India. Out of the 24 states in India, 6 of them have female literacy rates of below 60 percent. The rural state Rajasthan has a female literacy rate of less than 12 percent.

In India, higher education is defined as the education of an age group between 18 and 24, and is largely funded by the government. Despite women making up 24-50% of higher education enrollment, there is still a gender imbalance within higher education. Only one third of science students and 7% of engineering students, are women. In comparison however, over half the students studying education are women.

Vocational Education

Vocational education or *Vocational Education and Training* (VET), also called *Career and Technical Education* (CTE), prepares learners for jobs that are based in manual or practical activities, traditionally non-academic and totally related to a specific trade, occupation or *vocation*, hence the term, in which the learner participates. It is sometimes referred to as *technical education*, as the learner directly develops expertise in a particular group of techniques or technology.

Generally, vocation and career are used interchangeably. Vocational education might be classified as teaching procedural knowledge. This may be contrasted with declarative knowledge, as used in education in a usually broader scientific field, which might concentrate on theory and abstract conceptual knowledge, characteristic of tertiary education.

Vocational education can be at the secondary or post-secondary level and can interact with the apprenticeship system. Increasingly, vocational education can be recognised in terms of recognition of prior learning and partial academic credit towards tertiary education (e.g., at a university) as credit; however, it is rarely considered in its own form to fall under the traditional definition of a higher education.

Up until the end of the twentieth century, vocational education focused on specific trades such as for example, an automobile mechanic or welder, and was therefore associated with the activities of lower social classes. As a consequence, it attracted a level of stigma. Vocational education is related to the age-old apprenticeship system of learning.

However, as the labour market becomes more specialized and economies demand higher levels of skill, governments and businesses are increasingly investing in the future of vocational education through publicly funded training organizations and subsidized apprenticeship or traineeship initiatives for businesses. At the post-secondary level vocational education is typically provided by an institute of technology, or by a local community college.

Vocationalisation of Education in India

The greatest challenge in Indian education system today is to provide skill based education to the youth. This is exacerbated by a mismatch in demand and supply for the skilled workforce. The penetration of vocational education and training remains poor not only in rural areas, but also in urban regions where there is a higher installed capacity to impart the same.

A recent survey (61st round) conducted by the NSSO found that:

1. The percentage of population that completed primary education was 70%, but less than 10% went on to complete a graduation course and above. Almost 97% of individuals in the age bracket of 15–60 years had limited exposure to technical education, which is another indicator of low skills sets among Indians.

2. According to the occupational profile of India's workforce, 90% of the workforce population is employed in skill-based jobs, whereas more than 90% had no exposure to vocational education or training even though more than half of the seats remain unutilised in vocational education.
3. There is a lack of training facilities and skills development in as many as 20 high-growth industries such as logistics, healthcare, construction, hospitality and automobiles.
4. India has roughly close to 5,500 public (ITI) and private (ITC) institutes as against 500,000 similar institutes in China. As against India's 4% formally trained vocational workers, country like Korea had 96% vocationally trained workforce. Even relatively under-developed countries like Botswana had a surprisingly decent score of 22%.

Trends in the Labour market: Over the past decades, there has been a gradual decline in the labour force market for skilled workers that do not possess higher educational degrees. Today's industrial sector demands workers to possess at least a graduation degree in addition to vocational training. A diploma holder undergoing vocational training desires vertical mobility and hits a glass ceiling after a few years. Thus, while the employers complain that the worker does not stay longer, the employee complains that he does not see growth in the current job. The net result is a decrease in demand for skilled workers with lower degrees.

Current Scenario and key challenges: Skills in India are largely acquired through two main sources: formal training centres and the informal or hereditary mode of passing on cascading skill sets from one generation to the next. Nowadays vocational courses are becoming quite popular among youth because it is believed that taking these courses would provide more and better employment opportunities than those provided by conventional academic courses. While there remains a requirement for skilled professionals in the industry, the supply for the same is hampered by:

1. High dropout rate at Secondary level: Vocational Education is presently offered at senior secondary level but the students at this level aspire for higher education.
2. At present, the vocational system doesn't put much emphasis on the academic skills hence lower incidences of vertical mobility
3. There is a lack of participation by private players in the field of vocational education.

4. Vocationalisation of education is not in line with industry needs.
5. Lack of opportunities for continuous skill up-gradation.
6. There is no clear provision of certifications and degrees for the unorganised/informal sector.
7. Challenges faced by ITCs and ITIs are poor quality trainers, lack of flexibility and outdated infrastructure

New directions: Vocationalisation should not be attempted in an unsystematic or haphazard manner. Need of the hour is to understand the trainees' apprehensions and challenges regarding Vocational Education and training (VET). Thus there is a huge opportunity for a vocational training institute that can address these challenges. This will favour the organisations willing to enter the vocational education market as well as the students wanting to take up vocational courses to increase their employability. In summation, it is critical to redefine the essential elements of VET so that it becomes more flexible, inclusive, relevant and contemporary.

Over the past few years, various recommendations have been suggested by researchers and scholars.

Comprehensive Guidance and Counseling Programme

The Comprehensive Guidance and Counseling Programme is an approved district educational programme serving students from kindergarten through 12th grade. The programme is organized and implemented by licensed school counsellors and child development specialists in collaboration with parents, teachers and administrators. It addresses student development in academic achievement, career development, personal/social skills and community involvement. The Comprehensive Guidance and Counseling Programme focuses on activities and services in five areas:

- Guidance and Curriculum
- Individual Planning
- Responsive Services
- System Support
- Student Advocacy Student

Guidance and Curriculum

Curriculum is presented as classroom instruction, large and small group activities, school presentations, parent workshops and community events. Teachers, community members, support staff and administrators may also be involved. The elementary counseling and guidance curriculum focuses on:

- Academic Development - Learning to Learn
- Career Development - Learning to Work
- Personal/Social Development-Learning to Live
- Community Development-Learning to Contribute

Examples of programmes used in the guidance programme include:

- Second Step - violence prevention
- Steps to Respect - bullying prevention
- Kelso's Wheel - conflict management
- Growing up Lessons

Responsive Services

Responsive services are counseling activities that meet the immediate needs, concerns, or problems that distract students from their academic, personal/social and/or career involvement. Responsive services include individual and small group counseling, consultation with staff, parents, and community agencies on the student's behalf, referral to outside resources, crisis counseling for prevention, intervention and follow-up and peer facilitation. In responsive services, school counsellors use their unique expertise for immediate intervention and short term counseling. They do not provide therapy.

System Support

System support integrates the Comprehensive Guidance and Counseling Programme in to the school. To enhance student learning, school counsellors provide advocacy while over-seeing programme content and improvement. Advocacy is an essential support component in Newberg's school improvement design. System support activities include communication, programme coordination, programme review (data driven), providing staff instruction, consultation and feedback on emerging student needs, collaboration and participation on site councils, advisory committees, etc. and community outreach.

Individual Student Planning

Individual planning consists of activities that assist each and every student in developing and reviewing their own individual academic, career, and personal/social interests and plans. Individual planning begins at the elementary level and continues through high school. It includes discussion and strategizing for post high school plans. Students are supported in the development of individual education plans beginning in elementary school. Progress towards the plan is reviewed and updated annually and documented in the education profile.

Student Advocacy

Student advocacy focuses on the proactive involvement of counseling staff to ensure all students have equal access to achieving high standards. Counsellors are aware of potential barriers for students, including special needs, gender, race, language, sexual orientation, social and economic status, pregnancy, parenting, giftedness, disabilities and religion.

The school counselor must be an advocate in the school and community for all students to achieve.

2

Educational and Other Forms of Guidance

Educational Guidance, the helping of persons to do better in their studies and to select courses and schools that will be fitted to their tastes and abilities. Closely related is vocational guidance, the helping of persons to find the right kind of work.

Persons who give educational guidance are usually called counsellors. Many schools employ trained full-time counsellors. Their work often includes helping with students' emotional problems. In many schools the principal or one or more selected teachers serve as part-time counsellors. Home-room teachers often play a main part in a school's guidance programme. In colleges and universities, professors (called faculty advisors) and deans of students act as counsellors.

A counselor tries to help each student to understand himself better and make the most of his talents. The counselor first learns about his family background, the school subjects he likes or dislikes, and his interest in athletics or other activities. He studies the student's school record and may give him aptitude and other special tests. In working with the failing student, the counselor may advise on how to improve study habits. Counsellors provide information on college or graduate school entrance requirements and scholarships, and may also give vocational guidance.

At first glance, the field of education and guidance appears to be quite similar to the field of teaching. Both belong to the same spiritual talent group, since they involve the use of talents that have spiritual effects.

In truth, however, they are entirely different.

Educating and guiding is a difficult task, in general.

It involves harder work than the task of a teacher instructing his students.

Although teaching is also one of the hardest and most difficult types of labour, still and all, its difficulty is not at all comparable to the hardship of educating and guiding.

There are two reasons for this:

1. In teaching, an instructor is involved in [transmitting] intellectual matters:
   i) to clarify a concept, and explain it to a student by means of analogies and illustrations; 2) to develop a student's abilities in,
   a) conceiving ideas,
   b) comprehending the analogy and the rationale,
   c) with a settled and clear understanding.

In any event, the task of a teacher in his instruction is only in the area of intellect and knowledge, as even the most simple and basic concept is still within the realm of the intellect.

This is not so in the labour of education and guidance.

In most cases the main effort of an educator lies chiefly in [transforming] base and ignoble traits [of his pupil].

This is particularly true at the beginning of a pupil's education and guidance, since "man is born [like] a wild young donkey," with animalistic tendencies and behaviour, being drawn after that which is materially good, and that which is visually desirable.

2. Although teaching, too, carries with it great responsibility, it is not at all like the responsibility assumed in educating and guiding.

If one is ineffective when teaching, one at least does no harm.

This is not so in the work of education and guidance - which carries with it enormous responsibility.

If one's work in this field is not constructive, it is perforce, damaging.

Therefore the educator and guidance counsellor, both of older pupils and of younger pupils, must follow the general and indispensable provisions of education, without which not only will he fail to correct [any matter pertaining to a pupil], but he will do harm as well.

Vocational Guidance in American Colleges

A vocation is a career or calling and the word is derived from the Latin *vocare*, which means "to call." Vocational guidance means helping someone find his or her calling or at least a suitable career choice. Vocations or careers can be loosely categorized into areas such as service, technical, mechanical, creative, health and business.

Vocational training rather than vocational guidance is available at career colleges and this is usually for entry-level careers. For example, a career college with a health vocational curriculum may offer education and training programmes for nurse's aide and medical assistant careers, while business-oriented vocational schools may have marketing assistant and bookkeeping programme offerings. A career college or vocational school differs from regular colleges and universities as the focus isn't on academics, but rather on training students for a specific career. Vocational or career colleges are also sometimes referred to as community colleges or trade schools.

Vocational guidance is often started in high school although some high schools also have vocational training programmes. Vocational exploration courses offer students the opportunity to research different career possibilities as well as learn which vocational areas they have aptitude or talent in. For instance, many vocational guidance classes give tests to the students that test their ability with numbers, words, mechanical concepts and many more subjects. Tests designed to measure an individual's personality traits, intelligence quotient (IQ) as well as his or her main values and interests are administered and analysed by career counsellors.

Vocational guidance is one of the basic pillars in the life of contemporary societies as this process continues throughout the individual life, starting as he joins kindergarten and continues throughout his shift to the stages of general education, graduation in higher education stages, embarking on practical life till his pension. Guidance process has an important and constructive impact on the individual life as it helps him achieve harmony between the various factors of his personality, tendencies and preparedness and the reality of life. This helps him develop and grow in various psychological, social and economic aspects and consequently assist in achieving prosperity and progress of the society in which he lives.

The Concept of Guidance

It is a process to guide the individual to the various paths through which he is able to discover and utilize his potentials and capabilities, tendencies and desires to lead a pleasant life and contributes to the happiness of his society.

General Objectives of Guidance:

- To guide trainees in various psychological, moral, social, educational and occupational aspects in order to become active members in the nation building process.
- To discuss the personal, social or educational problems encountered by the trainees during their study and work towards finding appropriate solutions which enable them to progress in their study.
- To work towards discovering the skills, capabilities and tendencies of distinct or ordinary trainees and help them invest their skills.
- To encourage trainees to learn and give them an insight into the training unit system and help them utilize available programmes.
- To help trainees select the specialization and occupation which meet the society requirements.
- To guide trainees in cooperation with the students tutor and solve their problems and participate in various councils and committees.

Career Counseling

Career counseling, career guidance and career coaching are similar in nature to other types of counseling or coaching, e.g. marriage or psychological counseling. What unites all types of professional counseling is the role of practitioners, who combine giving advice on their topic of expertise with counseling techniques that support clients in making complex decisions and facing difficult situations. The focus of career counseling is generally on issues such as career exploration, career change, personal career development and other career related issues.

Around the globe, countless definitions, concepts and terminology exist for career counseling - particularly due to cultural and linguistic differences. This even affects the most central term *counseling* (or: *counselling* in British English) which is often substituted with the word *guidance* as in *career guidance*. For example, in the UK, *career counseling* would usually be referred to as *careers advice* or *guidance*. Due to the widespread reference to both *career guidance* and *career counseling* among policy-makers, academics and practitioners around the world, references to *career guidance and counselling* are becoming common. Accordingly, this article emphasizes a *broad understanding* of career counseling which involves a variety of professionals activities commonly associated with career counseling, guidance, coaching, and advise. More specific roles and activities associated with career counseling are explained below.

Related Professional Activities

Career counseling or career guidance includes a wide variety of professional activities which focus on supporting people in dealing with career-related challenges - both preventively and in difficult situations (such as unemployment). Career counsellors work with people from various walks of life, such as adolescents seeking to explore career options, experienced professionals contemplating a career change, parents who want to return to the world of work after taking time to raise their child, or people seeking employment. Career counselling is also offered in various settings, including in groups and individually, in person or by means of digital communication.

Several approaches have been undertaken to systemize the variety of professional activities related to career guidance and counseling. In the most recent attempt, the Network for Innovation in Career Guidance and Counselling in Europe (NICE) - a consortium of 45 European institutions of higher education in the field of career counseling - has agreed on a system of professional roles for guidance counsellors. Each of these five roles is seen as an important facet of the *career guidance and counselling profession*. Career counsellors performing in any of these roles are expected to behave professionally, e.g. by following ethical standards in their practice. The NICE Professional Roles (NPR) are:

- The *Career Educator* "supports people in developing their own career management competences"
- The *Career Information & Assessment Expert* "supports people in assessing their personal characteristics and needs, then connecting them with the labour market and education systems"
- The *Career Counsellor* "supports individuals in understanding their situations, so as to work through issues towards solutions"
- The *Programme & Service Manager* "ensures the quality and delivery of career guidance and counselling organisations' services"
- The *Social Systems Intervener & Developer* "supports clients (even) in crisis and works to change systems for the better"

The description of the NICE Professional Roles (NPR) draws on a variety of prior models to define the central activities and competences of guidance counsellors. The NPR can, therefore, be understood as a state-of-the-art framework which includes all relevant aspects of career counselling. For this reason, other models haven't been included here so far. Models which are reflected in the NPR include:

- BEQU: "Kompetenzprofil für Beratende" (Germany, 2011)
- CEDEFOP "Practitioner Competences" (2009)
- ENTO: "National Occupational Standards for Advice and Guidance" (Great Britain, 2006)
- IAEVG: "International Competences for Educational and Vocational Guidance" (2003)
- Savickas, M.: "Career Counselling" (USA, 2011)

Benefits

Professional career counsellors can support people with career-related challenges in many ways. Through their expertise in career development and labour markets, they can put a person's qualification, experience, strengths and weakness in a broad perspective taking into consideration their desired salary, personal hobbies and interests, location, job market and educational possibilities.

Through their counselling and teaching abilities, career counsellors can additionally support people in gaining a better understanding of what really matters for them personally, how they can plan their careers autonomously, or help them in making tough decisions and getting through times of crisis. Finally, career counsellors are often capable of supporting their clients in finding suitable placements/ jobs, in working out conflicts with their employers, or finding the support of other helpful services.

It is due to these various benefits of career counseling that policy-makers in many countries of the world publicly fund guidance services. For example, the European Union understands career guidance and counseling as an instrument to effectively combat social exclusion and increase citizens' employability.

History

Frank Parson's *Choosing a Vocation* (1909) was perhaps the first major work which is concerned with careers guidance. While until the 1970s a strongly normative approach was characteristic for theories (e.g. of Donald E. Super's *life-span approach*) and practice of career counseling (e.g. concept of *matching*), new models have their starting point in the individual needs and transferable skills of the clients while managing biographical breaks and discontinuities. Career development is no longer viewed as a linear process. More consideration is now placed on nonlinear, chance and unplanned influences.

Training

Up until now there is no standardized qualification path for professional career counsellors, although various certificates are offered nationally and internationally (e.g. by professional associations), and the number of academic degree programmes in career guidance and/ or career counseling is growing worldwide. Still, in most countries, basically anybody could call themselves a "career counselor" (unlike engineers or psychologists whose professions are protected legally). At the same time, policy makers agree that the competence of career counsellors is one of the most important factors in ensuring that people receive high quality support in dealing with their career questions. Depending on the country of their education, career counsellors may have a variety of academic backgrounds: In Europe, for instance, degrees in (vocational/ industrial/ organization) psychology and educational sciences are among the most common, but backgrounds in sociology, public administration and other sciences are also frequent. At the same time, many training programmes for career counsellors are becoming increasingly multidisciplinary.

Professional Career Guidance Centres

There are many career guidance and counseling centres all over the world. They give services of guidance and counseling on higher studies, possibilities, chances and nature of courses and institutes. Also that these services are offered either fixing up a meeting with the Experts or having telephonic conversations with the guide or even the online guidance which is very common these days with the people getting services on click of their mouse. There are many such service providers all over the world providing online counseling to people about their career or conducting a psychometric test to know the persons aptitude as well as interests.

Career Testing

People who participate in career counseling can benefit from the use of aptitude tests, or career testing. Career testing is often done online and provides insightful and relatively objective information about which jobs may be suitable for the test taker based on combination of their interests, values and skills. Career tests usually provide a list of recommended jobs that match the test takers attributes with those of people with similar personalities who enjoy/are successful at their jobs. There are various ways to test an individual for which field he is suitable, psychometric testing being one among them.

Psychometric testing covers a wide range of skills, interests and values of people and can be of use in career counseling in different ways. For example, the information won from such tests can be of help for the professionals who mentor, coach or counsel individuals. With psychometric testing, there is no pass or fail, but the quality of the information won from the tests can vary. Psychometric testing uses in-depth psychological profiles to assess personality and intellectual levels. Different test companies use different theoretical approaches to testing, such as the psychometric approach, the psychodynamic approach, the social learning approach and the humanist approach. Different test companies have their own methods of testing, some of them being protected with copyrights. Two commonly used assessments are the Strong Interest Inventory and the MBTI, for example. Usually, psychometric testing uses multiple sets of questions relating to personality type, how the test taker would handle aspects of work and home life, what his or her goals are for the future and his or her strengths and weaknesses. If the test taker is honest and the employed tests follow scientific standards, the results should be fairly accurate and useful for career counseling activities.

Challenges

One of the major challenges associated with career counseling is encouraging participants to engage in the process. For example in the UK 70% of people under 14 say they have had no careers advice while 45% of people over 14 have had no or very poor/limited advice.

In a related issue some client groups tend to reject the interventions made by professional career counsellors preferring to rely on the advice of peers or superiors within their own profession. Jackson et al. found that 44% of doctors in training felt that senior members of their own profession were best placed to give careers advice. Furthermore it is recognised that the giving of career advice is something that is widely spread through a range of formal and informal roles. In addition to career counsellors it is also common for teachers, managers, trainers and Human Resources (HR) specialists to give formal support in career choices. Similarly it is also common for people to seek informal support from friends and family around their career choices and to bypass career professionals altogether. Today increasingly people rely on career web portals to seek advice on resume writing and handling interviews; as also to research on various professions and companies. It has even become possible to take vocational assessments online.

Psychology and Vocational Guidance

Vast changes in the world of work spurred by rapid technological growth and globalization have called for a more inclusive, progressive, and forward thinking conceptualization of vocational theory, practice, training, and policy.

A vocation is an occupation to which a person is specially drawn or for which he or she is suited, trained, or qualified. Though now often used in non-religious contexts, the meanings of the term originated in Christianity.

Senses

Use of the word "vocation" before the sixteenth century referred firstly to the "call" by God to the individual, or calling of all humankind to salvation, particularly in the Vulgate, and more specifically to the "vocation to the priesthood", which is still the usual sense in Roman Catholicism. Roman Catholicism recognizes marriage and virginity or celibacy as the two vocations. Martin Luther, followed by John Calvin, placed a particular emphasis on vocations, or divine callings, as potentially including most secular occupations, though this idea was by no means new.

Calvinism developed complex ideas about different types of vocations of the first type, connected with the concepts of Predestination, Irresistible grace, and the elect. There are the *vocatio universalis*, the *vocatio specialis*, only extended to some. There were also complex distinctions between internal and external, and the "vocatio efficax" and "inefficax" types of callings. Hyper-Calvinism, unusually, rejects the idea of a "universal call" to repent and believe, held by virtually all other Christian groups.

In Protestantism the call from God to devote one's life to him by joining the clergy is often covered by the English equivalent term "call", whereas in Roman Catholicism "vocation" is still used.

Both senses of the word "call" are used in 1 Corinthians 7:20, where Paul says "Let every man abide in the same calling wherein he was called" (KJV).

Concept

The idea of vocation is central to the Christian belief that God has created each person with gifts and talents oriented towards specific purposes and a way of life. In the broadest sense, as stated in the Catechism of the Catholic Church, "*Love* is the fundamental and innate vocation of every human being" (CCC 2392). More specifically, in the Orthodox and Catholic Churches, this idea of vocation is especially associated with a divine call to service to the Church and humanity through particular vocational life commitments such as marriage to a particular person, consecration as a religious, ordination to priestly ministry in the Church and even a holy life as a single person. In the broader sense, Christian vocation includes the use of one's gifts in their profession, family life, church and civic commitments for the sake of the greater common good.

Christian Views on Work

Many Christian theologians appeal to the Old Testment Book of Genesis in regards to work. According to Genesis 1, human beings were created in the image of God, and according to Genesis 2, Adam was placed in the Garden of Eden to "work it and keep it" (2:15, ESV). Dorothy L. Sayers has argued that "work is the natural exercise and function of man – the creature who is made in the image of his Creator." Likewise, John Paul II said in *Laborem Exercens* that by his work, man shares in the image of his Creator.

Christian theologians see the Fall of man profoundly affecting human work. In Genesis 3:17, God said to Adam, "cursed is the ground because of you; in pain you shall eat of it all the days of your life" (ESV). Leland Ryken points out that, because of the Fall, "many of the tasks we perform in a fallen world are inherently distasteful and wearisome."

Through the Fall, work has become toil, but John Paul II says that work is a good thing for man in spite of this toil, and "perhaps, in a sense, because of it" because work is something that corresponds to man's dignity and through it he achieves fulfilment as a human being. The Fall also means that a work ethic is needed. As a result of the Fall work has become subject to the abuses of idleness on the one hand, and overwork on the other. Drawing on Aristotle, Ryken suggests that that the moral ideal is the golden mean between the two extremes of being lazy and being a workaholic.

Some Christian theologians also draw on the doctrine of redemption to discuss the concept of work. Oliver O'Donovan points out that although work is a gift of creation, it is "ennobled into mutual service in the fellowship of Christ."

Leland Ryken argues for seeing the call of God to a particular occupation as a reflection of the gospel call, and suggests that this implies vocational loyalty – "modern notions of job become deficient" and "the element of arbitrariness of one's choice of work" is removed.

Modern Vocation

Since the establishment of Vocational Guidance in 1908 by the engineer Frank Parsons, the use of the term "vocation" has evolved, with emphasis shifting to an individual's development of talents and abilities in the choice and enjoyment of a career. This semantic expansion has meant some diminishment of reference to the term's religious meanings in everyday usage.

Avocation

An avocation is an activity that one engages in as a hobby outside one's main occupation. There are many examples of people whose professions were the ways that they made their livings, but for whom their activities outside of their workplaces were their true passions in life. Occasionally, as with Lord Baden-Powell and others, a person who pursues an avocation is more remembered by history for their avocation than for their professional career.

Many times a person's regular vocation may lead to their avocation. Many forms of humanitarian campaigning, such as work for organizations such as Amnesty International and Greenpeace may be done by people involved in the law or human rights issues as part of their work. Many people involved with youth work pursue this as an avocation.

Volunteering

Volunteering is generally considered an altruistic activity and is intended to promote good or improve human quality of life. In return, this activity can produce a feeling of self-worth and respect. There is no financial gain involved. Volunteering is also renowned for skill development, socialization, and fun. It is also intended to make contacts for possible employment. Many volunteers are specifically trained in the areas they work, such as medicine, education, or emergency rescue. Others serve on an as-needed basis, such as in response to a natural disaster.

Moral Resources, Political Capital and Civil Society

Based on a case study in China, Xu and Ngai (2011) revealed that the developing arses grew likeroots volunteerism (a religion is many eastern countries) can be an enclave among various organizations and may be able to work towards the development of civil society in the developing countries. The researchers developed a "Moral Resources and Political Capital" approach to examine the contributions of volunteerism in promoting the civil society. Moral resource means the available morals could be chosen by NGOs. Political capital means the capital that will improve or enhance the NGOs' status, possession or access in the existing political system.

Moreover, Xu and Ngai (2011) distinguished two types of Moral Resources: Moral Resource-I and Moral Resource-II (ibid).

1. Moral Resource I: Inspired by Immanuel Kant's (1998 [1787]) argument of "What ought I to do," Moral Resource-I will encourage the NGOs' confidence and then have the courage to act and conquer difficulties by way of answering and confirming the question of "What ought I to do."
2. Moral Resource II: given that Adorno (2000) recognizes that moral or immoral tropes are socially determined, Moral Resource-II refers to the morals that are well accepted by the given society.

Thanks to the intellectual heritage of Blau and Duncan (1967), two types of political capital were identified:

1. Political Capital-I refers to the political capital mainly ascribed to the status that the NGO inherited throughout history (e.g., the CYL).
2. Political Capital-II refers to the Political Capital that the NGOs earned through their hard efforts.

Obviously, "Moral resource-I itself contains the self-determination that gives participants confidence in the ethical beliefs they have chosen", almost any organizations may have Moral Resource-I, while not all of them have the societal recognized Moral Resource-II. However, the voluntary service organizations predominantly occupy Moral Resource-II because a sense of moral superiority makes it possible that for parties with different values, goals and cultures to work together in promoting the promotion of volunteering. Thus the voluntary service organizations are likely to win the trust and support of the masses as well as the government more easily than will the organizations whose morals are not accepted by mainstream society. In other words, Moral Resource II helps the grassroots organizations with little Political Capital I to win Political Capital-II, which is a crucial factor for their survival and growth in developing countries such as China. Therefore, the voluntary service realm could be an enclave of the development of civil society in the developing nations.

Etymology and History

The verb *volunteer* was first recorded in 1755 from the noun, in C.1600, "one who offers himself for military service," by M.Fr. Voluntaire. In the non-military sense, the word was first recorded during the 1630s. The word *volunteering* has more recent usage—still predominantly military—coinciding with the word *community service.* In a military context, a volunteer army is a military body whose soldiers chose to enter service, as opposed to having been conscripted. Such volunteers do not work "for free" and are given regular pay.

If a student is engaged in some sort of volunteer work, taking a gap year after high school or during college is also one form of volunteering. Career break is also considered to be a form of volunteering, until involved in a voluntary work.

19th Century

During this time, America experienced the Great Awakening. People became aware of the disadvantaged and realized the cause for the movement against slavery. Younger people started helping the needy in their communities. In 1851, the first YMCA in the United States was started, followed seven years later by the first YWCA. During the American Civil War, women volunteered their time to sew supplies for the soldiers and the "Angel of the Battlefied" Clara Barton and a team of volunteers began providing aid to servicemen. Barton founded the American Red Cross in 1881 and began mobilizing volunteers for disaster relief operations, including relief for victims of the Johnstown Flood in 1889.

20th & 21st Centuries

The Salvation Army is one of the oldest and largest organization working for disadvantaged people. Though it is a charity organization, it has organized a number of volunteering programmes since its inception. Prior to the 19th century, few formal charitable organizations existed to assist people in need.

In the first few decades of the 20th century, several volunteer organizations were founded, including the Rotary International,

Kiwanis International, Association of Junior Leagues International, and Lions Clubs International.

The Great Depression saw one of the first large-scale, nationwide efforts to coordinate volunteering for a specific need. During World War II, thousands of volunteer offices supervised the volunteers who helped with the many needs of the military and the home front, including collecting supplies, entertaining soldiers on leave, and caring for the injured.

After World War II, the people shifted the focus of their altruistic passions to other areas, including helping the poor and volunteering overseas. A major development was the Peace Corps in the United States in 1960. When President Lyndon B. Johnson declared a *War on Poverty* in 1964, volunteer opportunities started to expand and continued into the next few decades. The process for finding volunteer work became more formalized, with more volunteer centres forming and new ways to find work appearing on the World Wide Web.

Types

Skills-based volunteering: *Skills-based volunteering* is leveraging the specialized skills and talents of individuals to strengthen the infrastructure of nonprofits, helping them build and sustain their capacity to successfully achieve their missions. This is in contrast to traditional volunteering, where specific training is not required. The average hour of traditional volunteering is valued by the Independent Sector at between $18–20 an hour. Skills-based volunteering is valued at $40–500 an hour depending on the market value of the time.

Volunteering in Developing Countries

An increasingly popular form of volunteering among young people, particularly gap year students, is to travel to communities in the developing world to work on projects. Activities include teaching English, working in orphanages, conservation, and so on. International volunteering is said to give participants valuable skills, knowledge, and the experience of a lifetime. However, "voluntourism" has been criticized by some as being paternalistic and reinforcing historic power imbalances. Some critics argue that in many cases, voluntourism does more harm to communities than good.

Virtual Volunteering

Also called *e-volunteering* or *online volunteering*, virtual volunteering is a term that describes a volunteer who completes tasks, in whole or in part, offsite from the organization being assisted. They use the Internet and a home, school, telecentre or work computer, or other Internet-connected device, such as a PDA or smartphone. Virtual volunteering is also known as cyber service, telementoring, and teletutoring, as well as various other names. Virtual volunteering is similar to telecommuting, except that instead of online employees who are paid, these are online volunteers who are not paid.

Micro-volunteering

Micro-volunteering is an unpaid task that is operated via an internet-connected device and completed in small increments of time. It is distinct from virtual volunteering in that it typically does not require an application process or training period.

Environmental Volunteering

Environmental volunteering refers to volunteers who contribute towards environmental management or conservation. Volunteers conduct a range of activities including environmental monitoring, ecological restoration such as re-vegetation and weed removal, protecting endangered animals, and educating others about the natural environment.

The Giant Panda Conservation programme in Xi'an and Sichuan, China, is a famous endangered animals protection programme. Sichuan Giant Panda Sanctuaries conservation programme attracts huge foreign support and volunteers.

Volunteering in an Emergency

Volunteering often plays a pivotal role in the recovery effort following natural disasters, such as tsunamis, floods, droughts, hurricanes, and earthquakes. For example, the 2004 Indian Ocean earthquake and tsunami attracted a large number of volunteers worldwide, deployed by non-governmental organizations, government agencies, and the United Nations.

Volunteering in Schools

Resource poor schools around the world rely on government support, or on efforts from volunteers and private donations, in order to run effectively. In some countries, whenever the economy is down, the need for volunteers and resources increases greatly. There are many opportunities available in school systems for volunteers. Yet, there are not many requirements in order to volunteer in a school system. Whether one is a high school or TEFL (Teaching English as a Foreign Language) graduate or college student, most schools require just voluntary and selfless effort.

Much like the benefits of any type of volunteering there are great rewards for the volunteer, student, and school. In addition to intangible rewards, volunteers can add relevant experience to their resumes. Volunteers who travel to assist may learn foreign culture and language.

Volunteering in schools can be an additional teaching guide for the students and help to fill the gap of local teachers. Cultural and language exchange during teaching and other school activities can be the most essential learning experience for both students and volunteers.

Corporate Volunteering

A majority of the companies at the Fortune 500 allow their employees to volunteer during work hours. These formalized Employee Volunteering Programmes (EVPs), also called Employer Supported Volunteering, are regarded as a part of the companies' sustainability efforts and their social responsibility activities. About 40% of Fortune 500 companies provide monetary donations, also known as volunteer grants, to nonprofits as a way to recognize employees who dedicate significant amounts of time to volunteering in the community.

According to information from Volunteer Match, a service that provides Employee Volunteering Programme solutions, the key drivers for companies that produce and manage EVPs are building brand awareness and affinity, strengthening trust and loyalty among consumers, enhancing corporate image and reputation, improving employee retention, increasing employee productivity and loyalty, and providing an effective vehicle to reach strategic goals.

Community Voluntary Work

Community volunteering refers to volunteers who work to improve community enhancement efforts in the area in which they live. Neighbourhood, church, and community groups play a key role in building strong cities from the neighbourhoods up. Supporting these understaffed groups can enable them to succeed in a variety of areas, which connect social, environmental, and economic boundaries. Volunteers can conduct a wide range of activities. Numerous community organizations exist to facilitate volunteering, some are affiliated with academic organizations (Harvard Alumni), some are corporate(Intel Employees), some religious based(Methodists) while others are more socially (One Brick).

International Work-camps

An international work-camp is an international voluntary project in which participants from different countries can meet, live, work, learn, and exchange with local people concerning issues about environmental conservation, cultural heritage, social justice, rural and human development, etc. Groups including CCIVS, NVDA, Group Work Foundation, and Service Civil International (SCI) are a few providing International work camps.

International work-camp volunteering can be divided into short term voluntary projects (STV) and long- or middle-term voluntary projects (LMTV). STV projects are international workcamps for less than two months, while LMTV projects are those lasting two months or more. The most common international workcamp lasts for two weeks with a group of 10-20 overseas and local work-camp participants.

Political View

Modern societies share a common value of people helping each other; not only do volunteer acts assist others, but they also benefit the volunteering individual on a personal level. Despite having similar objectives, tension can arise between volunteers and state-provided services. In order to curtail this tension, most countries develop policies and enact legislation to clarify the roles and relationships among governmental stakeholders and their voluntary counterparts; this regulation identifies and allocates the necessary legal, social, administrative, and financial support of each party. This is particularly necessary when some voluntary activities are seen as a challenge to the authority of the state, (e.g., on January 29, 2001, President Bush cautioned that volunteer groups should supplement—not replace—government agencies' work).

Volunteering that benefits the state but challenges paid counterparts angers labour unions that represent those who are paid for their volunteer work; this is particularly seen in combination departments, such as volunteer fire departments.

Difficulties in Cross-national Aid

Difficulties in the cross-national aid model of volunteering can arise when it is applied across national borders. The presence of volunteers who are sent from one state to another can be viewed as a breach of sovereignty and showing a lack of respect towards the national government of the proposed recipients. Thus, motivations are important when states negotiate offers to send aid and when these proposals are accepted, particularly if donors may postpone assistance or stop it altogether. Three types of conditionality have evolved:

1. Financial accountability: Transparency in funding management to ensure that what is done by the volunteers is properly targeted
2. Policy reform: Governmental request that developing countries adopt certain social, economic, or environmental policies; often, the most controversial relate to the privatization of services traditionally offered by the state
3. Development objectives: Asking developing countries to adjust specific time-bound economic objectives

Some international volunteer organizations define their primary mission as being an altruistic one: to fight poverty and improve the living standards of people in the developing world, (e.g., Voluntary Services Overseas has almost 2,000 skilled professionals working as volunteers to pass on their expertise to local people so that the volunteers' skills remain long after they return home). When these organizations work in partnership with governments, the results can be impressive. However, when other organizations or individual First World governments support the work of volunteer groups, there can be questions as to whether the organizations' or governments' real motives are poverty alleviation. Instead, a focus on creating wealth for some of the poor or developing policies intended to benefit the donor states is sometimes reported. Many low-income countries' economies suffer from industrialization without prosperity and investment without growth. One reason for this is that development assistance guides many Third World governments to pursue development policies that have been wasteful, ill-conceived, or unproductive; some of these policies have been so destructive that the economies could not have been sustained without outside support.

Indeed, some offers of aid have distorted the general spirit of volunteering, treating local voluntary action as contributions in kind, i.e., existing conditions requiring the modification of local people's behaviour in order for them to earn the right to donors' charity. This can be seen as patronizing and offensive to the recipients because the aid expressly serves the policy aims of the donors rather than the needs of the recipients.

Criticisms

In the 1960s, Ivan Illich offered an analysis of the role of American volunteers in Mexico in his speech entitled "To Hell With Good Intentions". His concerns, along with those of critics such as Paulo Freire and Edward Said, revolve around the notion of altruism as an extension of Christian missionary ideology. In addition, he mentions the sense of responsibility/obligation as a factor, which drives the concept of noblesse oblige—first developed by the French aristocracy as a moral duty derived from their wealth. Simply stated, these apprehensions propose the extension of power and authority over indigenous cultures around the world. Recent critiques of volunteering come from Westmier and Kahn (1996) and bell hooks (née Gloria Watkins) (2004). Also, Georgeou (2012) has critiqued the impact of neoliberalism on international aid volunteering.

The field of medical tourism (referring to volunteers who travel overseas to deliver medical care) has recently attracted negative criticism when compared to the alternative notion of sustainable capacities, i.e., work done in the context of long-term, locally-run, and foreign-supported infrastructures. A preponderance of this criticism appears largely in scientific and peer-reviewed literature. Recently, media outlets with more general readerships have published such criticisms as well.

Counseling Psychology

Counseling psychology is a psychological specialty that encompasses research and applied work in several broad domains: counseling process and outcome; supervision and training; career development and counseling; and prevention and health. Some unifying themes among counseling psychologists include a focus on assets and strengths, person–environment interactions, educational and career development, brief interactions, and a focus on intact personalities. In the United States, the premier scholarly journals of the profession are the *Journal of Counseling Psychology* and *The Counseling Psychologist*.

In Europe, the scholarly journals of the profession include the *European Journal of Counselling Psychology* (under the auspices of the European Association of Counselling Psychology) and the *Counselling Psychology Review* (under the auspices of the British Psychological Society). *Counselling Psychology Quarterly* is an international interdisciplinary publication of Routledge (part of the Taylor & Francis Group).

In the U.S., counseling psychology programmes are accredited by the American Psychological Association (APA), while counseling programmes are accredited through the Counsel for Accreditation of Counseling and Related Educational Programmes (CACREP). To become licensed as a counseling psychologist, one must meet the criteria for licensure as a psychologist (4-7 year doctoral degree post-bachelors, 1 year full-time internship, including 3,000 hours of supervised experience and exams). Both doctoral level counseling psychologists and doctoral level counsellors can perform both applied work, as well as research and teaching.

Holland's Theory of Psychology of Vocational Guidance

John Holland criticised the theories of vocational choice by Ginzberg and Donald e.s. He said that on the basis of these theories, it was very difficult to take decision about some vocation.

This criticism made Holland to formulate this theory of Vocational Choice in 1949.

According to his theory, Vocational choice is the result of the following factors:

- Heredity
- Culture and Civilization
- Friends
- Parents
- Matured person
- Social status
- Interaction of physical environment

On the basis of ones experiences and the above said factors, one learns to behave in some specific way with his environment. These behaviour acts as an basis through which one chooses ones vocation that satisfies oneself.

Holland termed these groups as occupational environment. Holland has mentioned 6 types of occupational environments or occupational groups as follows:

- Intellectual Environment: Chemistry, Mathematics, Physiology, Medical Science and such subjects were included in intellectual environment.
- Aesthetic Environment: Artists, poets, writers, sculptures, etc, were included.
- Realistic Environment
- Social Environment
- Conventional Environment
- Enterprising Environment

According to him, a definite life style is required for every occupational environment. If the life style coincides to the necessary traits of the vocation, then the person's job satisfication can be attained. This will maintain a person's personality balance.

Process of Vocational Choice

Process 1: Selection of main occupational environment according to one's own life-style.

Process 2: To select one occupation, according to one's own abilities, out of the main occupational environment or occupation group selected in the process 1.

Process 3: There should be proper co-ordination among a person's interests for the rapid vocational choice.

Process 4: Definite and correct self knowledge is must for quick vocational choice. Due to lack of self knowledge, the proper direction and stage of occupational choice remains uncertain.

Process5: For convenient vocational choice, correct knowledge of occupational environment or group is needed.

Process6: Age cannot be ignored for vocational choice because age affects vocational choice.

The theories of vocational choice can be applied only in the state of complete employment. But no state is in the state of providing full employment to its citizens, so one has to give up one's interest and satisfication towards one's occupations and take up one which one gets.

3

Vocational Education

Vocational education (education based on occupation or employment) (also known as vocational education and training or VET) is education that prepares people for specific trades, crafts and careers at various levels from a trade, a craft, technician, or a professional position in engineering, accountancy, nursing, medicine, architecture, pharmacy, law etc. Craft vocations are usually based on manual or practical activities, traditionally non-academic, related to a specific trade, occupation, or *vocation*. It is sometimes referred to as *technical education* as the trainee directly develops expertise in a particular group of techniques. In the UK some higher technician engineering positions that require 4-5 year apprenticeship require academic study to HNC / HND or higher City & Guilds level.

Vocational education may be classified as teaching procedural knowledge. This can be contrasted with declarative knowledge, as used in education in a usually broader scientific field, which might concentrate on theory and abstract conceptual knowledge, characteristic of tertiary education. Vocational education can be at the secondary, post-secondary level, further education level and can interact with the apprenticeship system. Increasingly, vocational education can be recognised in terms of recognition of prior learning and partial academic credit towards tertiary education (e.g., at a university) as credit; however, it is rarely considered in its own form to fall under the traditional definition of higher education.

Vocational education is related to the age-old apprenticeship system of learning. Apprenticeships are designed for many levels of work from manual trades to high knowledge work.

However, as the labour market becomes more specialized and economies demand higher levels of skill, governments and businesses are increasingly investing in the future of vocational education through publicly funded training organizations and subsidized apprenticeship or traineeship initiatives for businesses. At the post-secondary level vocational education is typically provided by an institute of technology, university, or by a local community college.

Vocational education has diversified over the 20th century and now exists in industries such as retail, tourism, information technology, funeral services and cosmetics, as well as in the traditional crafts and cottage industries.

VET Internationally

Australia: In Australia vocational education and training is mostly post-secondary and provided through the vocational education and training (VET) system by registered training organisations. There were 24 Technical Colleges in Australia but now only 4 independent Trade Colleges remain with two in Queensland; one in Brisbane and one on the Gold Coast and one in Adelaide and Perth. This system encompasses both public, TAFE, and private providers in a national training framework consisting of the Australian Quality Training Framework, Australian Qualifications Framework and Industry Training Packages which define the assessment standards for the different vocational qualifications.

Australia's apprenticeship system includes both traditional apprenticeships in traditional trades and "traineeships" in other more service-oriented occupations. Both involve a legal contract between the employer and the apprentice and provide a combination of school-based and workplace training. Apprenticeships typically last three to four years, traineeships only one to two years. Apprentices and trainees receive a wage which increases as they progress.

Since the states and territories are responsible for most public delivery and all regulation of providers, a central concept of the system is "national recognition" whereby the assessments and awards of any one registered training organisation must be recognised by all others and the decisions of any state or territory training authority must be recognised by the other states and territories. This allows national portability of qualifications and units of competency.

A crucial feature of the training package (which accounts for about 60% of publicly funded training and almost all apprenticeship training) is that the content of the vocational qualifications is theoretically defined by industry and not by government or training providers. A Training Package is "owned" by one of 11 Industry Skills Councils which are responsible for developing and reviewing the qualifications.

The National Centre for Vocational Education Research or NCVER is a not-for-profit company owned by the federal, state and territory ministers responsible for training. It is responsible for collecting, managing, analysing, evaluating and communicating research and statistics about vocational education and training (VET).

The boundaries between Vocational education and tertiary education are becoming more blurred. A number of vocational training providers such as NMIT, BHI and WAI are now offering specialised Bachelor degrees in specific areas not being adequately provided by Universities. Such Applied Courses include in the areas of Equine studies, Winemaking and viticulture, aquaculture, Information Technology, Music, Illustration, Culinary Management and many more.

Commonwealth of Independent States

The largest and the most unified system of vocational education was created in the Soviet Union with the Professional'no-tehnicheskoye uchilische and, Tehnikum. But it became less effective with the transition of the economies of post-Soviet countries to a market economy.

Finland

In Finland, vocational education belongs to secondary education. After the nine-year comprehensive school, almost all students choose to go to either a *lukio* (high school), which is an institution preparing students for tertiary education, or to a vocational school. Both forms of secondary education last three years, and give a formal qualification to enter university or *ammattikorkeakoulu*, i.e. Finnish polytechnics. In certain fields (e.g. the police school, air traffic control personnel training), the entrance requirements of vocational schools include completion of the *lukio*, thus causing the students to complete their secondary education twice.

The education in vocational school is free, and the students from low-income families are eligible for a state student grant. The curriculum is primarily vocational, and the academic part of the curriculum is adapted to the needs of a given course. The vocational schools are mostly maintained by municipalities.

After completing secondary education, one can enter higher vocational schools (*ammattikorkeakoulu*, or *AMK*) or universities.

It is also possible for a student to choose both lukio and vocational schooling. The education in such cases last usually from 3 to 4 years.

German-language Areas

Vocational education is an important part of the education systems in Austria, Germany, Liechtenstein and Switzerland (including the French and the Italian speaking parts of the country) and one element of the German model.

For example, in Germany a law (the *Berufsausbildungsgesetz*) was passed in 1969 which regulated and unified the vocational training system and codified the shared responsibility of the state, the unions, associations and chambers of trade and industry. The system is very popular in modern Germany: in 2001, two thirds of young people aged under 22 began an apprenticeship, and 78% of them completed it, meaning that approximately 51% of all young people under 22 have completed an apprenticeship. One in three companies offered apprenticeships in 2003; in 2004 the government signed a pledge with industrial unions that all companies except very small ones must take on apprentices.

The vocational education systems in the other German speaking countries are very similar to the German system and a vocational qualification from one country is generally also recognized in the other states within this area.

Hong Kong

In Hong Kong, vocational education is usually for post-secondary 3, 5 and 7 students. The Hong Kong Institute of Vocational Education (IVE) provides training in nine different vocational fields, namely: Applied Science; Business Administration; Child Education and Community Services; Construction; Design; Printing, Textiles and Clothing; Hotel, Service and Tourism Studies; Information Technology; Electrical and Electronic Engineering; and Mechanical, Manufacturing and Industrial Engineering.

Hungary

Normally at the end of elementary school (at age 14) students are directed to one of three types of upper secondary education: one academic track (gymnasium) and two vocational tracks. Vocational secondary schools (szakközépiskola) provide four years of general education and also prepare students for the maturata. These schools combine general education with some specific subjects, referred to as pre-vocational education and career orientation. At that point many students enrol in a post-secondary VET programme often at the same institution, to obtain a vocational qualification, although they may also seek entry to tertiary education.

Vocational training schools (szakiskola) initially provide two years of general education, combined with some pre-vocational education and career orientation, they then choose an occupation, and then receive two or three years of vocational education and training focusing on that occupation – such as bricklayer. Students do not obtain the maturata but a vocational qualification at the end of a successfully completed programme. Demand for vocational training schools, both from the labour market and among students, has declined while it has increased for upper secondary schools delivering the maturata.

India

Vocational training in India is provided on a full-time as well as part-time basis. Full-time programmes are generally offered through I.T.I.s Industrial training institutes. The nodal agency for granting the recognition to the I.T.I.s is NCVT, which is under the Min. of labour, Govt. of India. Part-time programmes are offered through state technical education boards or universities who also offer full-time courses. Vocational training has been successful in India only in industrial training institutes and that too in engineering trades. There are many private institutes in India which offer courses in vocational training and finishing, but most of them have not been recognized by the Government. India is a pioneer in vocational training in Film & Television, and Information Technology. AAFT, Audio Production & Recording ILM Academy. Maharashtra State Government also offers vocational Diplomas in various Trades . Vocational Higher Secondary schools are under MHRD in India. All the state governments runs vocational schools. In the state of Kerala, 389 vocational schools are there with 42 different courses. Commerce & Business, Tourism, Agriculture, Automobile, Air conditioning, Live stock management, Lab Technician are some prominent courses.

Japan

Japanese vocational schools are known as *senmon gakkô*. They are part of Japan's higher education system. They are two-year schools that many students study at after finishing high school (although it is not always required that students graduate from high school). Some have a wide range of majors, others only a few majors. Some examples are computer technology, fashion and English.

South Korea

Vocational high schools offer programmes in five fields: agriculture, technology/engineering, commerce/business, maritime/fishery, and home economics. In principle, all students in the first year of high school (10th grade) follow a common national curriculum, In the second and third years (11th and 12th grades) students are offered courses relevant to their specialisation. In some programmes, students may participate in workplace training through co-operation between schools and local employers. The government is now piloting Vocational Meister Schools in which workplace training is an important part of the programme. Around half of all vocational high schools are private. Private and public schools operate according to similar rules; for example, they charge the same fees for high school education, with an exemption for poorer families.

The number of students in vocational high schools has decreased, from about half of students in 1995 down to about one-quarter today. To make vocational high schools more attractive, in April 2007 the Korean government changed the name of vocational high schools into professional high schools. With the change of the name the government also facilitated the entry of vocational high school graduates to colleges and universities.

Most vocational high school students continue into tertiary education; in 2007 43% transferred to junior colleges and 25% to university. At tertiary level, vocational education and training is provided in junior colleges (two- and three-year programmes) and at polytechnic colleges. Education at junior colleges and in two-year programmes in polytechnic colleges leads to an Industrial Associate degree. Polytechnics also provide one-year programmes for craftsmen and master craftsmen and short programmes for employed workers. The requirements for admission to these institutions are in principle the same as those in the rest of tertiary sector (on the basis of the College Scholastic Aptitude Test) but candidates with vocational qualifications are given priority in the admission process. Junior colleges have expanded rapidly in response to demand and in 2006 enrolled around 27% of all tertiary students.

95% of junior college students are in private institutions. Fees charged by private colleges are approximately twice those of public institutions. Polytechnic colleges are state-run institutions under the responsibility of the Ministry of Labour; government funding keeps student fees much lower than those charged by other tertiary institutions. Around 5% of students are enrolled in polytechnic colleges.

Mexico

In Mexico, both federal and state governments are responsible for the administration of vocational education. Federal schools are funded by the federal budget, in addition to their own funding sources. The state governments are responsible for the management of decentralised institutions, such as the State Centres for Scientific and Technological Studies and Institutes of Training for Work (ICAT). These institutions are funded 50% from the federal budget and 50% from the state budget. The state governments also manage and fund "decentralised institutions of the federation", such as CONALEP schools.

Compulsory education (including primary and lower secondary education) finishes at the age of 15 and about half of those aged 15-to-19 are enrolled full-time or part-time in education. All programmes at upper secondary level require the payment of a tuition fee.

The upper secondary vocational education system in Mexico includes over a dozen subsystems (administrative units within the Upper Secondary Education Undersecretariat of the Ministry of Public Education, responsible for vocational programmes) which differ from each other to varying degrees in content, administration, and target group. The large number of school types and corresponding administrative units within the Ministry of Public Education makes the institutional landscape of vocational education and training complex by international standards.

Vocational education and training provided under the Upper Secondary Education Under secretariat includes three main types of programme:

- "Training for work" courses at ISCED 2 level are short training programmes, taking typically 3 to 6 months to complete. The curriculum includes 50% theory and 50% practice. After completing the programme, students may enter the labour market. This programme does not provide direct access to tertiary education. Those who complete lower secondary education may choose between two broad options of vocational upper secondary education at ISCED 3 level. Both programmes normally take three years to complete and offer a vocational degree as well as the baccalaureate, which is required for entry into tertiary education.

- The title "technical professional – baccalaureate" is offered by various subsystems though one subsystem (CONALEP) includes two thirds of the students. The programme involves 35% general subjects and 65% vocational subjects. Students are required to complete 360 hours of practical training.
- The programme awarding the "technological baccalaureate" and the title "professional technician" is offered by various subsystems. It includes more general and less vocational education: 60% general subjects and 40% vocational subjects.

The Netherlands

Nearly all of those leaving lower secondary school enter upper secondary education, and around 50% of them follow one of four vocational programmes; technology, economics, agricultural, personal/ social services & health care. These programmes vary from 1 to 4 years (by level; only level 2, 3 and 4 diplomas are considered formal 'start qualifications' for successfully entering the labour market). The programmes can be attended in either of two pathways. One either involving a minimum of 20% of school time (apprenticeship pathway; BBL-Beroeps Begeleidende Leerweg) or the other, involving a maximum of 80% schooltime (BOL -Beroeps Opleidende Leerweg). The remaining time is both cases is apprenticeship/work in a company. So in effect, students have a choice out of 32 trajectories, leading to over 600 professional qualifications. BBL-Apprentices usually receive a wage negotiated in collective agreements.

Employers taking on these apprentices receive a subsidy in the form of a tax reduction on the wages of the apprentice. (WVA-Wet vermindering afdracht). Level 4 graduates of senior secondary VET may go directly to institutes for Higher Profession Education and Training (HBO-Hoger beroepsonderwijs), after which entering university is a possibility. The social partners participate actively in the development of policy. As of January 1, 2012 they formed a foundation for Co operation Vocational Education and Entrepreneurship. Its responsibility is to advise the Minister on the development of the national vocational education and training system, based on the full consensus of the constituent members (the representative organisations of schools and of entrepreneurship and their centres of expertise). Special topics are Qualification & Examination, Apprenticeships and Efficiency of VET. The Centres of Expertices are linked to the four vocational education programmes provided in senior secondary VET on the content of VET programmes and on trends and future skill needs. The Local County Vocational Training represents the VET schools in this foundation and advise on the quality, operations and provision of VET.

New Zealand

New Zealand is served by 39 Industry Training Organisations (ITO). The unique element is that ITOs purchase training as well as set standards and aggregate industry opinion about skills in the labour market. Industry Training, as organised by ITOs, has expanded from apprenticeships to a more true lifelong learning situation with, for example, over 10% of trainees aged 50 or over. Moreover much of the training is generic. This challenges the prevailing idea of vocational education and the standard layperson view that it focuses on apprenticeships.

One source for information in New Zealand is the Industry Training Federation. Another is the Ministry of Education.

Polytechnics, Private Training Establishments, Wananga and others also deliver vocational training, amongst other areas.

Norway

Nearly all those leaving lower secondary school enter upper secondary education, and around half follow one of 9 vocational programmes. These programmes typically involve two years in school followed by two years of apprenticeship in a company. The first year provides general education alongside introductory knowledge of the vocational area. During the second year, courses become more trade-specific.

Apprentices receive a wage negotiated in collective agreements ranging between 30% and 80% of the wage of a qualified worker; the percentage increasing over the apprenticeship period. Employers taking on apprentices receive a subsidy, equivalent to the cost of one year in school. After the two years vocational school programme some students opt for a third year in the 'general' programme as an alternative to an apprenticeship. Both apprenticeship and a third year of practical training in school lead to the same vocational qualifications. Upper secondary VET graduates may go directly to Vocational Technical Colleges, while those who wish to enter university need to take a supplementary year of education.

The social partners participate actively in the development of policy. The National Council for Vocational Education and Training advises the Minister on the development of the national vocational education and training system. The Advisory Councils for Vocational Education and Training are linked to the nine vocational education programmes provided in upper secondary education and advise on the content of VET programmes and on trends and future skill needs. The National Curriculum groups assist in deciding the contents of the vocational training within the specific occupations. The Local County Vocational Training Committees advise on the quality, provision of VET and career guidance.

Paraguay

In Paraguay, vocational education is known as *Bachillerato Técnico* and is part of the secondary education system. These schools combine general education with some specific subjects, referred to as pre-vocational education and career orientation. After nine years of *Educación Escolar Básica* (Primary School), the student can choose to go to either a *Bachillerato Técnico* (Vocational School) or a *Bachillerato Científico* (High School). Both forms of secondary education last three years, and are usually located in the same campus called *Colegio*.

After completing secondary education, one can enter to the universities. It is also possible for a student to choose both Técnico and Científico schooling.

Russia

Sweden: Nearly all of those leaving compulsory schooling immediately enter upper secondary schools, and most complete their upper secondary education in three years. Upper secondary education is divided into 13 vocationally oriented and 4 academic national programmes. Slightly more than half of all students follow vocational programmes. All programmes offer broad general education and basic eligibility to continue studies at the post-secondary level. In addition, there are local programmes specially designed to meet local needs and 'individual' programmes.

A 1992 school reform extended vocational upper secondary programmes by one year, aligning them with three years of general upper secondary education, increasing their general education content, and making core subjects compulsory in all programmes. The core subjects (which occupy around one-third of total teaching time in both vocational and academic programmes) include English, artistic activities, physical education and health, mathematics, natural science, social studies, Swedish or Swedish as a second language, and religious studies. In addition to the core subjects, students pursue optional courses, subjects which are specific to each programme and a special project.

Vocational programmes include 15 weeks of workplace training over the three-year period. Schools are responsible for arranging workplace training and verifying its quality. Most municipalities have advisory bodies: programme councils and vocational councils composed of employers' and employees' representatives from the locality. The councils advise schools on matters such as provision of workplace training courses, equipment purchase and training of supervisors in APU.

Switzerland

Nearly two thirds of those entering upper secondary education enter the vocational education and training system. At this level, vocational education and training is mainly provided through the 'dual system'. Students spend some of their time in a vocational school; some of their time doing an apprenticeship at a host company; and for most programmes, students attend industry courses at an industry training centre to develop complementary practical skills relating to the occupation at hand. Common patterns are for students to spend one- two days per week at the vocational school and three-four days doing the apprenticeship at the host company; alternatively they alternate between some weeks attending classes at the vocational school and some weeks attending industry courses at an industry training centre. A different pattern is to begin the programme with most of the time devoted to in-school education and gradually diminishing the amount of in-school education in favour of more in-company training.

Switzerland draws a distinction between vocational education and training (VET) programmes at upper-secondary level, and professional education and training (PET) programmes, which take place at tertiary B level. In 2007, more than half of the population aged 25–64 had a VET or PET qualification as their highest level of education. In addition, universities of applied sciences (Fachhochschulen) offer vocational education at tertiary A level. Pathways enable people to shift from one part of the education system to another.

Turkey

Students in Turkey may choose vocational high schools after completing the 8-year-long compulsory primary education. Vocational high school graduates may pursue 2 year-long polytechnics or may continue with a related tertiary degree. Municipalities in Turkey also offer vocational training. The metropolitan municipality of Istanbul, the most populous city in Turkey, offers year long free vocational programmes in a wide range of topics through ISMEK, an umbrella organization formed under the municipality.

United Kingdom

The first "Trades School" in the UK was *Stanley Technical Trades School* (now Harris Academy South Norwood) which was designed, built and set up by William Stanley. The initial idea was thought of in 1901, and the school opened in 1907.

The system of vocational education in the UK initially developed independently of the state, with bodies such as the RSA and City & Guilds setting examinations for technical subjects. The Education Act 1944 made provision for a Tripartite System of grammar schools, secondary technical schools and secondary modern schools, but by 1975 only 0.5% of British senior pupils were in technical schools, compared to two-thirds of the equivalent German age group.

Successive recent British Governments have made attempts to promote and expand vocational education. In the 1970s, the Business And Technology Education Council was founded to confer further and higher education awards, particularly to further education colleges in the United Kingdom. In the 1980s and 1990s, the Conservative Government promoted the Youth Training Scheme, National Vocational Qualifications and General National Vocational Qualifications. However, youth training was marginalised as the proportion of young people staying on in full-time education increased.

In 1994, publicly funded Modern Apprenticeships were introduced to provide "quality training on a work-based (educational) route". Numbers of apprentices have grown in recent years and the Department for Children, Schools and Families has stated its intention to make apprenticeships a "mainstream" part of England's education system.

United States

In the United States, vocational education varies from state to state. The majority of postsecondary technical and vocational training is provided by proprietary (privately owned) career schools. About 30 percent of all credentials in career training are provided by two-year community colleges, which also offer courses transferable to four-year universities; other programmes are offered through military technical training government-operated adult education centres. Several states operate their own institutes of technology which are on an equal accreditational footing with other state universities.

Historically, middle schools and high schools have offered vocational courses such as home economics, wood and metal shop, typing, business courses, drafting, and auto repair, though schools have put more emphasis on academics for all students because of standards based education reform. School-to-Work is a series of federal and state initiatives to link academics to work, sometimes including spending time during the day on a job site without pay.

National Programmes

Federal involvement is principally carried out through the Carl D. Perkins Career and Technical Education Act. Accountability requirements tied to the receipt of federal funds under this Act help provide some overall leadership. The Office of Vocational and Adult Education within the US Department of Education also supervises activities funded by the Act, along with grants to individual states and other local programmes.

The Association for Career and Technical Education (ACTE) is the largest private association dedicated to the advancement of education that prepares youth and adults for careers. Its members include CTE teachers, administrators, and researchers.

Accreditation

There is however an issue with vocational or "career" schools who have national accreditation instead of regional accreditation. Regionally accredited schools are predominantly academically oriented, non-profit institutions. Nationally accredited schools are predominantly for-profit and offer vocational, career or technical programmes. Every college has the right to set standards and refuse to accept transfer credits. However, if a student has gone to a nationally accredited school it may be particularly difficult to transfer credits (or even credit for a degree earned) if he or she then applies to a regionally accredited college.

Some regionally accredited colleges have general policies against accepting any credits from nationally accredited schools, others are reluctant to because regional schools feel that national schools academic standards are lower than their own or they are unfamiliar with the particular school. Students who are planning to transfer to a regionally accredited school after studying at a nationally accredited school should ensure that they will be able to transfer the credits before attending the nationally accredited school. There have been lawsuits regarding nationally accredited schools who led prospective students to believe that they would have no problem transferring their credits to regionally accredited schools, most notably Florida Metropolitan University and Crown College, Tacoma, Washington. The U.S. Department of Education has stated, however, that its criteria for recognition of accreditors "do not differentiate between types of accrediting agencies, so the recognition granted to all types of accrediting agencies — regional, institutional, specialized, and programmatic — is identical." However the same letter states that "the specific scope of recognition varies according to the type of agency recognized."

Job retraining

In many states, vocational training is available to workers who have been previously laid off or whose previous employer is defunct; such training was expanded under the American Recovery and Reinvestment Act of 2009. Though results have been for the most part inconclusive, job retraining programmes have been noted to retain a positive effect on employee morale. Even in cases of displacement, those who underwent job retraining programmes exhibited a more positive outlook on their circumstances than those employees who did not partake in job retraining programmes. Several studies have also suggested that in cases of layoffs, employees who remain with the company exhibit positive morale and are more motivated in their work environment if the layoffs are handled effectively by the company. Job retraining programmes in the United States are often criticized for their lack of proper focus on skills that are required in existing jobs. A 2009 study by the United States Department of Labour showed that the difference in earnings and chances of being re-hired between those who had been trained and those who had not been was small.

History

In the early years of the twentieth century, a number of efforts were made to imitate German-style industrial education in the United States. Researchers such as Holmes Beckwith described the relationship between the apprenticeship and continuation school models in Germany, and suggested variants of the system that could be applied in an American context. The industrial education system evolved, after large-scale growth following World War I, into modern vocational education.

New York City's New CTE High Schools: In 2008, New York City's Department of Education began to rethink vocational training in high schools. Mayor Bloomberg in his State of the City 2008 address said, "This year, we're going to begin dramatically transforming how high school students prepare for technical careers in a number of growing fields. Traditionally, such career and technical education has been seen as an educational dead-end. We're going to change that. College isn't for everyone, but education is. Building on work by the State Education Department, we'll do what no other public school system in the nation has done- create rigorous career and technical programmes that start in high schools and continue in our community colleges" A hallmark of New York City public education is school choice. One category of schools students could choose since the early 20th Century has been the vocational high school. In recent years, several new CTE high schools have been started in New York City or reforged with a new perspective.

The idea behind this reconfiguration of CTE is that vocational positions are becoming increasingly sophisticated and a high school degree will not be sufficient training. Future vocational technicians will need college training. The new CTE schools prepare students for success college in addition to providing a vocational certification. A new vocational high school, called City Polytechnic High School, will allow students to take college courses while still in high school. While many high schools in New York City offer college courses as part of their curriculum, City Poly, as the school is known, is the first to offer programmes in technical fields. Students will graduate in five years instead of the usual four, with a high school diploma and an associate's degree.

Some famous New York City CTE schools include—

- Aviation High School (New York), founded in 1925, known for supplying 12 percent of all of the workers on aircraft worldwide and sending several graduates to high level engineering programmes, such as Columbia School of Engineering and Applied Science and Massachusetts Institute of Technology. Famous alumni include Whitey Ford and Michael Bentt.
- High School of Art and Design, founded 1936, whose famous alumni include Tony Bennett, Lenny White, Tom Sito, and several others.
- Urban Assembly New York Harbor School, founded 2003, known for being the first non-U.S. Military organization to be housed on Governors Island in New York City Harbor since the Lenape. The school is also known for sending graduates to Cornell

University and other prestigious schools in addition to supplying well-trained workers on New York City's 600 mile waterfront. This school has the second certified SCUBA training programme in a high school in the U.S.

Apprenticeship

Apprenticeship is a system of training a new generation of practitioners of a structured competency a basic set of skills. Apprenticeships ranged from craft occupations or trades to those seeking a professional license to practice in a regulated profession. Apprentices (or in early modern usage "prentices") or protégés build their careers from apprenticeships. Most of their training is done while working for an employer who helps the apprentices learn their trade or profession, in exchange for their continuing labour for an agreed period after they have achieved measurable competencies. For more advanced apprenticeships, theoretical education was also involved, with jobs and farming over a period of 4–6 years.

To be successful, the individual must have perseverance, ambition, and initiative. Like a college education, the successful completion of an apprenticeship term does not come easily, but is the result of hard work on the part of the apprentice. In practically every skilled occupation, more than fundamental knowledge of arithmetic is essential. The ability to read, write and speak well is beneficial in any walk of life, but in some apprenticeship occupations it is more important than in others.

Development

Figure: *A medieval baker with his apprentice. The Bodleian Library, Oxford.*

The system of apprenticeship first developed in the later Middle Ages and came to be supervised by craft guilds and town governments. A master craftsman was entitled to employ young people as an inexpensive form of labour in exchange for providing food, lodging and formal training in the craft. Most apprentices were males, but female apprentices were found in crafts such as seamstress, tailor, cordwainer, baker and stationer. Apprentices usually began at ten to fifteen years of age, and would live in the master craftsman's household. Most apprentices aspired to becoming master craftsmen themselves on completion of their contract (usually a term of seven years), but some would spend time as a journeyman and a significant proportion would never acquire their own workshop.

In Coventry those completing seven-year apprenticeships with stuff merchants were entitled to become freemen of the city.

Subsequently governmental regulation and the licensing of technical colleges and vocational education formalized and bureaucratized the details of apprenticeship.

Educational Theory of Apprenticeship

The Apprentice Perspective is an educational theory of apprenticeship concerning the process of learning through physical integration into the practices associated with the subject, such as workplace training. By developing similar performance to other practitioners, an apprentice will come to understand the tacit (informally taught) duties of the position. In the process of creating this awareness, the learner also affect their environment; as they are accepted by master practitioners, their specific talents and contributions within the field are taken into account and integrated into the overall practice.

The Apprenticeship Perspective can be used to teach procedures to students. For example, tying a shoe, building a fire, and taking blood can all use the Apprenticeship Perspective to teach students these skills. However, it can be used to develop master practitioners in fields that involve increased complexity, numerous webs of interaction, or shifting environments demanding constant attention. Driver education, flight training and sports training all use the Apprenticeship Perspective for learners to learn a specific skill.

Educational Theory of Apprenticeship

Unlike most other perspectives of education, the Apprenticeship Perspective is rarely formally taught. This is because the concepts communicated through apprenticeship are often practical, tacit strategies for achieving goals that do not always conform to standard procedure. For example, in an office environment lunch breaks may be limited to thirty minutes, but through apprenticeship one learns that up to forty-five minutes is acceptable. It would be inconvenient for the company to formally allow that allotment, but through informal training the message may still be communicated.

Educational theories of apprenticeship often involve the combination of formal and information training for the development of schema, mental structures that represent individual understanding of experiences that frame a person's conceptualization of reality. For example, a bicycle mechanic accustomed to road cycling may study texts covering mountain biking, but he will probably find it difficult to apply that formal training on a rough course. Educational theory's response to this is apprenticeship; by riding with a friend on the mountain side, the cyclist can watch and learn, constantly reiterating his performance to meet the demands of the sport. In this way he is developing his schema through formal and informal training.

The Apprentice Perspective is a holistic field of learning because it involves the education of both the student and the teacher. As the learner develops a schema that begins to incorporate the intricacies of the environment, they will be more capable of performing similarly to their peers. Once this is recognized by the trainer, the student will become accepted as a peer; at this point, as the new worker tackles problems through their new and previously existing schema, their individual talents may start to be applied within the group practices. In this way, apprenticeship retains fresh information and ideas within a common body of knowledge.

Factors of Success in Apprenticeship

According to Pratt (1998), successful development through apprenticeship involves three key factors. To become a master of the field, the learning process must be active, social, and authentic. These points will lead to the learner's greater understanding of the field and improved future contributions:

- Activity concerns the level to which the learner is physically and mentally stimulated within the environment. Successful trainers allow the student to be highly involved in the processes of decision making and action because they know that it is the doing that will have the most effect on the student's schema. In training to drive an automobile, students will never be able to pass without a physical examination of driving ability. To prepare for this, learners are given the opportunity to drive in safe areas. This active use of the tool prepares the student for its later, tested use.

- Second is the concept of sociality. Students must interact constantly with the tools for success, the teachers and the beneficiaries of the work. This holistic approach will further integrate the student into the interrelated web of action and consequence within the field. For example, a server training at a restaurant will not only follow a more experienced server, but interact with the customers, fellow employees, and management in the same time frame. The server will thus establish connections between all these groups and the personnel that embody them, preparing the server for day to day activities.
- Finally, authenticity is essential to apprenticeship. This is the establishment of a mental connection between the work of the student in a particular field and the comprehension of the greater public. An electrical engineer may understand the intricacies and challenges of computer panels, but this is only half of the required knowledge. They must also learn how most people perceive these panels and their interaction with them. From this understanding of the other end of spectrum, the engineer will better understand the achievement and thus authenticity of the community of electrical engineering.

Apprenticeship Phases

The Apprenticeship Perspective includes a series of phases that help articulate the roles of the learner and teacher during the process of observing and enacting concepts.

- Phase I: Modelling - The complete act is observed and contemplated. This means that the smaller parts that make up the whole are not yet examined in depth. The observer first frames the larger experience and will be able to specify from there(). "Modelling occurs in two parts: behavioural modelling allows learners to observe performance of an activity by experienced members to share "tricks of the trade" with news members" (Hansman, 2001, p. 47). The learner is using articulation and domain-specific heuristics in this phase (Brandt et al., 1993).
- Phase II: Approximating - In private or in non-critical scenarios, the observer begins to mimic the actions of the teacher. Through

close guidance, the learner begins to articulate more clearly the teacher's actions. This phase allows the learner to try the activity and lets them think about what they plan to do and why they plan to do it. Then after the activity the learner reflects about the activity. They examine what the did in comparison to what the expert did.

- Phase III: Fading - The learner, still within the safety net, starts operating in a more detailed manner, playing within the structure that has been taught. The learner's capabilities are increased as the experts assistance decreases (Hansman, 2001).
- Phase IV: Self-directed Learning - The learner attempts the actions within real society, limiting him/herself to the scope of actions in the field that are well-understood(). The learner is performing the actual task and only seeking assistance when needed from the expert (Hansman, 2001).
- Phase V: Generalizing - The learner generalizes what has been learned, trying to apply those skills to multiple scenarios and continuing to grow in ability in the field. The learner uses discussion in this phase to relate that they have learned to other relevant situations (Hansman, 2001).

Goals of Apprenticeship

There are three main goals of apprenticeship learning according to Brandt et al. (1993).

- The first goal is for the adult learner to discover what works. This does not mean for the learner to use problem solving learning and figure out the situation on their own. There is guidance provided. The learner uses skills learned from the expert in order to successfully solve a problem.
- Secondly, the learner recognizes tasks, problems or situations and knows how to handle them.

  The learner learns the appropriate practical and theoretical knowledge. Learners are not learning this knowledge in isolation from other students. Students are working in a social setting with lifelike scenarios in order to learn a specific task.
- Finally, the learner is able to perform at an acceptable level. The learner is not learning basic skills at a novice level but working with an expert in order to perform at an acceptable level. Students are not learning skills at a basic level but rather at a level that is accepted in the specific industry.

These three goals have been accomplished based on published literature, learners feel apprenticeship "learning experience expands their awareness of the factors that should be considered' helps them organize and pay attention to their thought processes while handling difficult tasks, problems, and problematic situations; and emphasizes the importance of particular aspects of such tasks, problems, and problematic situations previously ignored or regarded as unimportant" (Brandt et al., 1993). Clearly the three goals of apprenticeship learning have been accomplished. Learners have been able to discover what works in situations, and knows how to handles problems and finally the learner can perform at a satisfactory level.

Analogs at Universities and Professional Development

The modern concept of an internship is similar to an apprenticeship. Universities still use apprenticeship schemes in their production of scholars: bachelors are promoted to masters and then produce a thesis under the oversight of a supervisor before the corporate body of the university recognises the achievement of the standard of a doctorate. Another view of this system is of graduate students in the role of apprentices, post-doctoral fellows as journeymen, and professors as masters.

Also similar to apprenticeships are the professional development arrangements for new graduates in the professions of accountancy, Chartered Engineer and the law. A British example was training contracts known as 'articles of clerkship'. The learning curve in modern professional service firms, such as law firms or accountancies, generally resembles the traditional master-apprentice model: the newcomer to the firm is assigned to one or several more experienced colleagues (ideally partners in the firm) and learns his skills on the job.

Australia

Australian Apprenticeships encompass all apprenticeships and traineeships. They cover all industry sectors in Australia and are used to achieve both 'entry-level' and career 'upskilling' objectives. There were 470,000 Australian Apprentices in-training as at 31 March 2012, an increase of 2.4% from the previous year. Australian Government employer and employee incentives may be applicable, while State and Territory Governments may provide public funding support for the training element of the initiative. Australian Apprenticeships combine time at work with formal training and can be full-time, part-time or school-based.

Information and resources on potential apprenticeship and traineeship occupations are available in over sixty industries.

The distinction between the terms apprentices and trainees lies mainly around traditional trades and the time it takes to gain a qualification. The Australian government uses Australian Apprenticeships Centres to administer and facilitate Australian Apprenticeships so that funding can be disseminated to eligible businesses and apprentices and trainees and to support the whole process as it underpins the future skills of Australian industry. Australia also has a fairly unique safety net in place for businesses and Australian Apprentices with its Group Training scheme.

This is where businesses that are not able to employ the Australian Apprentice for the full period until they qualify, are able to lease or hire the Australian Apprentice from a Group Training Organisation. It is a safety net, because the Group Training Organisation is the employer and provides continuity of employment and training for the Australian Apprentice.

In addition to a safety net, Group Training Organisations (GTO) have other benefits such as additional support for both the Host employer and the trainee/apprentice through an industry consultant who visits regularly to make sure that the trainee/apprentice are fulfilling their work and training obligations with their Host employer. There is the additional benefit of the trainee/apprentice being employed by the GTO reducing the Payroll/Superannuation and other legislative requirements on the Host employer who pays as invoiced per agreement.

Austria

Apprenticeship Training in Austria is organized in a Dual education system: company-based training of apprentices is complemented by compulsory attendance of a part-time vocational school for apprentices (Berufsschule). It lasts two to four years – the duration varies among the 250 legally recognized apprenticeship trades.

About 40 percent of all Austrian teenagers enter apprenticeship training upon completion of compulsory education (at age 15). This number has been stable since the 1950s.

The five most popular trades are: Retail Salesperson (5,000 people complete this apprenticeship per year), Clerk (3,500 / year), Car Mechanic (2,000 / year), Hairdresser (1,700 / year), Cook (1,600 / year). There are many smaller trades with small numbers of apprentices, like "EDV-Systemtechniker" (Sysadmin) which is completed by fewer than 100 people a year.

The Apprenticeship Leave Certificate provides the apprentice with access to two different vocational careers.

On the one hand, it is a prerequisite for the admission to the Master Craftsman Exam and for qualification tests, and on the other hand it gives access to higher education via the TVE-Exam or the Higher Education Entrance Exam which are prerequisites for taking up studies at colleges, universities, "Fachhochschulen", post-secondary courses and post-secondary colleges.

The person responsible for overseeing the training inside the company is called "Lehrherr" or "Ausbilder". An Ausbilder must prove he has the professional qualifications needed to educate another person. The "Ausbilder" must also prove he does not have a criminal record and is an otherwise respectable person. According to the laws: *the person wanting to educate a young apprentice must prove that he has an ethical way of living and the civic qualities of a good citizen.*

Switzerland

Switzerland has an apprenticeship similarly to Germany and Austria. The educational system is ternar, which is basically Dual education system with mandatory practical courses. The length of an apprenticeship can be 2, 3 or 4 years.

Length

Apprenticeship with a length of 2 years are for persons with weaker school results. The certificated after successfully completing an 2 year apprenticeship is called "Eidgenössisches Berufsattest" (EBA).

Apprenticeship with a length of 3 or 4 years are the most common ones. The certificated after successfully completing an 3 or 4 year apprenticeship is called "Certificat Fédérale de Capacité" (CFC) or "Eidgenössisches Fähigkeitszeugnis" (EFZ).

Some crafts like Electrician are educated in length of 3 and 4 years. In this case, an Electrician with 4 years apprenticeship gets more theoretical background than one with 3 years apprenticeship. Also, but that is easily lost in translation, the profession has a different name.

Each of the over 300 nationwide defined vocational profiles has defined framework - conditions as length of education, theoreticla and practical learning goals and certification conditions.

Age of the Apprentices

Typically an apprenticeship is started at age of 15 and 18 after finishing general education. Some apprenticeships have a recommend or required age of 18, which obviously leads to a higher average age. There is formally no maximum age, however for persons above 21 it is hard to find company.

Canada

In Canada, each province has its own apprenticeship programme. At the completion of the provincial exam they may write the Interprovincal Standard exam. British Columbia is one province that uses these exams as the provincial exam. This means a qualification for the province will satisfy the whole country. The interprovincal exam questions are agreed upon by all provinces.

France

In France, apprenticeships also developed between the ninth and thirteenth centuries, with guilds structured around apprentices, journeymen and master craftsmen, continuing in this way until 1791, when the guilds were suppressed.

The first laws regarding apprenticeships were passed in 1851. From 1919, young people had to take 150 hours of theory and general lessons in their subject a year. This minimum training time rose to 360 hours a year in 1961, then 400 in 1986.

The first training centres for apprentices (*centres de formation d'apprentis*, CFAs) appeared in 1961, and in 1971 apprenticeships were legally made part of professional training. In 1986 the age limit for beginning an apprenticeship was raised from 20 to 25. From 1987 the range of qualifications achieveable through an apprenticeship was widened to include the *brevet professionnel* (certificate of vocational aptitude), the *bac professionnel* (vocational baccalaureate diploma), the *brevet de technicien supérieur* (advanced technician's certificate), engineering diplomas, masters degree and more.

On January 18, 2005, President Jacques Chirac announced the introduction of a law on a programme for social cohesion comprising the three pillars of employment, housing and equal opportunities. The French government pledged to further develop apprenticeship as a path to success at school and to employment, based on its success: in 2005, 80% of young French people who had completed an apprenticeship entered employment. In France, the term apprenticeship often denotes manual labour but it also include other jobs like secretary, manager, engineer, shop assistant... The plan aimed to raise the number of apprentices from 365,000 in 2005 to 500,000 in 2009. To achieve this aim, the government is, for example, granting tax relief for companies when they take on apprentices. (Since 1925 a tax has been levied to pay for apprenticeships.) The minister in charge of the campaign, Jean-Louis Borloo, also hoped to improve the image of apprenticeships with an information campaign, as they are often connected with academic failure at school and an ability to grasp only practical skills and not theory.

After the civil unrest end of 2005, the government, led by prime minister Dominique de Villepin, announced a new law. Dubbed "law on equality of chances", it created the First Employment Contract as well as manual apprenticeship from as early as 14 years of age. From this age, students are allowed to quit the compulsory school system in order to quickly learn a vocation. This measure has long been a policy of conservative French political parties, and was met by tough opposition from trade unions and students.

Germany

Apprenticeships are part of Germany's dual education system, and as such form an integral part of many people's working life. Finding employment without having completed an apprenticeship is almost impossible. For some particular technical university professions, such as food technology, a completed apprenticeship is often recommended; for some, such as marine engineering it may even be mandatory.

In Germany, there are 342 recognized trades (*Ausbildungsberufe*) where an apprenticeship can be completed. They include for example doctor's assistant, banker, dispensing optician, plumber or oven builder. The dual system means that apprentices spend about 50-70% of their time in companies and the rest in formal education. Depending on the profession, they may work for three to four days a week in the company and then spend one or two days at a vocational school (*Berufsschule*). This is usually the case for trade and craftspeople. For other professions, usually which require more theoretical learning, the working and school times take place blockwise e.g. in a 12–18 weeks interval. These *Berufsschulen* have been part of the education system since the 19th century.

In 2001, two thirds of young people aged under 22 began an apprenticeship, and 78% of them completed it, meaning that approximately 51% of all young people under 22 have completed an apprenticeship. One in three companies offered apprenticeships in 2003, in 2004 the government signed a pledge with industrial unions that all companies except very small ones must take on apprentices.

The latent decrease of the German population due to low birth rates is now causing a lack of young people available to start an apprenticeship.

Apprenticeship after General Education

After graduation from school at the age of fifteen to nineteen (depending on type of school), students start an apprenticeship in their chosen professions. Realschule and Gymnasium graduates usually have better chances for being accepted as an apprentice for sophisticated craft professions or apprenticeships in white-collar jobs in finance or administration. An apprenticeship takes between 2.5 and 3.5 years. Originally, at the beginning of the 20th century, less than 1% of German students attended the Gymnasium (the 8-9 year university-preparatory school) to obtain the Abitur graduation which was the only way to university back then. In the 1950 still only 5% of German youngsters entered university and in 1960 only 6% did. Due to the risen social wealth and the increased demand for academic professionals in Germany, about 24% of the youngsters entered college/university in 2000. Of those, who did not enter university many started an apprenticeship. The apprenticeships usually end a person's education by age 18-20, but also older apprentices are accepted by the employers under certain conditions. This is frequently the case for immigrants from countries without a compatible professional training system.

History

In 1969, a law (the *Berufsbildungsgesetz*) was passed which regulated and unified the vocational training system and codified the shared responsibility of the state, the unions, associations and the chambers of trade and industry. The dual system was successful in both parts of the divided Germany. In the GDR, three quarters of the working population had completed apprenticeships.

Business and Administrative Professions

The precise skills and theory taught on German apprenticeships are strictly regulated. The employer is responsible for the entire education programme coordinated by the German chamber of commerce. Apprentices obtain a special apprenticeship contract until the end of the education programme. During the programme it is not allowed to assign the apprentice to a regularly employment and he is well protected from abrupt dismissal until the programme ends. The defined content and skillset of the apprentice profession must be fully provided and taught by the employer. The time taken is also regulated. Each profession takes a different time, usually between 24 and 36 months.

Thus, everyone who had completed an apprenticeship e.g. as an industrial manager (*Industriekaufmann*) has learned the same skills and has attended the same courses in procurement and stocking up, controlling, staffing, accounting procedures, production planning, terms of trade and transport logistics and various other subjects. Someone who has not taken this apprenticeship or did not pass the final examinations at the chamber of industry and commerce is not allowed to call himself an *Industriekaufmann*. Most job titles are legally standardized and restricted. An employment in such function in any company would require this completed degree.

Trade and Craft Professions

The rules and laws for the trade and craftswork apprentices such as mechanics, bakers, joiners, etc. are as strict as and even broader than for the business professions. The involved procedures, titles and traditions still strongly reflect the medieval origin of the system. Here, the average duration is about 36 months, some specialized crafts even take up to 42 months.

After completion of the dual education, e.g. a baker is allowed to call himself a bakery journeyman (*Bäckergeselle*). After the apprenticeship the journeyman can enter the master's school (*Meisterschule*) and continue his education at evening courses for 3–4 years or full-time for about one year. The graduation from the master's school leads to the title of a master craftsman (*Meister*) of his profession, so e.g. a bakery master is entitled as *Bäckermeister*. A master is officially entered in the local trade register, the craftspeople's roll (*Handwerksrolle*). A master craftsman is allowed to employ and to train new apprentices. In some mostly safety-related professions, e.g. that of electricians only a master is allowed to found his own company.

License for Educating Apprentices

To employ and to educate apprentices requires a specific license. The AdA - *Ausbildung der Ausbilder* - "Education of the Educators" license needs to be acquired by a training at the chamber of industry and commerce.

The masters complete this license course within their own master's coursework. The training and examination of new masters is only possible for masters who have been working several years in their profession and who have been accepted by the chambers as a trainer and examiner. Academic professionals, e.g. engineers, seeking this license need to complete the AdA during or after their university studies, usually by a one-year evening course.

The holder of the license is only allowed to train apprentices within his own field of expertise. For example a mechanical engineer would be able to educate industrial mechanics, but not e.g. laboratory assistants or civil builders.

After the Apprenticeship of Trade and Craft Professions

When the apprenticeship is ended, the former apprentice now is considered a journeyman. He may choose to go on his journeyman years-travels.

India

In India, the Apprentices Act was enacted in 1961. It regulates the programme of training of apprentices in the industry so as to conform to the syllabi, period of training etc. as laid down by the Central Apprenticeship Council and to utilise fully the facilities available in industry for imparting practical training with a view to meeting the requirements of skilled manpower for industry.

The Apprentices Act enacted in 1961 and was implemented effectively in 1962. Initially the Act envisaged training of trade apprentices. The Act was amended in 1973 to include training of graduate and diploma engineers as "Graduate" & "Technician" Apprentices. The Act was further amended in 1986 to bring within its purview the training of the 10+2 vocational stream as "Technician (Vocational)" Apprentices. Overall responsibility is with the Directorate General of Employment & Training (DGE&T) in the Union Ministry of Labour. DGE&T is also responsible for implementation of the Act in respect of Trade Apprentices in the Central Govt. Undertakings & Departments. This is done through six Regional Directorates of Apprenticeship Training located at Kolkata, Mumbai, Chennai, Hyderabad, Kanpur & Faridabad.

State Apprenticeship Advisers are responsible for implementation of the Act in respect of Trade Apprentices in State Government Undertakings/ Departments and Private Establishments. Department of Education in the Ministry of HRD is responsible for implementation of the Act in respect of Graduate, Technician & Technician (Vocational) Apprentices. This is done through four Boards of Apprenticeship Training located at Kanpur, Kolkata, Mumbai & Chennai.1

Pakistan

In Pakistan, special apprenticeship programmes running to fulfill the needs of IT industry in the coming years. So, for this purpose Pakistan Software Export Board formerly PSEB has launched a very attractive programme for young IT graduates.

Under the IT Industry Apprenticeship Programme, PSEB offers financial subsidy for the companies to recruit graduates possessing the basic skills and knowledge in Information Technology and other related disciplines to provide IT/ITeS services. These recruits, generally graduates with some experience rather than traditional apprentices, are hired by companies as full-time employees and put through a 12-month programme, consisting of in-company training, on-the-job training and mentoring. Since its launch, the IT Industry Apprenticeship Programme has been awarded to 7 companies, approved by PSEB and ICT R&D Fund's Project Committee, which will result in the creation of over 700 job opportunities in the IT industry.

Turkey

In Turkey, apprenticeship has been part of the small business culture for centuries since the time of Seljuk Turks who claimed Anatolia as their homeland in 11th century. There are three levels of apprenticeship. First level is the apprentice, i.e. the "çýrak" in Turkish. The second level is pre-master which is called, "kalfa" in Turkish. The mastery level is called as "usta" and is the highest level of achievement. An 'usta' is eligible to take in and accept new 'ciraks' to train and bring them up. The training process usually starts when the small boy is of age 10-11 and becomes a full grown master at the age of 20-25. Many years of hard work and disciplining under the authority of the master is the key to the young apprentice's education and learning process.

In Turkey today there are many vocational schools that train children to gain skills to learn a new profession. The student after graduation looks for a job at the nearest local marketplace usually under the authority of a master.

United Kingdom

Early history: Apprenticeships have a long tradition in the United Kingdom, dating back to around the 12th century and flourishing by the 14th century. The parents or guardians of a minor would agree with a Guild's Master craftsman the conditions for an apprenticeship which would bind the minor for 5–9 years (e.g. from age 14 to 21). They would pay a premium to the craftsman and the contract would be recorded in an indenture. In 1563, the Statute of Artificers and Apprentices was passed to regulate and protect the apprenticeship system, forbidding anyone from practising a trade or craft without first serving a 7-year period as an apprentice to a master (though in practice Freemen's sons could negotiate shorter terms).

From 1601, 'parish' apprenticeships under the Elizabethan Poor Law came to be used as a way of providing for poor, illegitimate and orphaned children of both sexes alongside the regular system of skilled apprenticeships, which tended to provide for boys from slightly more affluent backgrounds. These parish apprenticeships, which could be created with the assent of two Justices of the Peace, supplied apprentices for occupations of lower status such as farm labouring, brickmaking and menial household service.

In the early years of the Industrial Revolution entrepreneurs began to resist the restrictions of the apprenticeship system, and a legal ruling established that the Statute of Apprentices did not apply to trades that were not in existence when it was passed in 1563, thus excluding many new 18th century industries. In 1814 compulsory apprenticeship by indenture was abolished.

System Introduced in 1964

The mainstay of training in industry has been the apprenticeship system, and the main concern has been to avoid skill shortages in traditionally skilled occupations and higher technician and engineering professionals, e.g. through the UK Industry Training Boards (ITBs) set up under the 1964 Act. The aims were to ensure an adequate supply of training at all levels; to improve the quality and quantity of training; and to share the costs of training among employers. The ITBs were empowered to publish training recommendations, which contained full details of the tasks to be learned, the syllabus to be followed, the standards to be reached and vocational courses to be followed. These were often accompanied by training manuals, which were in effect practitioners' guides to apprentice training, and some ITBs provide training in their own centres. The ITBs did much to formalize what could have been a haphazard training experience and greatly improved its quality. The years from the mid-1960s to the mid-1970s saw the highest levels of apprentice recruitment, yet even so, out of a school leaving cohort of about 750,000, only about 110,000 (mostly boys) became apprentices. The apprenticeship system aimed at highly developed craft and higher technician skills for an elite minority of the workforce, the majority of whom were trained in industries that declined rapidly from 1973 onwards, and by the 1980s it was clear that in manufacturing this decline was permanent.

Since the 1950s the UK high technology industry (Aerospace, Nuclear, Oil & Gas, Automotive, Telecommunications, Power Generation and Distribution etc.) trained its higher technicians and professional engineers via the traditional indentured apprenticeship system of learning - usually a 4 - 6 year process from age 16–21. There were 4 types of traditional apprenticeship; craft, technician, higher technician, and graduate. Craft, technician and higher technician apprenticeships usually took 4 to 5 years while a graduate apprenticeship was a short 2 year experience usually while at university or post graduate experience. Non graduate technician apprenticeships were often referred to as technical apprenticeships.

The traditional Apprenticeship Framework in the 1950s, 60's and 70's was designed to allow young people (16 years old) an alternative path to GCE A Levels to achieve both an academic qualification at level 4 or 5 NVQ along with competency based skills for knowledge work. Often referred to as the "Golden Age" of work and employment for bright young people, the traditional technical apprenticeship framework was open to young people who had a minimum of 4 GCE "O" Levels to enroll in an Ordinary National Certificate or Diploma or a City & Guilds engineering technician course. Apprentices could progress to the Higher National Certificate, Higher National Diploma or advanced City and Guilds course such as Full Technological Certification. Apprenticeship positions at elite companies often had hundreds of applications for a placement. Academic learning during an apprenticeship was achieved either via block release or day release at a local technical institute.

An OND or HND were usually obtained via the block release approach whereby an apprentice would be released for periods of up to 3 months to study academic courses full-time and then return to the employer for applied work experience. For entrance into the higher technical engineering apprenticeships "O"Levels had to include Mathematics, Physics, and English language. The academic level of subjects such as mathematics, physics, chemistry on ONC / OND and some City & Guilds advanced technicians courses was equivalent to A level mathematics, physics and chemistry. The academic science subjects were based on applied science in subjects such as thermodynamics, fluid mechanics, mechanics of machines, dynamics and statics, electrical science and electronics. These are often referred to as the engineering sciences . HNC and HND were broadly equivalent to subjects in the first year of a Bachelors degree in engineering but not studied to the same intensity or mathematical depth. HNC was accepted as entrance into the first year of an engineering degree and high performance on an HND course could allow a student direct entry into the second year of a degree. Few apprentices followed this path since it would have meant 10 –12 years in further and higher education. For the few that did follow this path they accomplished a solid foundation of competency based work training via apprenticeship and attained a higher academic qualifications at a university or Polytechnic combining both forms of education; vocational plus academic. During the 1970s City and Guilds assumed responsibility for the administration of HNC and HND courses.

The City and Guilds of London Institute the forerunner of Imperial College engineering school has been offering vocational education through apprenticeships since the 1870s from basic craft skills (mechanic, hairdresser, chef, plumbing, carpentry, bricklaying etc.) all the way up to qualifications equivalent to university masters degrees and doctorates. The City and Guilds diploma of fellowship is awarded to individuals who are nationally recognized through peer review as having achieved the very highest level in competency based achievement. The first award of FCGI was approved by Council in December 1892 and awarded in 1893 to Mr H A Humphrey, Engineering Manager of the Refined Bicarbonate and Crystal Plant Departments of Messrs Brunner, Mond & Co. His award was for material improvements in the manufacture of bicarbonate of soda. The system of nomination was administered within Imperial College, with recommendations being passed to the Council of the Institute for approval. Approximately 500 plus people have been awarded Fellowship since its inception.

The traditional apprenticeship framework's purpose was to provide a supply of young people seeking to enter work-based learning via apprenticeships by offering structured high value learning and transferable skills and knowledge. Apprenticeship training was enabled by linking industry with local technical colleges and professional engineering institutions. The apprenticeship framework offered a clear pathway and competency outcomes that addressed the issues facing the industry sector and specific companies. This system was in place since the 1950s. The system provided young people with an alternative to staying in full-time education post- 16/18 to gain purely academic qualifications without work-based learning. The apprenticeship system of the 1950s 60's and 70's provided the necessary preparation for young people to qualify as a Craft trade (Machinist, Toolmaker, Fitter, Plumber, Welder, Mechanic, Millwright etc.), or Technician (quality inspector, draughtsman, designer, planner, work study, programmer, or Technician Engineer (tool design, product design, methods, stress and structural analysis, machine design etc.) and even enabled a path to full Chartered Engineer registration (Mechanical, Electrical, Civil. Aeronautical, Chemical, Manufacturing etc.). Chartered Engineer registration was usually achieved in the late 20's early 30's. Apprentices undertook a variety of job roles in numerous shop floor and office technical functions to assist the work of master craftsmen, technicians, engineers, and managers in the design, development, manufacture and maintenance of products and production systems.

It was possible for apprentices to progress from national certificates and diplomas to engineering degrees if they had the aptitude. Reference "The social production of technical work: the case of British engineers" Peter Whalley, SUNY Press 1986. The system allowed young people to find their level and still achieve milestones along the path from apprenticeship into higher education via a polytechnic or university. Though rare, it was possible for an apprentice to advance from vocational studies, to undergraduate degree, to graduate study and earn a masters degree or a PhD. The system was effective; industry was assured of a supply of well educated and fit for work staff, local technical colleges offered industry relevant courses that had a high measure of academic content and an apprentice was prepared for professional life or higher education by the age of 21. With the exception of advanced technology companies particularly in aerospace (BAE systems, Rolls Royce, Bombardier) this system declined with the decline of general manufacturing industry in the UK.

Traditional apprenticeships reached their lowest point in the 1980s: by that time, training programmes declined. The exception to this was in the high technology engineering areas of aerospace, chemicals, nuclear, automotive, power and energy systems where apprentices continued to served the structured four- to five-year programmes of both practical and academic study to qualify as engineering technician or Incorporate Engineer (engineering technologist) and even go on to earn a master of engineering degree and qualify as a Chartered Engineer; the UK gold standard engineering qualification. Engineering technicians and technologists continued in the traditional approach from the golden age attended the local technical college (1 day and 2 evenings per week) on a City & Guilds programme or Ordinary National Certificate / Higher National Certificate course. In effect becoming a chartered engineer via the apprenticeship route involved 10 – 12 years of both academic and vocational training at an employer, college of further education and university. In 1986 National Vocational Qualifications (NVQs) were introduced, in an attempt to revitalize vocational training. Still, by 1990, apprenticeship took up only two-thirds of one percent of total employment.

Revitalisation from 1990s on

In 1994, the Government introduced Modern Apprenticeships (since renamed 'Apprenticeships' in England, Wales and Northern Ireland; Scotland has retained Modern Apprenticeship), based on frameworks that are now devised by Sector Skills Councils. Apprenticeship frameworks contain a number of separately certified elements:

- a knowledge-based element, typically certified through a qualification known as a 'Technical Certificate' (this component is not mandatory in the Scottish Modern Apprenticeship);
- a competence-based element, typically certified through an NVQ (in Scotland this can be through an SVQ or an alternative Competence Based Qualification);
- Key Skills (in Scotland, Core Skills); and
- Employment Rights and Responsibilities (known as ERR) to show that the Apprentice has had a full induction to the company or training programme, and is aware of those right and responsibilities that are essential in the workplace; this usually requires the creation of a personal portfolio of activities, reading and instruction sessions, but is not examined.

In Scotland, Modern Apprenticeship Frameworks are approved by the Modern Apprenticeship Group (MAG) and it, with the support of the Scottish Government, has determined that from January 2010, all Frameworks submitted to it for approval, must have the mandatory elements credit rated for the Scottish Credit and Qualifications Framework (SCQF).

As of 2009 there are over 180 apprenticeship frameworks. The current scheme extends beyond manufacturing and high technology industry to parts of the service sector with no apprenticeship tradition. In 2008 Creative & Cultural Skills, the Sector Skills Council, introduced a set of Creative Apprenticeships awarded by EDI. A freelance apprenticeship framework was also approved and uses freelance professionals to mentor freelance apprentices. The Freelance Apprenticeship was first written and proposed by Karen Akroyd (Access To Music) in 2008. In 2011 Freelance Music Apprenticeships are available in music colleges in Birmingham, Manchester and London. The Department for Children, Schools and Families has stated its intention to make apprenticeships a "mainstream" part of England's education system.

Employers who offer apprenticeship places have an employment contract with their apprentices, but off-the-job training and assessment is wholly funded by the state for apprentices aged between 16 and 18. In England, Government only contributes 50% of the cost of training for apprentices aged 19 – 24. Employers of apprentices over the age of 25 may only get a contribution.

Government funding agencies (in England, the Learning and Skills Council) contract with 'learning providers' to deliver apprenticeships, and may accredit them as a Centre of Vocational Excellence or National Skills Academy. These organisations provide off-the-job tuition and manage the bureaucratic workload associated with the apprenticeships. Providers are usually private training companies but might also be Further Education colleges, voluntary sector organisations, Chambers of Commerce or employers themselves.

United States

Apprenticeship programmes in the United States are regulated by the Smith-Hughes Act (1917), The National Industrial Recovery Act (1933), and National Apprenticeship Act, also known as the "Fitzgerald Act."

In the modern era, the number of apprenticeships have declined greatly in the United States. Free traditional apprenticeship job training has largely been replaced with on-the-job training (pay as you work), vocational classes, or college courses, which requires the student or an organization to pay for tuition.

American Apprenticeship Educational Regime

In the United States, education officials and nonprofit organizations who seek to emulate the apprenticeship system in other nations have created school to work education reforms. They seek to link academic education to careers. Some programmes include job shadowing, watching a real worker for a short period of time, or actually spending significant time at a job at no or reduced pay that would otherwise be spent in academic classes or working at a local business. Some legislators raised the issue of child labour laws for unpaid labour or jobs with hazards.

In the United States, school to work programmes usually occur only in high school. American high schools were introduced in the early 20th century to educate students of all ability and interests in one learning community rather than prepare a small number for college. Traditionally, American students are tracked within a wide choice of courses based on ability, with vocational courses (such as auto repair and carpentry) tending to be at the lower end of academic ability and trigonometry and pre-calculus at the upper end.

American education reformers have sought to end such tracking, which is seen as a barrier to opportunity. By contrast, the system studied by the NCEE (National Centre on Education and the Economy) actually relies much more heavily on tracking. Education officials in the U.S., based largely on school redesign proposals by NCEE and other organizations, have chosen to use criterion-referenced tests that define one high standard that must be achieved by all students to receive a uniform diploma. American education policy under the "No Child Left Behind Act" has as an official goal the elimination of the achievement gap between populations. This has often led to the need for remedial classes in college.

Many U.S. states now require passing a high school graduation examination to ensure that students across all ethnic, gender and income groups possess the same skills. In states such as Washington, critics have questioned whether this ensures success for all or just creates massive failure (as only half of all 10th graders have demonstrated they can meet the standards).

The construction industry is perhaps the heaviest user of apprenticeship programmes in the United States, with the US Department of Labour reporting 74,164 new apprentices accepted in 2007 at the height of the construction boom. Most of these apprentices participated in what are called "joint" apprenticeship programmes, administered jointly by construction employers and construction labour unions. For example, the International Union of Painters and Allied Trades (IUPAT) has opened the Finishing Trades Institute (FTI). The FTI is working towards national accreditation so that it may offer associate and bachelor degrees that integrate academics with a more traditional apprentice programmes. The IUPAT has joined forces with the Professional Decorative Painters Association (PDPA) to build educational standards using a model of apprenticeship created by the PDPA.

School-to-work Transition

School-to-work transition is a phrase referring to on-the-job training, apprenticeships, cooperative education agreements or other programmes designed to prepare students to enter the job market. This education system is primarily employed in the United States, partially as a response to work training as it is done in Asia.

School to Work is a system to introduce the philosophy of school-based, work-based, and connecting activities as early as kindergarten to expose students to potential future careers. School to Work emphasizes lifelong learning.

School to Work is funded and sponsored at the federal level by the U.S. Department of Labour and U.S. Department of Education. At the state level in states like Arizona, the grant is administered by the Arizona Department of Commerce, School to Work Division. This grant was funded for a maximum of five years with decreasing funds years three through five;

An example of county level involvement is the Cochise County School to Work Consortia in Arizona. It is composed of more than fifty Cochise County public and private schools, kindergarten through four-year university level, local and community-based organizations, and more than one hundred supporting business partners.

STW is part of a comprehensive education reform movement which includes formulating new standards which emphasize higher order thinking skills, new standards based assessments, and graduation exams, such as the Certificate of Initial Mastery which insure that students are ready for job training or college prep by age 16. Reformers believe that it is important and egalitarian that all students graduate ready for jobs and ready for college, rather than tracking students one way or the other.

Critics

"Back to basics" traditionalists observe that in Europe, apprenticeships typically mean that the worker essentially ends their formal education after age 16, and works full-time at reduced pay in exchange for learning "job skills" such as assembling automobiles.

Some believe that it was better to have students who were not bound for college concentrate on career schools, while academic students should spend class time learning core academic subjects such as history or science rather than job-shadowing at a hospital or auto dealer. A student in North Dakota would have little opportunity to learn to be an auto designer, while one in Alabama would have little opportunity to do job shadowing at a major software company if job training were allocated according to local human resource needs, as many programmes are structured. Local businesses also need to structure their operations to accommodate student workers, and transportation since typically schools are situated close to homes, and not businesses which are typically a car or transit commute away from homes.

The Michigan STW Initiative states "students work without pay for two to three hours each day" and "students are able to perform what might otherwise be hazardous order work." which would contradict child labour laws. Data would be shared with state STW partnership network and local labour market areas which might be an invasion of privacy. The state would utilize the national industry-recognized skill certificates when developed, which would be the Certificate of Initial Mastery. Critics call this a government-controlled passport to work. Michigan Rep. Harold J. Voorhees expressed concern that, with full implementation, a child would not be employed without this Certificate.

Outcome-based Education

Methods of outcome-based education (OBE) are student-centred learning methods that focus on empirically measuring student performance (the "outcome"). OBE contrasts with traditional education, which primarily focuses on the resources that are available to the student, which are called *inputs*. While OBE implementations often incorporate a host of many progressive pedagogical models and ideas, such as reform mathematics, block scheduling, project-based learning and whole language reading, OBE in itself does not specify or require *any* particular style of teaching or learning. Instead, it requires the students to demonstrate what they have learned the required skills and content.

However in practice, OBE generally promotes curricula and assessment based on constructivist methods and discourages traditional education approaches based on direct instruction of facts and standard methods.

Each independent education agency specifies its own outcomes and its own methods of measuring student achievement according to those outcomes. The results of these measurements can be used for different purposes. For example, one agency may use the information to determine how well the overall education system is performing, and another may use its assessments to determine whether an individual student has learned required material.

Outcome-based methods have been adopted for large numbers of students in several countries. In the United States, the Texas Assessment of Academic Skills started in 1991. In Australia, implementation of OBE in Western Australia was widely criticised by parents and teachers and was mostly dropped in January 2007. In South Africa, OBE was dropped in mid-2010. On a smaller scale, some OBE practices, such as not passing a student who does not know the required material, have been used by individual teachers around the world for centuries.

OBE was a popular term in the United States during the 1980s and early 1990s. It is also called mastery education, performance-based education, and other names.

The effort, often by a state or local education agency, to organize all the features of schooling (including aims, curriculum, instruction, and assessment) so as to produce specifically delineated results (often including noncognitive as well as cognitive results) and generally with the expectation that all students will demonstrate such results.

Outcome-based education is an effort of education that converges the traditional focus on what the school provides (Means + Ends) to students, in favour of making students demonstrate that they "know and are able to do" whatever the required outcomes are.

OBE reforms emphasize setting clear standards for observable, measurable outcomes. A significant body of deductive sources at ERIC Database provide peer-reviewed research material about OBE requirements that enhance the adoption of specific outcomes. For example, many countries write their OBE standards so that they focus on mathematics, language, science, and history, without referring to attitudes, social skills, or moral values. Yet, a body of exceptions is gaining here: social skills for labour & job market, the reduction of youth unemployment is a moral value (International Labour Office ILO on Youth Employment Crisis).

The key features which may be used to judge if a system has implemented an outcomes-based education systems are:

- Creation of a curriculum framework that outlines specific, measurable outcomes. The standards included in the frameworks are usually chosen through the area's normal political process.
- A commitment not only to provide an opportunity of education, but to require learning outcomes for advancement. Promotion to the next grade, a diploma, or other reward is granted upon achievement of the standards, while extra classes, repeating the year, or other consequences entail upon those who do not meet the standards.
- Standards-based assessments that determines whether students have achieved the stated standard. Assessments may take *any* form, so long as the assessments actually measure whether the student knows the required information or can perform the required task.
- A commitment that all students of all groups will ultimately reach the same minimum standards. Schools may not "give up" on unsuccessful students.

Outcomes

The emphasis in an OBE education system is on measured outcomes rather than "inputs," such as how many hours students spend in class, or what textbooks are provided. Outcomes may include a range of skills and knowledge, reduction of youth unemployment, return-on-investment. Generally, outcomes are expected to be concretely measurable, that is, "Student can run 50 metres in less than one minute" instead of "Student enjoys physical education class." A complete system of outcomes for a subject area normally includes everything from mere recitation of fact ("Students will name three tragedies written by Shakespeare") to complex analysis and interpretation ("Student will analyse the social context of a Shakespearean tragedy in an essay"). Writing appropriate and measurable outcomes can be very difficult, and the choice of specific outcomes is often a source of local controversies.

Each educational agency is responsible for setting its own outcomes. Under the OBE model, education agencies may specify any outcome (skills and knowledge), but not inputs (field trips, arrangement of the school day, teaching styles). Some popular models of outcomes include the National Science Education Standards and the NCTM's Principles and Standards for School Mathematics, as well as European Union's Rethinking Education.

Approaches to Grading, Reporting, and Promoting

An important by-product of this approach is that students are assessed against external, absolute objectives, instead of reporting the students' relative achievements. The traditional model of grading on a curve (top student gets the best grade, worst student always fails (even if they know all the material), everyone else is evenly distributed in the middle) is never accepted in OBE or standards-based education. Instead, a student's performance is related in absolute terms: "Jane knows how to write the letters of the alphabet" or "Jane answered 80% of questions correctly" instead of "Jane answered more questions correctly than Mary."

Under OBE, teachers can use any objective grading system they choose, including letter grades. In fact, many schools adopt OBE methods and use the same grading systems that they have always used. However, for the purposes of graduation, advancement, and retention, a fully developed OBE system generally tracks and reports not just a single overall grade for a subject, but also give information about several specific outcomes within that subject. For example, rather than just getting a passing grade for mathematics, a student might be assessed as level 4 for number sense, level 5 for algebraic concepts, level 3 for measurement skills, etc. This approach is valuable to schools and parents by specifically identifying a student's strengths and weaknesses.

In one alternate grading approach, a student is awarded "levels" instead of letter grades. From Kindergarten to year 12, the student will receive either a Foundational level (which is pre-institutional) or be evidenced at levels 1 through to 8. In the simplest implementation, earning a "level" indicates that the teacher believes that a student has learned enough of the current material to be able to succeed in the next level of work. A student technically cannot flunk in this system: a student who needs to review the current material will simply not achieve the next level at the same time as most of his same-age peers. This acknowledges differential growth at different stages, and focuses the teacher on the individual needs of the students.

In this approach, students and their parents are better able to track progress from year to year, since the levels are based on criteria that remain constant for a student's whole time at school. However, this experience is perceived by some as a flaw in the system: While it is entirely normal for some students to work on the same level of outcomes for more than one year parents and students have been socialized into the expectation of a constant, steady progress through schoolwork. Parents and students therefore interpret the normal experience as failure.

This emphasis on recognizing positive achievements, and comparing the student to his own prior performance, has been accused by some of "dumbing down" education (and by others as making school much too hard), since it recognises achievement at different levels. Even those who would not achieve a passing grade in a traditional age-based approach can be recognized for their concrete, positive, individual improvements.

OBE-oriented teachers think about the individual needs of each student and give opportunities for each student to achieve at a variety of levels. Thus, in theory, weaker students are given work within their grasp and exceptionally strong students are extended. In practice, managing independent study programmes for thirty or more individuals is difficult. Adjusting to students' abilities is something that good teachers have always done: OBE simply makes the approach explicit and reflects the approach in marking and reporting.

Differences with Traditional Education Methods

In a traditional education system and economy, students are given grades and rankings compared to each other. Content and performance expectations are based primarily on what was taught in the past to students of a given age. The basic goal of traditional education was to present the knowledge and skills of the old generation to the new generation of students, and to provide students with an environment in which to learn, with little attention (beyond the classroom teacher) to whether or not any student ever learns any of the material. It was enough that the school presented an opportunity to learn. Actual achievement was neither measured nor required by the school system.

In fact, under the traditional model, student performance is expected to show a wide range of abilities. The failure of some students is accepted as a natural and unavoidable circumstance. The highest-performing students are given the highest grades and test scores, and the lowest performing students are given low grades. (Local laws and traditions determine whether the lowest performing students were socially promoted or made to repeat the year.) Schools used norm-referenced tests, such as inexpensive, multiple-choice computer-scored questions with single correct answers, to quickly rank students on ability. These tests do not give criterion-based judgements as to whether students have met a single standard of what every student is expected to know and do: they merely rank the students in comparison with each other. In this system, grade-level expectations are defined as the performance of the median student, a level at which half the students score better and half the students score worse. By this definition, in a normal population, half of students are expected to perform above grade level and half the students below grade level, no matter how much or how little the students have learned.

Claims in Favour of OBE

Proponents view OBE as a valuable replacement of the traditional model of relative ranking by ability and getting credit for merely sitting through class. OBE proponents support OBE because of its vision of high standards for all groups. OBE proponents endorse measuring outputs rather than inputs (such as money spent, number of hours of lecture given, new EU outcome requirements focus on reducing the youth unemployment rate) and requiring that student demonstrate learning rather than just showing up.

OBE proponents believe that all students can learn, regardless of ability, race, ethnicity, socioeconomic status, and gender. Furthermore, OBE recognizes that a complex organization is more likely to produce what it measures, and to downplay anything it considers unimportant. The adoption of measurable standards is seen as a means of ensuring that the content and skills covered by the standards will be a high priority in the education of students.

The standards-based education approach rejects social promotion and the inevitability of inferior performance by disadvantaged groups. While recognizing that some students will learn certain material faster than others, the standards movement rejects the idea that only a few can succeed. All students are capable of continuous improvement.

The opportunities that were previously afforded to those at the top of a bell curve are opened up to the diversity of all students, in a democratic vision, sometimes connected to social justice.

The approach presents the following positions and viewpoints on OBE:

- All students will complete rigorous academic coursework so that they leave high school prepared for college or technical training, without remedial courses.
- All students, including those who live in poverty, will meet district, state, and national standards.

- Staff will maintain high expectations and standards, believing all students will succeed if kept to high expectations
- Students should be measured against a fixed yardstick, a finish line, or "against the mountain" rather than against other students.
- Higher world class standards are required for 21st Century Skills.
- Students should demonstrate that they have met standards, not just put in seat time to advance to the next level.

> *We haven't taught many of them even up to middle school standards. It only punishes them more to give them an empty piece of paper we call a diploma when their high school experience hasn't prepared for any of the skills they'll need after high school. We give them a diploma that is a doorway to a street corner or unemployment line.*
>
> —(Russlynn Ali of Education Trust-West)

In essence, OBE seeks to reject a rank-ordered definition of success by essentially requiring that all students shall be required to cross the finish line, at least as well as the specified standards. In practice, OBE results in accountable spending, thus also enabling jobless-rate risk-prevention of students who were previously allowed to graduate while being functionally illiterate and innumerate. OBE's objective standards finally put a brake on useless & popgun grade inflation, clearly to the distress of students who prefer high, but meaningless, grades.

Deductive Evidence that OBE Actually Works

The ERIC Database provides a Thesaurus Descriptor "Outcome-based Education" with presently over 369 peer-reviewed hits. Meanwhile, OBE is a coherent bound collection of ideas, with uniformity in the way it is implemented from case to case. This enhances testability for OBE's effectiveness in a way that applies universally. The concreteness of OBE's conception of a "measurable outcome" is welcoming, both in implementing an OBE regime and in testing its effectiveness.

Criticism

Criticism of OBE falls into a few major groups:

- Opposition to standardized testing
- Criticism of inappropriate outcomes

- Extra burden on instructors and educational institutions
- Dislike of something that is not OBE

Though it is claimed the focus is not on "inputs", OBE is criticised for being used to justify increased funding requirements, increased graduation and testing requirements, and additional preparation, homework, and continuing education time spent by students, parents and teachers in supporting learning. It is also criticized for not being able to measure certain skills, much like IQ tests.

Opposition to Testing

Critics claim that existing tests do not adequately measure student mastery of the stated objectives. Some parents also object to the use of standardized tests (all students take the same test under the same conditions) because they think it unfair for schools to require the same level of work or to use the achievement tests for impoverished or disadvantaged students as they do for more advantaged students.

The OBE philosophy insists that assessment models be carefully matched to the stated objectives. High-stakes tests are *not* required in an OBE system; norm-referenced tests are prohibited. Portfolios, daily assessments, teacher opinions, and other methods of assessment are perfectly compatible with OBE models. Furthermore, the OBE approach does not permit special, lower standards for students who have been badly served by public education in the past.

Inappropriate Outcomes

Many people oppose OBE reforms because they dislike the proposed outcomes. They may think that the standards are too easy, too hard, or wrongly conceived. Finally, some so-called OBE critics oppose non-OBE reforms that were presented as a part of a wide-ranging reform "package", rather than opposing OBE itself. Standards can be set too low: Most fear that the focus on achievement by all students will result in "dumbing down" the definition of academic competence to a level that is achievable by even the weakest students. Critics are unhappy with having all students meet a minimum standard, instead of most students meeting a somewhat higher standard.

Some critics also question whether even such low goals are realistic or attainable, and whether success can only be framed in terms of high test scores and high incomes. The emphasis on higher reading standards and algebra for all appears to devalue vocational training and the achievement of those who do not get high test scores, but who are likely to become competent blue-collar workers.

Standards can be set too high: Others object that the standards are too high. OBE models do not approve of social promotion, so non-disabled students who perform significantly below the stated standard may be held back or required to take additional instruction. Especially when the standards are relatively new, and the schools are just beginning to adjust to the new standards, a majority of students struggle with at least some of the requirements. Parents are understandably unhappy to learn that their children have not acquired the necessary skills, and occasionally respond by demanding that the standards be lowered until their children are declared to be passing.

Sometimes this demand that the standards be lowered is justified, because standards can be found developmentally inappropriate for all but the brightest students. The State of Washington found that some fourth grade WASL math problems were much more difficult than what is typically expected of nine-year-old students. A 2008 draft mathematics standard proposed that Kindergartners multiply to 30 by skip counting (also known as *counting by twos*: 2, 4, 6, 8...), and that second graders solve simple algebra story problems.

Committees often set standards without considering how many students are currently achieving at that level. For example, in the 1998 North Carolina Writing Assessment, less than 1 percent of fourth graders received the highest possible score for writing content. While a majority of students passed easily, parents were upset that so few were rated as being best. Dislike of specific outcomes: Finally, many complaints are directed against the nature of certain standards. For example, a politician might propose that standards be included for education about sex or creationism. Opponents say that many educational agencies have adopted outcomes which focus too much on attitudes (e.g., "Students will enjoy physical education class") rather than academic content. Similarly, the "Who Controls Our Children" campaign in Pennsylvania claimed that an OBE reform effort was part of a federal programme that was "stressing values over academic content, and holding students accountable for goals that are so vague and fuzzy they can't be assessed at all." The Western Australian outcomes were criticised for being too vague.

Controversial standards are opposed because of their content, not simply because they are standards. OBE models always leave the choice of the exact standards to the educational authority, so that families can influence the choice of standards according to their community's preferences.

Extra Burden on Instructors and Educational Institutions

Critics sometimes oppose OBE because of the burden it imposes on instructors and educational institutions more broadly, a burden that they regard as unjustified by any evidence showing that OBE actually improves learning outcomes. Rather than issuing a single letter or number to summarize an entire term's achievements, an OBE system may require that the teacher track and report dozens of separate outcomes. It takes longer to report that a student can add, subtract, multiply, divide, solve story problems, and draw graphs than to report "passed mathematics class," but the burden imposed by OBE does not owe primarily to the *reporting* of more data. The burden is spread across the entire educational institution, in the form of (1) a new layer of assessment placed atop the old familiar one, (2) a new bureaucracy responsible for the institution-wide collection and presentation of data, and (3) the altering and curtailing of classroom instruction to make room for more intrusive testing. In view of the paucity of evidence showing that OBE actually works, many regard this extra burden as an unjustified drain on pedagogical resources.

Criticism of Educational Reforms Associated with OBE

Many criticisms of OBE are actually criticisms of other things that are introduced with an OBE system. Many people oppose OBE reforms because the OBE reforms are packaged with other reforms.

OBE reform is often packaged as part of a comprehensive school reform model which promotes constructivism, enquiry-based science, tax reform, teacher training, and more. Other educational reforms, including changes to the school calendar, the age of students that attend school in a certain building, or the way tax revenues are divided, may all be inappropriately labelled "OBE" reforms simply because they were proposed on the same day as an OBE programme.

School to work may also be a component of these multi-faceted reform programmes. School-to-work programmes require students to spend time in an internship or other form of career training or experience.

OBE Programmes

Australia: One of the problems of OBE for students wishing to attend university is that it does not lend itself well to forming a competitive Tertiary Entrance Rank (TER). The suggested model for mapping levels to a TER has been attacked because it results in a score with more significant digits than the measures from which it is derived and so is charged with being mathematically unsound. William Spady promoted the OBE method as a way of getting beyond 'meaningless' percentages and marks, aiming for education for life beyond school, giving children and young adults a broader and more transformative education. Arguably inelegant implementation makes the future of OBE unclear, and at odds with the Australian Government in Canberra.

Western Australia

The current OBE controversy in Western Australia relates specifically to the introduction of OBE in upper school (year 11 and 12) classes. Many Western Australian schools have been using some form of OBE for K-10 students for several years. (OBE is only one part of the current changes to upper school education currently being implemented. Other aspects of the new courses of study that form the upper school review have received little public attention.)

As part of the debate over further introduction of OBE into the teaching practice of Western Australia, various groups of concerned citizens and those in the teaching profession formed various single-issue lobby and action groups to progress their viewpoints. One such group was *People Lobbying Against Teaching Outcomes* formed by Greg Williams.

The core view of this group was their disagreement with the former Western Australian Minister for Education (Ljiljanna Ravlich) in respect to her commitment to implement OBE. Another such group was Parents Against Outcomes Based Education, who took the position that the implementation of OBE would pose significant problems and potentially lead to the decreased knowledge and performance of school students. Their objection was not to OBE itself, but to the bundle of reforms, of which OBE was the most mentioned. The "Fuzzy Outcomes" criticism above applies.

In January 2007, the Western Australian Government responded to the massive opposition by teachers and parents to its implementation of an OBE system by stating that it would allow year 11 and 12 students to be graded traditionally.

South Africa

OBE was introduced to South Africa in the late 1990s by the post-apartheid government as part of its Curriculum 2005 programme, but it was widely viewed as a failure, and was eventually scrapped in 2010.

United States

In the early 1990s, several standards-based reform measures were passed in various states, creating the Texas Assessment of Academic Skills (1991), Washington Assessment of Student Learning (1993), the CLAS in California (1993), and the Massachusetts Comprehensive Assessment System (1993).

At the national level, Congress passed the Goals 2000 act in 1994. The best-known and most far-reaching standards-based education law in the U.S. is the No Child Left Behind Act, which mandated certain measurements as a condition of receiving federal education funds. States are free to set their own standards, but the federal law mandates public reporting of math and reading test scores for disadvantaged demographic subgroups, including racial minorities, low-income students, and special education students. Various consequences for schools that do not make "adequate yearly progress" are included in the law.

At the state level, exit examinations have proliferated, and now more than half of US high school students will be required to pass a high-stakes test to get a normal high school diploma. In some states, fewer than half of students and one-quarter of ethnic minorities have met these standards.

In some communities, such as Littleton, Colorado, organized opposition groups have forced educational agencies to rescind reforms. In Littleton, community members felt that vague, nonacademic outcomes were replacing content, and that technically unsound assessments would be used to determine something as important as high school graduation. They also objected to students being refused a high school diploma if they could not perform 36 separate mathematics skills, despite being given good grades in class.

OBE Diplomas

A certificate of initial mastery was a programme to provide students with an interim certification around the age of 16. The certificate was earned by taking and passing a written test, which had been designed to determine whether a student was performing at about the tenth grade level. A student who passed the 10th grade test would receive a Certificate of Initial Mastery.

The CIM concept was patterned after nations like Germany's hauptschule system, in which the students who are not going to elite universities end their school-based education around age 16 and start career-oriented training in fields like construction technology, allied health professions, and business. In a typical US proposal, a student who received a CIM would then take two more years of career-based training. A national standards board was proposed to create similar tests for eight career fields, with the hope that employers would prefer certificated employees.

The CIM has been essentially abandoned; however, in its place, states frequently require passing the same exam as a condition of receiving a high school diploma. Oregon had proposed a CAM for "advanced mastery" at the 12th grade.

OBE's Relationship to College

One effect of high school exit examinations is that it may become more difficult to graduate from high school than enter college. There is no set passing level for college entry tests like the SAT, and such tests are often not required by the lowest-rated colleges.

In the future, some states may require criterion-based standards either for admission to or graduation from public universities. States are attempting to align high school curricula with the minimum standards for beginning college in an effort to reduce college dropouts and the number of remedial classes being taught at universities.

European Union

In December 2012, the European Commission stated that it "presented a] new strategy in 22 languages: The youth unemployment rate is close to 23% across the European Union – yet at the same time there are more than 2 million vacancies that cannot be filled. Europe needs a radical rethink on how education and training systems can deliver the skills needed by the labour market. ... Rethinking Education calls for a fundamental shift in education, with more focus on 'learning outcomes' - the knowledge, skills and competences that students acquire. Merely having spent time in education is no longer sufficient."

Treaties

Washington Accord: The Washington Accord is an international accreditation agreement for professional engineering academic degrees, between the bodies responsible for accreditation in its signatory countries. The Washington Accord covers undergraduate engineering degrees under Outcome-based education approach.

Performance-based Economy

Outcome-based methods are used in some businesses. For whole companies, outcome-based evaluations are the basis of stock exchange prices: Companies which produce higher profit growth are more valuable than companies which perform poorly. Employees who are paid for piecework or by commission are examples of traditional employment use of outcome-based pay. Alternatives include seniority systems (oldest worker gets highest pay).

Many private employers give standards-based tests to determine whether job applicants have necessary job skills (such as typing speed), and nearly all government employees have to take and pass a civil service examination. Furthermore, nearly all licensed professionals, from nurses to truck drivers to beauticians, already take such tests as a condition of entering their professions. Often these tests have disproportionate failure rates for disadvantaged subgroups, such as school dropouts and impoverished people.

Standards-based Education Reform in the United States

Education reform in the United States since the 1980s has been largely driven by the setting of academic standards for what students should know and be able to do. These standards can then be used to guide all other system components. The SBE (standards-based education) reform movement calls for clear, measurable standards for all school students. Rather than norm-referenced rankings, a standards-based system measures each student against the concrete standard. Curriculum, assessments, and professional development are aligned to the standards.

Standards are an evolution of the earlier OBE (outcomes-based education) which was largely rejected in the United States as unworkable in the 1990s, and is still being implemented by some and abandoned by other governments in Australia by the hito completely change the structure of education and grading by massively individualizing instruction. In contrast, the more modest "standards" reform has been limited to the core goals of the OBE programmes:

- the creation of curriculum frameworks which outline specific knowledge or skills which students must acquire,
- an emphasis on criterion-referenced assessments which are aligned to the frameworks, and
- the imposition of some high-stakes tests, such as graduation examinations requiring a high standard of performance to receive a diploma.

In the process of establishing standards for each individual curriculum area, such as mathematics and science, many other reforms, such as enquiry-based science may be implemented, but these are not core aspects of the standards programme.

The standards movement can be traced to the efforts of Marc Tucker's NCEE which adapted aspects of William Spady's OBE movement into a system based on creating standards and assessments for a Certificate of Initial Mastery. This credential has since been abandoned by every state which first adopted the concept, including Washington and Oregon and largely replaced by graduation examinations. His organization had contracts with states and districts covering as many as half of all American school children by their own claims, and many states enacted education reform legislation in the early 1990s based on this model, which was also known at the time as "performance-based education" as OBE (and the non-OBE progressive reforms co-marketed with it) had been too widely attacked to be saleable under that name. Though the standards movement has a stronger backing from conservatives than OBE by adopting a platform of raising higher academic standards, other conservatives believe that it is merely a re-labelling of a failed, unrealistic vision. It is believed to be the educational equivalent of a planned economy which attempts to require all children to perform at world-class levels merely by raising expectations and imposing punishments and sanctions on schools and children who fall short of the new standards.

Vision

The vision of the standards-based education reform movement is that every teenager will receive a meaningful high school diploma that serves essentially as a public guarantee that they can read, write, and do basic mathematics (typically through first-year algebra) at a level which might be useful to an employer. To avoid a surprising failure at the end of high school, standards trickle down through all the lower grades, with regular assessments through a variety of means.

No student, by virtue of poverty, age, race, gender, cultural or ethnic background, disabilities, or family situation will ultimately be exempt from learning the required material, although it is acknowledged that individual students may learn in different ways and at different rates.

Standards are chosen through political discussions that focus on what students will need to learn to be competitive in the job market, instead of by textbook publishers or education professors or tradition. Standards are normally published and freely available to parents and taxpayers as well as professional educators and textbook writers.

Standards focus on the goal of a literate and economically competitive workforce.

- Standards outline *what students need to know, understand, and be able to do.*
- Standards should be developmentally appropriate and relevant to future employment and education needs. Standards should generally be written so that all students are capable of achieving them, and so that talented students will exceed them.
- All students are believed to be capable of learning and of meeting high expectations. Both advanced and struggling students can learn new things in their own ways and at their own rates.
- Instruction that helps an individual student learn the information and skills listed in the standards is emphasized.
- Both *excellence and equity* are valued. Subgroups are carefully measured to identify and reduce systemic racism, bias, and the tyranny of low expectations.
- Professional teachers are empowered to make the decisions essential for effective learning, rather than having a teaching style prescribed under traditional education models.
- Social promotion is discouraged. Students advance or are retained based on their actual learning achievements instead of based on their age, their friends' achievements, or tradition.

Components

Some of the common components of standards-based education reform are:

- Creation of specific, concrete, measurable standards in an integrated curriculum framework. These standards apply to all schools in a state or country, regardless of race or relative wealth.
- Criterion-referenced tests based on these standards rather than norm-based relative rankings (which compare one student with another).
- An assertion that the new standards are higher than the pre-reform expectations for middle-class or upper-middle-class students.
- A requirement that attention be paid to narrowing academic gaps between groups such as races, income, or gender.

- High school graduation examinations, which are a form of high-stakes testing that denies diplomas to students who do not meet the stated standards, such as being able to read at the eighth-grade level or do pre-algebra mathematics. The Regents Examination in New York, first given in 1878, is the oldest high school graduation exam in the U.S. In most educational systems, students who can not pass the test are given a certificate of attendance instead of a normal diploma.

History

Standards-based education reform in the United States began with the publication of *A Nation at Risk* in 1983. In 1989, an education summit involving all fifty state governors and President George H. W. Bush resulted in the adoption of national education goals for the year 2000; the goals included content standards. That same year, the National Council of Teachers of Mathematics published the *Curriculum and Evaluation Standards for School Mathematics*, a standards-based document.

A standards based vision was enacted under the Clinton Administration in 1994. A reauthorization of the Elementary and Secondary Education Act(ESEA)was passed to ensure that all states had rigorous standards for all subject areas and grade levels. This vision was then carried forward by the Bush Administration in 2001 with the passing of No Child Left Behind(NCLB).

Standards-based school reform has become a predominant issue facing public schools. By the 1996 National Education Summit, 44 governors and 50 corporate CEOs set the priorities (Achieve, 1998)

- High academic standards and expectations for all students.
- Tests that are more rigorous and more challenging, to measure whether students are meeting those standards.
- Accountability systems that provide incentives and rewards for educators, students, and parents to work together to help students reach these standards.

By 1998, almost every state had implemented or was in the process of implementing academic standards for their students in math and reading. Principals and teachers have received bonuses or been fired, students have been promoted or retained in their current grade, and legislation has been passed so that high school students will graduate or be denied a diploma based on whether or not they had met the standards, usually as measured by a criterion-referenced test.

The standards-based National Education Goals (Goals 2000) were set by the U.S. Congress in the 1990s. Many of these goals were based on the principles of outcomes-based education, and not all of the goals were attained by the year 2000 as was intended. The movement resulted in the No Child Left Behind Act of 2001, which as of 2009 is still an active nation-wide mandate in the United States.

Example of a U.S. Apprenticeship Programme

Persons interested in learning to become electricians can join one of several apprenticeship programmes offered jointly by the International Brotherhood of Electrical Workers and the National Electrical Contractors Association. No background in electrical work is required. A minimum age of 18 is required. There is no maximum age. Men and women are equally invited to participate. The organization in charge of the programme is called the National Joint Apprenticeship and Training Committee.

Apprentice electricians work 32 to 40+ hours per week at the trade under the supervision of a journeyman wireman and receive pay and benefits. They spend an additional 8 hours every other week in classroom training. At the conclusion of training (five years for inside wireman and outside lineman, less for telecommunications), apprentices reach the level of journeyman wireman. All of this is offered at no charge, except for the cost of books (which is approximately $200–600 per year(depending on grades). Persons completing this programme are considered highly skilled by employers and command high pay and benefits. Other unions such as the United Brotherhood of Carpenters and Joiners of America, United Association of Plumbers, Fitters, Welders and HVAC Service Techs, Operating Engineers, Ironworkers, Sheet Metal Workers, Plasterers, Bricklayers and others offer similar programmes.

Trade associations such as the Independent Electrical Contractors and Associated Builders and Contractors also offer a variety of apprentice training programmes. Registered programmes also are offered by the Aerospace Joint Apprenticeship Committee (AJAC) to fill a shortage of aerospace and advanced manufacturing workers in Washington State.

Example of a Professional U.S. Apprenticeship

A modified form of apprenticeship is required for before an engineer is licensed as a Professional Engineer in any of the states of the United States. In the United States, regulation of professional engineering licenses is the right and responsibility of the federated state. That is, each of the 50 states sets its own licensing requirements and issues (and, if needed, revokes) licenses to practice engineering in that state.

Although the requirements can vary slightly from state to state, in general to obtain a Professional Engineering License in a given state, one must a graduate with Bachelor of Science in Engineering from an accredited college or university, pass the Engineer-in-Training (Engineer Intern) exam, work in that discipline for at least four years under a Licensed Professional Engineer, and then pass the Professional Engineers exam.

In most cases the states have reciprocity agreements so that once an individual becomes licensed in one state can also become licensed in other states with relative ease.

Internship

An internship is a method of on-the-job training for white-collar and professional careers. Internships for professional careers are similar to apprenticeships for trade and vocational jobs. Although interns are typically college or university students, they can also be high school students or post-graduate adults. On occasion, they are middle school or even elementary students. In some countries, internships for school children are called work experience. Internships may be paid or unpaid, and are usually understood to be temporary positions.

Generally, an internship consists of an exchange of services for experience between the student and an organization. Students can also use an internship to determine if they have an interest in a particular career, create a network of contacts, or gain school credit. Some interns find permanent, paid employment with the organizations with which they interned. This can be a significant benefit to the employer as experienced interns often need little or no training when they begin regular employment. Unlike a trainee programme, however, employment at the completion of an internship is not guaranteed.

Types of Internships

Internships exist in a wide variety of industries and settings. An internship may be paid, unpaid or partially paid (in the form of a stipend). Paid internships are common in professional fields including medicine, architecture, science, engineering, law, business (especially accounting and finance), technology, and advertising. Non-profit charities and think tanks often have unpaid, volunteer positions.

Internships may be part-time or full-time. A typical internship lasts 6–12 weeks, but can be shorter or longer, depending on the organization involved. The act of job shadowing may also constitute interning.

The two primary types of internships that exist in the United States are:

- *Work experience internship:* Most often this will be in the second or third year of the school period. The placement can be from 2 months to one full school year. During this period, the student is expected to use the things he/she has learned in school and put them into practice. This way the student gains work experience in their field of study. The gained experience will be helpful to finish the final year of study.
- *Research internship (graduation) or dissertation internship:* This is mostly done by students who are in their final year. With this kind of internship a student does research for a particular company. The company can have something that they feel like they need to improve, or the student can choose a topic within the company themselves. The results of the research study will be put in a report and often will have to be presented. Due to strict labour laws, European internships are mostly unpaid, although they are still popular among non-Europeans in order to gain international exposure on one's résumé and for foreign language improvement.

Another type of internship growing in popularity is the virtual internship, in which the intern works remotely, and is not physically present at the job location. It provides the capacity to attain the same results without the conventional means of being physically present at a job. Usually the internship is conducted via virtual means, such as phone, email, and web communication. Virtual interns generally have the opportunity to work at their own pace.

The practice of a mid-career person taking an internship is relatively new to the U.S. but becoming more common due to the current economic crisis.

Fees for Internship and Charity Auctions

Some companies now find and place students in mostly unpaid internships for a fee. These companies charge to assist with a search, promising to refund their fees if no internship is found. These programmes vary, but they claim to provide internship placements at reputable companies, provide controlled housing in a new city, mentorship and support throughout the summer, networking, weekend activities in some programmes, and sometimes academic credit.

Another form of paying for internships is through charity auctions. A company with an internship will select a charity who will obtain an internship position funded by the auction. In some cases, companies have created internships simply to help a charity.

Some claim that fee-based programmes and charity auctions restrict internship opportunities to students in wealthier families. These companies respond that "the average student comes from the middle class, and their parents "dig deep" to pay for it." Some companies specifically fund scholarships and grants for low-income applicants.

Critics of internships also decry the practice of requiring certain college credits to be obtained only through unpaid internships. Depending on the cost of the school, this is often seen as an unethical practice, as it requires students to exchange paid-for and often limited tuition credits in order to work an uncompensated job. Even if the school does not require credit for an internship, companies offering the internship often pressure colleges to give college credit so interns cannot complain that they receive nothing for their efforts.

Internships by Region

Internship laws and practices vary widely from country to country, and region to region.

Asia and Australia

Australia: Internships in Australia are often referred to as "work experience" when undertaken by high school students and "industry experience" when undertaken by university students.

Some degree programmes such as engineering require a minimum amount of industry experience (usually 12 weeks) to attain professional accreditation with industry bodies such as Engineers Australia.

Unpaid internships are legal and allowed for under the Fair Work Act 2009. There are a number of criteria used to determine if the engagement forms a legitimate internship, including:

- benefit to the individual
- commercial gain for the company
- period of placement, and/or
- relationship to a course of study.

India

Internship opportunities in India are career specific, college students often choose internships based on their major at University. Students often see it as a way to develop their capabilities by practically applying the academic elements of their degree and as an opportunity to learn about the work environment.

Malaysia

Some courses offered in public universities of Malaysia require the student to attend an industrial training programme for a minimum ten weeks. This includes, for example, engineering and architecture. However, this period can vary from ten weeks to as long as six months.

New Zealand

In New Zealand, there are a number of colleges where students can undertake an internship whilst studying. Students studying adventure tourism or hospitality management must complete an internship in order to complete their course studies. Most of these internships are paid by the employer. Students studying for careers in educational psychology in New Zealand must complete a one year Internship - the Internship programme at Massey University for example is a one year post masters Post Graduate Diploma in Educational Psychology and the majority of Internships are carried out on placement with the Ministry of Education. Some funding is available through the Ministry of Education Study Awards programme to support Interns in their applied practice. The funds are contestable each year. In 2013 there were 10 study awards each worth NZ$15,000.

Nigeria

Internship in Nigeria is called S.I.W.E.S(Student Industrial Work Experience Scheme) or IT(Industrial Training). Students usually spend six month in their third year for four courses or fourth year for five year courses. Student of Veterinary Medicine usually use their semester break period for IT. This case particular for Ahmadu Bello University, Zaria and other universities as well with little or no difference.

Europe

Croatia: Internships are possible in Croatia.

Denmark

Work without pay is inappropriate in Denmark. One way it can be done is as part of a work-trial where a person is tested by the authorities in conjunction with putting the individual back into the workplace.

It is also common within most Danish universities to place students in "free work" jobs. The company is then compensated and the intern receives welfare during this period. This normally lasts about three months.

The Danish Trade Unions monitor this type of work very closely so the hiring of an intern does not result in the loss of a paid job.

In 2008, a new system established by the Department of Education may lower the motivation of students who take time to work for charity.

Students/ citizens of the EEA/EU area can freely move and reside in Denmark under EU rules. If their stay exceeds three months then an application for registration with the Regional State Administration will have to be filed. If the student comes from outside the European Union than the following rules to apply for residence and work permit for an internship apply:

> *- you must be between 18 and 34 years old (excluded from this are health care students) - the internship must contribute to your studies - the respective internship provide must be able to offer appropriate work - salary and employment conditions must comply with the regulations of the Danish collective agreements - detailed description of the internship and its objective must be handed in with the application*

Furthermore there are special rules for agricultural, healthcare and architectural internships.

European Union

The European Commission operates a sizeable traineeship programme.

France

At French universities, internships, known as "stages", are common. They occur during the third or fourth year of studies. The duration of French internships varies from 2 to 6 months. As of 1 January 2012, French labour law requires that all internships of 2 months or longer include minimum pay of 436,05€ per month. In France, it is also becoming more popular to perform internships after studies are completed.

Internships in France are also popular for international students. The primary reason international students intern in France is to learn to speak French fluently. French companies greatly appreciate employees who speak multiple languages and thus international opportunities are available.

Germany

As in most other countries, most students take their internship (German: "Praktikum") between the fourth or fifth semester of their degree at a university of applied sciences. In some fields of study it is common to write the final thesis in a company as part of an internship. Some degrees don't require practical training in order to graduate.

Another type of internship has emerged in recent years is the post graduation internship. The purpose of a post graduation internship is to equip the student with knowledge and tools to be successful in their future position. These post graduation internships should last between six and ten months.

Italy

Since the Italian University System entered the Bologna process, an internship experience (commonly referred to by the French term *stage*) has been made compulsory for almost all those who are studying for a bachelors or a master's degree (especially in technical, economic or scientific faculties). The goal of this process is to reduce the gap between companies' demands and the often very theoretical learning offered by Italian universities. However, since the internship is usually completed at university as well and since only few companies who employ student interns rarely offer proper training, these internships are generally not considered real work experience. Almost all students therefore have to do a second or a third internship after they have completed their studies, hoping to receive appropriate professional training and possibly getting employed afterwards in the same company or in another company in a close or related business.

Italian internships can last up to 6 months can be extended for further 6 months. The total period can be up to 12 months. Internships in Italy can be both paid or unpaid. Students internships, especially the ones not involved with the development of a thesis, are usually not paid.

Almost all the graduate internships are paid, but the remuneration is usually extremely low, around 600 euros gross per month (that is about 1/4 of the gross monthly remuneration of an hired young graduate employee) and without benefits other than lunch and a few paid days for sickness/vacation (so no 13th/14th mensilities, no parental leave etc.). This poses a big problem for graduates, considering as well that some companies use graduate interns just to save money, making them work for 6 to 12 months without giving them a decent remuneration, without offering them proper training/formation, and without hiring them after the internship even if they showed to be productive, fast-learning and trustworthy. In other words, a significant percentage of Italian graduates, after one or even two years from the end of their studies (in some cases even masters studies), are still searching for a real job, that can offer stability and a decent remuneration. This, together with the long time necessary to graduate in Italy, is part of the reason why graduate Italians leave the family home very late, usually in their early 30s.

In order to get an internship, graduates have to go to interviews, which might be held in cities far from the ones in which graduates have been studying.

Netherlands

In the Netherlands it is also common to perform internships during college which, just like in Belgium and France, is called a *stage*. Most student internships last between 3 and 9 months. Companies are not obligated to pay the student, so sometimes small companies won't pay anything. The normal internship compensation rate in the Netherlands is around €300 per month, depending on education level and company generosity.

Spain

At Spanish universities, internship during the education period are uncommon. "Real" work experience for students begins only when they are done with their study.

Some Spanish companies are getting more used to having student internships—mostly these are international students from other European countries. Often, students want to learn Spanish. Placement organizations may be needed as Spanish companies are harder to contact directly. The normal stage compensation rate in Spain is around 500€/month. Retribution is regulated in many universities starting from 6€/hr. Given these rates, Spanish employers who do hire interns often may be taking advantage of unpaid interships in order to get free labour.

United Kingdom

In the United Kingdom, work experience is offered as part of the national curriculum to secondary school students in years 10 and 11. Generally, these placements are unpaid.

During their degree programme, students may apply for internships during the summer holidays. University staff give students access, and students apply direct to employers. Some students opt to apply for year-long placements, often referred to as 'sandwich placements', between the penultimate and final year of their degree. This is done as part of a degree programme. Some universities and employers hold fairs and exhibitions to encourage students to consider the option and to enable students to meet potential employers. In the modern labour market, graduates with internship work experience are deemed more desirable to employers. Research has demonstrated they attain higher level degree classifications than those graduates without such experience.

The purpose of these placements is varied. Some university students see it as a way to develop their employability by utilizing the academic elements of their degree in a practical setting. International students may also seek to get understanding about how work is conducted in the English-speaking world and to experience cultural diversity. Organisations such as the Trades Union Congress and Intern Aware have been lobbying for a change in British internships to make interns aware of their employment law rights, especially in relation to whether they are entitled to minimum wage and paid holidays.

North America

Canada: In Canada, high school, college, and university student placements are typically referred to as "Co-ops" (co-operative education) programmes. University co-op programmes are often highly competitive; students must apply to and compete for admission, as enrollment is limited. Partnering employers will post placement opportunities through the university. These positions typically span a four month term taking place either during summer break or during the school year.

While some internships are unpaid (particularly in media, advertising, PR, and communications), many Canadian organizations do offer paid internships. Not all internships are entry-level positions; organizations may also offer internships for mid-level professionals. For example, in the province of Ontario, paid internships are available for immigrants who have extensive experience in other countries but lack relevant Canadian experience.

The nature and scope of unpaid internships in Canada is difficult to estimate. This is in part because there are no written regulations defining internships directly. Minimum wage for labour is covered by employment standards legislation and is governed at the provincial level. Ontario provides for a 6-point test to be applied to determine if an employee-employer relationship does not exist, where all of the conditions must be met:

1. The training is similar to that which is given in a vocational school.
2. The training is for the benefit of the individual.
3. The person providing the training derives little, if any, benefit from the activity of the individual while he or she is being trained.
4. The individual does not displace employees of the person providing the training.
5. The individual is not accorded a right to become an employee of the person providing the training.
6. The individual is advised that he or she will receive no remuneration for the time that he or she spends in training.

United States

Many internships in the United States are career specific. Students often choose internships based on their major at the university/college level. It is not uncommon for former interns to acquire full-time employment at an organization once they have enough necessary experience. The challenging job market has made it essential for college students to gain real world experience prior to graduation. In the US, company internships are at the centre of NIGMS funded biotechnology training programmes for science PhD students. One example is the Biotechnology Training Programme - University of Virginia.

Not all internships are paid. Many internships that are unpaid involve receiving college credit, especially if an internship is correlated with a specific class. The U.S. Department of Labour's Wage and Hour Division allows an employer not to pay a trainee if all of the following are true:

1. The training, even though it includes actual operation of the facilities of the employer, is similar to what would be given in a vocational school or academic educational instruction;

2. The training is for the benefit of the trainees;
3. The trainees do not displace regular employees, but work under their close observation;
4. The employer that provides the training derives no immediate advantage from the activities of the trainees, and on occasion the employer's operations may actually be impeded;
5. The trainees are not necessarily entitled to a job at the conclusion of the training period; and
6. The employer and the trainees understand that the trainees are not entitled to wages for the time spent in training.

An exception is allowed for individuals who volunteer their time, freely and without anticipation of compensation for religious, charitable, civic, or humanitarian purposes to non-profit organizations. An exception is also allowed for work performed for a state or local government agency.

Some states have their own laws on the subject. Laws in the state of California, for example, require an employer to pay its interns working in California unless the intern receives college credit for the labour.

South America

Brazil: Internships in Brazil are known as *estágios* (lit. "stages") and internship workers are known as *estagiários*. They are regulated by the *Lei do Estágio* ("Law of Internship"). This law demands that companies pay a monthly income, although some internships are unpaid. It also requires that companies provide Personal Injury Service. The *Lei do Estágio* further stipulates a 30-hour limit of hours worked per week, which is normally divided into six hours per day from Monday to Friday. *Estagiários* have the right to 30 days of paid holiday for each year worked.

Mentorship

Mentorship is a personal developmental relationship in which a more experienced or more knowledgeable person helps to guide a less experienced or less knowledgeable person. However, true mentoring is more than just answering occasional questions or providing ad hoc help. It is about an ongoing relationship of learning, dialogue, and challenge.

The person in receipt of mentorship may be referred to as a *protégé* (male), a *protégée* (female), an apprentice or, in recent years, a mentee.

"Mentoring" is a process that always involves communication and is relationship based, but its precise definition is elusive. One definition of the many that have been proposed, is:

Mentoring is a process for the informal transmission of knowledge, social capital, and the psychosocial support perceived by the recipient as relevant to work, career, or professional development; mentoring entails informal communication, usually face-to-face and during a sustained period of time, between a person who is perceived to have greater relevant knowledge, wisdom, or experience (the mentor) and a person who is perceived to have less (the protégé)".

Mentoring in Europe has existed since at least Ancient Greek times. Since the 1970s it has spread in the United States of America mainly in training contexts and it has been described as "an innovation in American management".

Historical

The roots of the practice are lost in antiquity. The word itself was inspired by the character of Mentor in Homer's *Odyssey*. Though the actual Mentor in the story is a somewhat ineffective old man, the goddess Athena takes on his appearance in order to guide young Telemachus in his time of difficulty. Historically significant systems of mentorship include the guru - disciple tradition practiced in Hinduism and Buddhism, Elders, the discipleship system practiced by Rabbinical Judaism and the Christian church, and apprenticing under the medieval guild system.

Mentoring Techniques

The focus of mentoring is to develop the whole person and so the techniques are broad and require wisdom in order to be used appropriately. A 1995 study of mentoring techniques most commonly used in business found that the five most commonly used techniques among mentors were:

1. *Accompanying:* making a commitment in a caring way, which involves taking part in the learning process side-by-side with the learner.
2. *Sowing:* mentors are often confronted with the difficulty of preparing the learner before he or she is ready to change. Sowing is necessary when you know that what you say may not be understood or even acceptable to learners at first but will make sense and have value to the mentee when the situation requires it.

3. *Catalyzing:* when change reaches a critical level of pressure, learning can escalate. Here the mentor chooses to plunge the learner right into change, provoking a different way of thinking, a change in identity or a re-ordering of values.
4. *Showing:* this is making something understandable, or using your own example to demonstrate a skill or activity. You show what you are talking about, you show by your own behaviour.
5. *Harvesting:* here the mentor focuses on "picking the ripe fruit": it is usually used to create awareness of what was learned by experience and to draw conclusions. The key questions here are: "What have you learned?", "How useful is it?".

Different techniques may be used by mentors according to the situation and the mindset of the mentee, and the techniques used in modern organizations can be found in ancient education systems, from the Socratic technique of harvesting to the accompaniment method of learning used in the apprenticeship of itinerant cathedral builders during the Middle Ages. Leadership authors Jim Kouzes and Barry Posner advise mentors to look for "teachable moments" in order to "expand or realize the potentialities of the people in the organizations they lead" and underline that personal credibility is as essential to quality mentoring as skill.

Typology

There are two broad types of mentoring relationships: formal and informal. Informal relationships develop on their own between partners. Formal mentoring, on the other hand, refers to a structured process supported by the organization and addressed to target populations. Youth mentoring programmes assist at-risk children or youth who lack role models and sponsors. In business, formal mentoring is part of talent management addressed to populations such as key employees, newly hired graduates, high potentials and future leaders. The matching of mentor and mentee is often done by a mentoring coordinator or by means of an (online) database registry.

There are formal mentoring programmes that are values-oriented, while social mentoring and other types focus specifically on career development. Some mentorship programmes provide both social and vocational support. In well-designed formal mentoring programmes, there are programme goals, schedules, training (for both mentors and protégés), and evaluation. In 2004 Metizo created the first mentoring certification for companies and business schools in order to guarantee the integrity and effectiveness of formal mentoring. Certification is attributed jointly by the organization and an external expert.

There are many kinds of mentoring relationships from school or community-based relationships to e-mentoring relationships. These mentoring relationships vary and can be influenced by the type of mentoring relationship that is in effect. That is whether it has come about as a formal or informal relationship. Also there are several models have been used to describe and examine the sub-relationships that can emerge. For example, Buell describes how mentoring relationships can develop under a cloning model, nurturing model, friendship model and apprenticeship model. The cloning model is about the mentor trying to "produce a duplicate copy of him or her self." The nurturing model takes more of a "parent figure, creating a safe, open environment in which mentee can both learn and try things for him-or herself." The friendship model are more peers "rather than being involved in a hierarchical relationship." Lastly, the apprenticeship is about less "personal or social aspects... and the professional relationship is the sole focus".

Contemporary Research and Practice in the US

Research in the 1970s, partly in response to a study by Daniel Levinson, led some women and African Americans to question whether the classic "white male" model was available or customary for people who are newcomers in traditionally white male organizations. In 1978 Edgar Schein described multiple roles for successful mentors. Two of Schein's students, Davis and Garrison, undertook to study successful leaders of both genders and at least two races. Their research presented evidence for the roles of: cheerleader, coach, confidant, counsellor, developer of talent, "griot" (oral historian for the organization or profession), guardian, guru, inspiration, master, "opener of doors", patron, role model, pioneer, "seminal source", "successful leader", and teacher. They described multiple mentoring practices which have since been given the name of "mosaic mentoring" to distinguish this kind of mentoring from the single mentor approach.

Mosaic mentoring is based on the concept that almost everyone can perform one or another function well for someone else — and also can learn along one of these lines from someone else. The model is seen as useful for people who are "non-traditional" in a traditional setting, such as people of colour and women in a traditionally white male organization. The idea has been well received in medical education literature. There are also mosaic mentoring programmes in various faith-based organizations.

Corporate Mentorship Programmes

Corporate mentoring programmes are used by mid to large organizations to further the development and retention of employees. Mentoring programmes may be formal or informal and serve a variety of specific objectives including acclimation of new employees, skills development, employee retention and diversity enhancement.

Formal Mentoring Programmes

Formal mentoring programmes offer employees the opportunity to participate in an organized mentoring programme. Participants join as a mentor, mentee or both by completing a mentoring profile. Mentoring profiles are completed as written forms on paper or computer or filled out via an online form as part of an online mentoring system. Mentees are matched with a mentor by a programme administrator or a mentoring committee, or may self-select a mentor depending on the programme format.

Informal mentoring takes places in organizations that develop a culture of mentoring but do not have formal mentoring in place. These companies may provide some tools and resources and encourage managers to accept mentoring requests from more junior members of the organization.

New-hire Mentorship

New-hire mentoring programmes are set up to help new employees acclimate more quickly into the organization. In new-hire mentoring programmes, newcomers to the organization (protégés) are paired with more experienced people (mentors) in order to obtain information, good examples, and advice as they advance. It has been claimed that new employees who are paired with a mentor are twice as likely to remain in their job than those who do not receive mentorship.

These mentoring relationships provide substance for career growth, and benefit both the mentor and the mentee. For example, the mentor gets to show leadership by giving back and perhaps being refreshed about their own work. The organization receives an employee that is being gradually introduced and shaped by the organization's culture and operation because they have been under the mentorship of an experienced member. The person being mentored networks, becomes integrated easier in an organization, gets experience and advice along the way. It has been said that "joining a mentor's network and developing one's own is central to advancement" and this is possibly why those mentored tend to do well in their organizations.

In the organizational setting, mentoring usually "requires unequal knowledge", but the process of mentorship can differ. Bullis describes the mentoring process in the forms of phase models. Initially, the "mentee proves himself or herself worthy of the mentor's time and energy". Then cultivation occurs which includes the actual "coaching...a strong interpersonal bond between mentor and mentee develops". Next, under the phase of separation "the mentee experiences more autonomy". Ultimately, there is more of equality in the relationship, termed by Bullis as Redefinition.

High-potential Mentorship

High-potential mentoring programmes are used to groom up-and-coming employees deemed to have the potential to move up into leadership roles. Here the employee (protégé) is paired with a senior level leader (or leaders) for a series of career-coaching interactions. These programmes tend to be smaller than more general mentoring programmes and mentees must be selected to participate.

A similar method of high-potential mentoring is to place the employee in a series of jobs in disparate areas of an organization, all for small periods of time, in anticipation of learning the organization's structure, culture, and methods. A mentor does not have to be a manager or supervisor to facilitate the process.

Matching Mentors and Mentees

Mentees are matched with mentors by a designated mentoring committee or mentoring administrator usually consisting of senior members of the Training, Learning and Development and Human Resources departments. The matching committee reviews the mentoring profiles and makes matches based on areas for development, mentor strengths, overall experience, skill set, location and objectives for the mentorship. Mentoring technology can be used to facilitate matches allowing mentees to search and select a mentor based on their own development needs and interests. This mentee-driven methodology increases the speed in which matches are created and reduces the amount of administrative time required to manage the programme. The quality of matches increases as well with self-match programmes because the greater the involvement of the mentee in the selection of their mentor, the better the outcome of the mentorship. There are a variety of online mentoring technology programmes available that can be utilized to facilitate this mentee-driven matching process.

Mentorship in Education

In many secondary and post-secondary schools, mentorship programmes are offered to support students in programme completion, confidence building and transitioning to further education or the workforce. There are also many peer mentoring programmes designed specifically to bring under-represented populations into science and engineering. The Internet has brought university alumni closer to graduating students. Graduate university alumni are engaging with current students in career mentorship through interview questions and answers. The students with the best answers receive professional recommendations from industry experts build a more credible CV. Websites such as, Endorse me and GapJumpers are leading the way in online career mentorship.

Blended Mentoring

The blended mentoring is a mix of on-site and online events, projected to give to career counselling and development services the opportunity to adopt mentoring in their ordinary practice.

Reverse Mentoring

In the reverse mentoring situation, the mentee has more overall experience (typically as a result of age) than the mentor (who is typically younger), but the mentor has more knowledge in a particular area, and as such, reverses the typical constellation. Examples are when young internet or mobile savvy Millennial Generation teens train executives in using their high end Smart Phones. They in turn sometimes offer insight in business processes.

Business Mentoring

The concept of mentoring has entered the business domain as well. This is different from being an apprentice, a business mentor provides guidance to a business owner or an entrepreneur on the entrepreneur's business. An apprentice learns a trade by working on the job with the "employer".

A 2012 literature review by EPS-PEAKS investigated the practice of business mentoring, with a focus on the Middle-East and North Africa region. The review found strong evidence to suggest that business mentoring can have real benefits for entrepreneurs, but highlights some key factors that need to be taken into account when designing mentoring programmes for this to be the case, such as the need to balance a formal and informal approach and to appropriately match mentors and mentees.

4

State Interest in Vocational Education

Vocational Education and Training (VET) is an important element of the nation's education initiative. In order for Vocational Education to play its part effectively in the changing national context and for India to enjoy the fruits of the demographic dividend, there is an urgent need to redefine the critical elements of imparting vocational education and training to make them flexible, contemporary, relevant, inclusive and creative. The Government is well aware of the important role of Vocational education and has already taken a number of important initiatives in this area. School-based vocational education in India is currently covered by a centrally sponsored scheme which was mooted in 1988 and was aimed at providing an alternative to the pursuit of higher academic education. One of the objectives of the Vocational Education Programme of NIOS is to meet the need for skilled and middle-level manpower for the growing sectors of economy, both organized and unorganized. The range of Vocational Education courses has been expanding over the years depending upon needs of learners and market demands.

Vocational education consists basically of practical courses through which one gains skills and experience directly linked to a career in future. It helps students to be skilled and in turn, offers better employment opportunities. These trainings are parallel to the other conventional courses of study (like B. Sc., M. Sc. etc.). Time management and meeting deadlines play an important role in success in a vocational course and during their studies students normally produce a portfolio of evidence (plans, reports, drawings, videos, placements), which is taken as a demonstration of students' capabilities for a job. After finishing the courses, students are often offered placements in jobs.

Vocational trainings in a way give students some work related experiences that many employers look for. According to a National Sample Survey Organization (NSSO) report (No. 517, 61/10/03) two types of vocational trainings are available in India: a) Formal and; b) Non-formal. Formal vocational training follows a structured training programme and leads to certificates, diplomas or degrees, recognized by State/Central Government, Public Sector and other reputed concerns.

Non-formal vocational training helps in acquiring some marketable expertise, which enables a person to carry out her/his ancestral trade or occupation. In a way through such non-formal vocational training, a person receives vocational training through 'hereditary' sources. Often 'Non-formal' vocational trainings are also received through 'other sources'. In such cases training received by a person to pursue a vocation, is not ancestral and is different from the trade or occupation of his/her ancestors.

Type of Institutions for Vocational training according to National Sample Survey Organization (NSSO):

Different institutions which impart vocational training can be classified into five categories:

(i) Government,

(ii) Local body,

(iii) Private aided,

(iv) Private unaided, and

(v) not known.

According to a NSSO report vocational training is received by only 10% of persons aged between 15-29 years. Out of this only 2% receive formal training, while non-formal training constitutes the remaining 8%. Out of the formal training received by that particular age group only 3% are employed. Most sought after field of training is computer related training. Only 20% of formal vocational training is received from ITI/ITCs. In India, technical education and vocational training system follows patterns like graduate - post graduate, engineer - technologists through training colleges, diploma from polytechnics and certificate level training in ITIs through formal apprenticeships.

The Vocational Training in India is imparted by mainly two types of bodies:

- Public Industrial Training Institutes (ITIs)
- Private owned Industrial Training Centres (ITCs)

The Indian Government has invested a lot for the development of skills through ITIs. The DGE&T generally regulates these ITIs and ITCs at national level and implements policies for vocational training.

Training statistics of ITI/ITCs - main formal vocational training institutes in India:

Some of the principal training schemes are:

- The Craftsmen Training Scheme (CTS)
- Apprenticeship Training Scheme (ATS).

According to the Planning commission report for the 11th Five year plan there are about 5,114 Industrial Training Institutes (ITIs) imparting training in 57 engineering and 50 non-engineering trades. Of these, 1,896 are State Government-run ITIs while 3,218 are private. The total seating capacity in these ITIs is 7.42 lakh (4 lakh seats in government ITIs and the remaining 3.42 lakh in private ITCs). Figures below this text represent detailed information on the number and capacity of ITIs/ITCs in different states/UTs. A number of vocational training institutes are being run by private training providers. The formal training system of India starts at Grade 8 and above. According to a report of ILO, the quality of DGE&T's skills development programmes compete with other programmes, such as high vocational schools (10 plus 2 stream), colleges, polytechnics, etc. The share of ITI-based training seems to capture around 10-12 per cent of the total number of school pass outs at Grade10 level.

Some training schemes provide by DGE&T other than Craftsmen Training Scheme (CTS) and Apprenticeship Training Scheme (ATS) are:

- Craft Instructors' Training Scheme(CITS),Advanced Vocational Training Scheme(AVTS)
- Supervisory/Foremen Training Scheme, Staff Training and Research Programme
- Instructional Media Development Programme
- Women's Training Scheme
- Hi-Tech Training Scheme

From the above graphs we may conclude that Tamil Nadu holds the majority stake in private owned ITCs and Maharashtra holds a similar position for Government owned ITIs.

Details about the nature of the training in ITIs etc. are available on the website of

- Ministry of Labour
- National Council for Vocational Training (NCVT)

National Council for Vocational Training', an advisory body, was set up by the Government of India in the year 1956. The National Council is chaired by the Minister of Labour, with members from different Central and State Government Departments, Employers and Workers organizations, Professional and Learned Bodies, All India Council for Technical Education, Scheduled castes and Scheduled tribes, All India Women's Organization, etc.

And State Councils for Vocational Training at the State level and Trade Committees have been established to assist the NCVT. Main mandate of the NCVT, according to DGE&T, is to establish and award National Trade Certificates in engineering, non-engineering, building, textile, leather trades and such other trades which are brought within its scope by the Government of India.

It also prescribes standards in respect of syllabi, equipment, scales of accommodation, duration of courses and methods of training. It also conducts tests in various trade courses and lays down standards of proficiency required for passing the examination leading to the award of National Trade Certificate etc.

Statistics on persons (per thousand) who attend vocational training, according to duration of training and age groups of trained people:

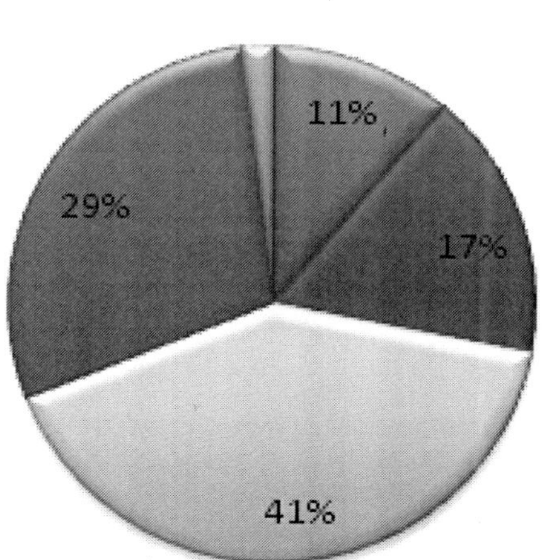

Figure: *Percentage of persons who received vocational training in Rural India (per thousand person) (duration of training wise)*

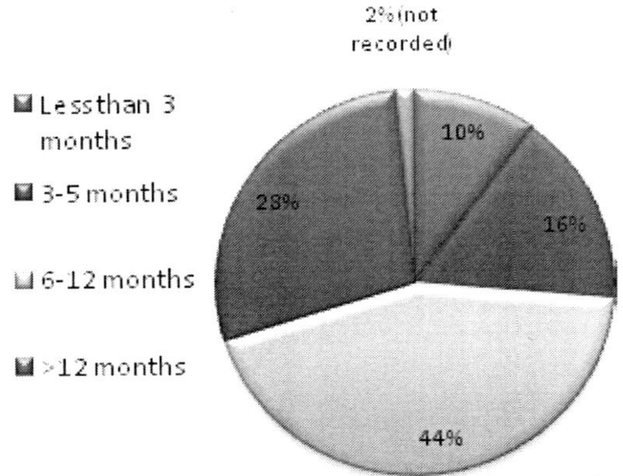

Figure: *Percentage of persons who received vocational training in Urban India(per thousand person)(duration of training wise)*

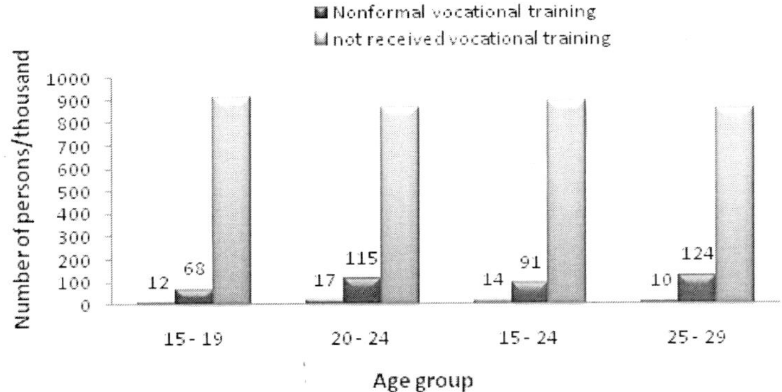

Figure: *Number of person getting vocational training per thousand persons age group wise in India*

Despite efforts made to popularize these courses, several problems prevent ITIs/ITCs from reaching common masses and youth.

Paramedical Training Status for Rural India

Paramedical courses are one of the largest sources of vocational educated persons in the field of medical industry. Status of the total paramedical manpower in rural India is given in following graph.

From the Figure below, it is clear that out of total 315,746 paramedical workers in rural India, 47% are female health workers. But extension workers are very few; almost 1%. We also need to focus on the availability of Radio Graphers, Pharmacists and Laboratory Technicians for rural India. To disseminate knowledge of basic health facilities we need to train more paramedical workers for rural India. But unfortunately at present they are few compared to the large size of the rural population.

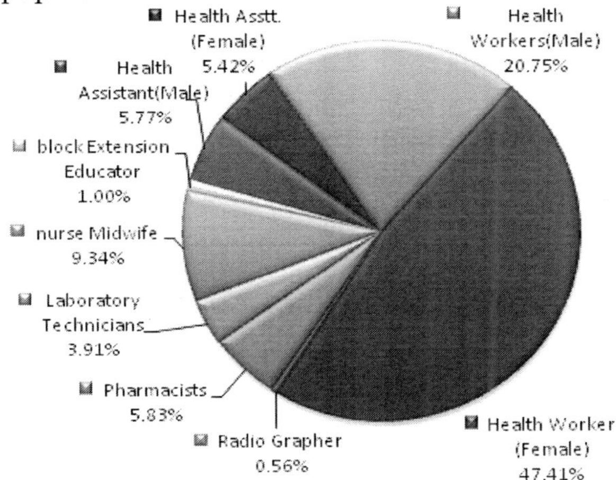

Figure: *Trained paramedical practitioners available in rural India*

Status in Schools

Schools also provide vocational training formally at 10 and 12th level. The percentage stake of all major states, providing vocational training in India. It is observed that states like Punjab, Orissa Tamil Nadu etc. hold approximately 79% stake in number of schools which impart vocational training. And Maharashtra is the foremost, holding more than 16%. Schools have an important role in vocational studies because one can start learning a vocation from his/her schools days. More coverage in school with proper infrastructure can create a large technical group in future, which at present is deficient.

Other Government and private bodies providing vocational training in India:

Khadi and Village Industries Commission (KVIC): The Khadi and Village Industries Commission (KVIC) impart training and awards vocational certificates for the unorganized sectors. The list of such training has been given. KVIC (established in April 1957) is a statutory body established by an Act of Parliament. It took over the work of former All India Khadi and Village Industries Board.

It has the main objective of generating employment; the other objective of producing saleable products; and the wider objective of creating self-reliance amongst the people and building up of strong rural community spirit.

- KVIC is assigned with the proper planning, promotion, organizational implementation of programmes for the development of Khadi and other village industries in rural areas in coordination with other agencies engaged in rural development and are also charged with the responsibility of encouraging and promoting research in the KVI sector.
- KVIC is also entrusted with the task of providing financial assistance to institutions engaged in rural development.

Rural Employment Generation Programme (REGP) is the major programme of KVIC. The main objective of this programme is employment generation in rural areas by setting up new village industries (except those on negative list) by availing loans from banks and margin money (middle end subsidy) being provided by KVIC. Beneficiaries own contributions should be minimum 10% of project cost for general category and 5% of project cost for special category. Banks will sanction 90% of the project cost in case of general category and 95% for project cost for special category beneficiary.

Prime Minister's Employment Generation Programme (PMEGP) as a central scheme to be monitored by the Ministry of Micro, Small and Medium Enterprises (MoMSME). The implementation body will be Khadi and Village Industries Commission (KVIC), a statutory organization under the administrative control of the Ministry of MSME as the single nodal agency at the National level. At the State level, the Scheme will be implemented through State KVIC Directorates, State Khadi and Village Industries Boards (KVIBs) and District Industries Centres (DICs) and banks.

The Government subsidy under the scheme is routed by KVIC through the Banks for similar distribution to the beneficiaries / entrepreneurs in their Bank accounts. The Implementing Agencies, such as KVIC, KVIBs and DICs will associate with different Non Government Organizations (NGOs)/reputed autonomous institutions/ Self Help Groups (SHGs)/ National Small Industries Corporation (NSIC)/Udyami Mitras empanelled under Rajiv Gandhi Udyami Mitra Yojana (RGUMY), Panchayati Raj institutions and other relevant bodies in the implementation of the Scheme. Here training, formally or informally, plays a crucial role for success for the schemes.

List of training institutes providing support for the schemes: Micro, Small and Medium Enterprises Development Institutes (MSME-DIs), Tool Rooms and Technical Development Centres (Development Commissioner), National Small Industries Corporation's (NSIC) offices,

Incubators and Training cum Incubation Centres (TICs) set up in Public Private Partnership Mode. National level Entrepreneurship Development Institutes like National Institute for Entrepreneurship and Small Business Development (NIESBUD), National Institute for Micro, Small and Medium Enterprises (NIMSME) and Indian Institute of Entrepreneurship (IIE), Guwahati (under MoMSME), and the Entrepreneurship Development Centres (EDCs).

According to the Annual Reports of KVIC in the year 2001-02 and 2004-05, three different categories of training namely, Khadi, Village Industries and EDP training existed. It is also observed that women's participation has also increased for Khadi training from 52% to 82.1%. But the women's participation fell from 47% to 30.9% and from 41.5% to 20% for Village industries and Other EAP/EDP trainings respectively. Karnataka, Kerala, Madhya Pradesh Maharashtra Orissa, Tamil Nadu, West Bengal, Uttaranchal and UP are the main states where KVIC imparts maximum number of trainings.

Tool Room & Training Centres (DC, MSME): Govt. of India has set up a few Tool Room & Training Centres of large size involving estimated cost of over Rs. 50 crores each, in order to provide facilities for design and manufacture of tools. Govt. of India have decided to assist the State governments by setting up Mini Tool Room and Training Centres.

The main objective of the Mini Tool Room & Training Centres would be-

- Manufacturing jigs, fixtures, cutting tools, gauges, press tools, plastic moulds, forging dies, pressure casting dies and other tools for Small Scale Industries. To provide training facility in tool manufacturing and tool design to generate a work force of skilled workers, supervisors, engineers/designers etc.
- To work as a Nucleus Centre for providing consultancy, information service, documentation etc, for solving problems related to tooling of industries in the region. And to act as a Common Facility Centre for small scale industries and to assist them in product and prototype development.

National Manufacturing Competitive Council (NMCC): This Body was set up by Govt. of India in the year of 2004 as a part of National Common Minimum Programme to help in accelerated growth of GDP, primarily focusing on manufacturing Industry. According to the strategy for National Manufacturing-2006, vocational training plays a key role on this. According to a report by NMCC, if Indian manufacturing has to grow at around 12 percent per annum, it will be necessary for the education and training system to produce at least 1.5 million technically skilled people every year. It is estimated that the country would need an incremental requirement of about 20 million skilled technicians by 2015.

To support the growth of manufacturing, the policy highlights of NMCC on vocational training system are:

- The public sector driven initiative, through The Apprentices Act, 1961 and ITIs (Industrial Training Institutes) has not been able to keep pace with changing requirements. So we need to be taken care of the up-gradation of the Industrial Training Institutes through public-private partnerships, with training authorities de-linked from certifying ones.
- To initiate some PPP mode operations to establish and operate new demand driven technical training centres through financial and other incentives, with designed industry-managed and government supported, quality control and accreditation systems.
- Two major themes to be taken up on priority basis, namely; 'National Vocational Education Qualification System' and setting up a Vocational Education & Training Institute in each State.
- Private sector manufacturing/engineering organizations will be encouraged to adopt Vocational Education Institutes to meet the challenges. The diploma-holders form the backbone of the manufacturing sector at the 'hands on' level. But for keeping focus on the rapid changes in manufacturing technology it is essential that the polytechnic institutions be strengthened both in terms of the equipment and teaching faculty; with curricula changing to match the emerging needs of the manufacturing sector.

CAPART (Council for Advancement of Rural Technology): CAPART is playing a crucial role in implementing development activities through funding of different voluntary organizations. These voluntary organizations help rural people to enhance livelihood by giving them support through different modes of vocational training and related activities. CAPART has been formed by amalgamating the 'Council for Advancement of Rural Technology' (CART) and 'People's Action for Development India' (PADI). CAPART is an autonomous body registered under the Societies Registration Act 1860, under the aegis of the Ministry of Rural Development, Government of India and it has been a major promoter of rural development in India, assisting over 12,000 voluntary organizations. (Details available on http://capart.nic.in)

SRI, Ranchi (Society for Rural Industrialization): This society has major programme to impart training for the rural people. It mainly focuses on skill development of village youths. Training of trainers and management training are offered to other organizations including the government. The skill training includes courses on communication, personality building and enterprise management. It also offers short training courses on programme management for various National schemes for functionaries of NGOs and of Governments. SRI's tie up with Indian Institute of Science, IIT-Kharagpur and CBRI-Roorkee on cost-effective construction is well known.(Details available on http://sriranchi.org/index.php)

Ramakrishna Math and Ramakrishna Mission: Ramakrishna Math was established by Sri Ramakrishna (1836-1886). Ramakrishna Mission is a society (registered) in which monks and devotees of Ramakrishna Math cooperate in conducting various types of social services, mainly in India. It was founded by Sri Ramakrishna's chief apostle, Swami Vivekananda (1863-1902), one of the foremost thinkers and religious leaders of the present age. Ramakrishna Math and Ramakrishna Mission are legally and financially separate from each other but they are closely inter-related in several other ways, and are to be regarded as twin organizations. Vocational training is one of their most valuable inputs in development activity. The rural and tribal activities are mainly classified as: (i) General; (ii) Agricultural; (iii) Educational and Self-reliance training; and (iv) Medical. Within the classification of Educational and self-reliance training, free schools are run for children. Adult and non-formal education centres have been set up. Audio-visual shows, farmers' fairs and the like are also organized. And a major activity is to help the formation of self-help groups and training schemes are organized for teaching lathe-turning, carpentry, bee-keeping, pisciculture, dairy-farming and poultry-farming, weaving, incense-stick rolling, etc to enable the rural and tribal community to achieve minimum livelihood.

Some other institutes which impart vocational training like Gandhi Ashram in Wardha and Madurai are also important in this field. We could name a few like Nanaji Deshmukh and many other personalities who had done remarkable work in the vocational education field in rural areas.

Initiatives: The Eleventh Plan has taken an initiative to launch a National Skill Development Mission that may bring some changes in 'Skill Development' programmes and initiatives. The Mission will be operative under Prime Minister's *National Council on Skill Development* for apex level policy directions, and under the *National Skill Development Coordination Board*, and a *National Skill Development Corporation/Trust*. The State governments will engage some of their Departments/Agencies for constituting a State Skill Development Mission. Some chosen private sectors (mainly twenty high growth sectors), will play an important part as the private arm of the Mission with an outlay of Rs 22,800 crores.

Constituents of *Prime Minister's National Council on Skill Development* and *National Skill Development Coordination Board* will be the following:

- *Prime Minister's National Council on Skill Development:* Prime Minister as Chairman; Ministers of Finance, HRD, Industries, Rural Development, Labour & Employment and Housing & Urban Poverty Alleviation; Deputy Chairman, Planning Commission; Chairperson, National Manufacturing Competitive Council; Chairperson of the National Skill Development Corporation; six experts in the area of Skill Development as Members and Private Secretary to Prime Minister as Member-Secretary.
- *National Skill Development Coordination Board:* Deputy Chairman, Planning Commission as Chairman; Chairperson/ Chief Executive Officer of the National Skill Development Corporation, Secretaries of Ministries of Finance, Human Resource Development, Labour and Employment, Rural Development, Housing and Employment, Rural Development, Housing & Urban Poverty Alleviation; Secretaries of Four States by rotation, for a period of two years, three Distinguished Academicians/Subject Area Specialists as Members and Secretary, Planning Commission as the Member-Secretary.

The National Skill Development Corporation will be constituted as Government Equity with a view to obtaining about Rs 15,000 crore from the public and private sectors, and other bilateral and multilateral sources for the promotion of skill development. It will act as a non-profit company under the Companies Act, with appropriate governance structures (board of directors being drawn from outstanding professionals/experts).

The National Commission for Enterprises in the Unorganized Sector (NCEUS): It has been set up as an advisory body for the informal sector to bring about improvement in the productivity of these enterprises and for generation of large scale employment opportunities on a sustainable basis, particularly in rural areas.

Public Private Partnership (PPP): Major emphasis has been given on the PPP mode in the Eleventh Five Year Plan. It focuses on the following:

- Private Investment in Skill Training.
- National framework for domain specific standards and common principles.
- National database for location wise availability (and shortage) of skilled personnel will be established.
- The system should provide the options of multiple entry and exit points and total mobility between vocational, general and technical streams.
- Special emphasis on economically weaker section.
- To overcome the regional disparities due to diverse socio-economic factors, VGF approach would be adopted to address regional imbalances through PPP.

The eleventh five year plan also envisions setting up an Apex skill development institute which will take initiatives on programme testing, certification, curriculum setting faculty development, introduction of new elective courses in IITs /IIMs etc.

State Govt. initiatives to be taken up in the 11th Five year plan are:

- Modernization of employment exchanges, which can act as career counselling centres.
- Modernization of existing it is.
- Giving institutes more autonomy.
- Execution of PPP mode.
- Personnel Policy to ensure accountability and outcomes.

Main focus of the 11th five year plan is to forge a joint collaboration between the States and the Centre and also boost private partnerships to create an estimated 58.6 million new jobs in the domestic economy and about 45 million jobs in the international economy.

World Bank also has taken initiative through its Millennium Development Goal to impart training and elementary education in India.

Points to focus on:

- The training courses lack focus on the changing job market. As a result it was seen from various reports that the number of students is declining for long term vocational courses, mainly in ITIs. The training policy should be focused on the changing job market in order to attract young people. More autonomy needs to be provided to institutes and they should have market linked infrastructure. For publicly funded training, equity distribution is also a problem. But job creation must be done regionally, not centrally; otherwise it will create regional imbalances of trained manpower. According to NSSO report (No. 470, 55th round) about 27 per cent of the Indian population were migrants. The proportion of migrants was higher (33 per cent) in urban areas than (24 per cent) in the rural areas. It was mainly in search of jobs. Creating job opportunities regionally can help maintain the equilibrium in future days.
- Funding for the public ITIs is very low compared to other countries like China and USA which have restructuring-funds, whose share goes for improvement of vocational training systems in order to achieve international quality. Although things have changed for the better in the 11th five year plan with the introduction of the National Skill Development Mission. But it is also desirable to have mechanisms to raise funds privately for up gradation of ITIs.
- ITIs must focus on low-literate youth and provide new vocational qualifications/training programmes and also on unorganised sector, otherwise it will cause long term losses. To take an example automobile industry is a technology intensive industry but most of the workshops are running without formally trained staff (we have currently no database of that). Sometimes, lack of training skills may harm the delicate instrument of vehicles. A vital challenge is to formally train workers for the crafts industry where a considerable number of informally trained craftsman work together.
- Lack of accountability and training/supply management are also major problems for ITI institutes.
- In our country different institutes impart vocational training but they do not have coordination among themselves. Information about this sector is not available from a single source. In fact we need to create a central database from where

one can get full access on vocational training system right from school level to ITI/ITC institutes.

- In rural sector, radiographer and other trained para-medical persons are very less in comparison to the large number of the rural population. Policy makers should focus on the paramedical vocational studies, so that incremental change in number of trained paramedical worker can benefit rural masses.
- A central vocational training standardization system, accredited nationally and globally, for maintaining the quality of the vocational education can enhance credibility of vocationally trained persons in the industry.
- To attract more students from school level, reorientation of vocational courses is needed.
- There should be a bridge organization to relate R&D institutes and vocational education system. It would help the vocationally trained person to get the benefits of R&D.

Smith–Hughes Act

The Smith-Hughes National Vocational Education Act of 1917 was an act of the United States Congress that promoted vocational agriculture to train people "who have entered upon or who are preparing to enter upon the work of the farm," and provided federal funds for this purpose. As such, it is the basis both for the promotion of vocational education, and for its isolation from the rest of the curriculum in most school settings. The act is an expansion and modification of the 1914 Smith-Lever Act and both were based largely on a report and recommendation from Charles Allen Prosser's *Report of the National Commission on Aid to Vocational Education.* Woodlawn High School (Woodlawn, Virginia) became the first public secondary school in the United States to offer agricultural education classes under the Smith–Hughes Act.

Separate State Boards for Vocational Education

Several specific elements of the Act contributed to the isolation of vocational education from other parts of the comprehensive high school curriculum. Topowers to cooperate ... with the Federal Board for Vocational Education." Each State board was required to establish a plan:

> *"... showing the kinds of vocational education for which it is proposed that the appropriation shall be used; the kinds of schools and equipment; courses of study;*

methods of instruction; qualifications of teachers; ... plans for the training of teachers. ... Such plans shall be submitted by the State Board to the Federal Board of Vocational Education. The State Board shall make an annual report to the Federal Board for Vocational Education ... on the work done in the State and the receipts and expenditures of money under the provisions of this Act." (Section 8)

The term "state plan" has been a misnomer from the outset. The plan does not arise from state policy and leadership, but from the mandates contained in the Federal law. Rather than establish state priorities, describe organizational systems, or identify state goals, activities, or accountability mechanisms, the purpose of a state plan was to serve as a contract between the state and Federal governments, assuring adherence to Federal requirements and procedures.

The requirement to establish a Board of Vocational Education led some States to the establish a board separate from the State Board of Education. Thus some states had two separate governance education structures. This in turn fostered the notion of vocational schools as separate and distinct from general secondary schools, and of vocational education as separate from "academic" education. This was the case dido act.

Separation of Funds

Smith-Hughes spelled out the Federal Government's intent that vocational teachers should be "...persons who have had adequate vocational experience or contact in the line of work..." (Section 12) in which they were to hold classes. Federal funds, as well as State and local funds for vocational education, as specified in the State plans, could be spent on salaries of teachers with vocational experience, but not on salaries of academic teachers. Although the Act's intent was to avoid "raiding" of vocational funds by other segments of the comprehensive high school, the result was to separate the vocational education programme from the mainstream of a school's operations.

Segregation of Vocational Education Students

The key restrictive section of the Act applied, however, not to teachers but to students. Smith-Hughes required that schools or classes giving instruction "to persons who have not entered upon employment shall require that at least half of the time of such instruction shall be given to practical work of a useful or productive basis, such instruction to extend over not less than nine months per year and not less than thirty hours per week." (Section 12) Thus, the law required the following: If a high-school student was taught one class by a teacher paid in full or in part from Federal vocational funds, that same student could receive no more than fifty per cent academic instruction.

The Federal Vocational Board was quickly able to extend the control of students' time to what came to be known as the 50-25-25 rule: fifty percent of the time in shop work; twenty-five percent in closely related subjects, and twenty-five percent in academic course work. This rule became a universal feature of State plans from the 1920s to the early 1960s.

The 1917 Act was virtually silent on manpower projections and on centralized assignment of training quotas to school districts. If the driving force of the Act was labour shortages, one would expect it to contain processes to identify shortages and time-controlled means to meet them. Surely the 50-25-25 pro-ration of students' time fits the development of some kinds of skills better than others.

The ultimate effect of the Act, though never stated explicitly, was to identify certain students and teachers as "vocational," and to protect the salaries of the latter by reserving for them (exclusively) certain amounts of Federal money matched by state and local contributions. Some critics infer that the authorities saw programmes of practical instruction so endangered from a dominant academic elite that they required such protection by Federal law. The result, however, was to segregate academic teachers and students from vocational teachers and students and to strengthen the social alienation that early critics of these steps had feared.

Segregation of the Curriculum

Predictably, vocational teachers emphasized job-specific skills to the almost complete exclusion of theoretical content. One result was that the intellectual development of vocational students tended to be limited at a relatively early age. Another result was that students so trained were ill-equipped to pass skills along in the workplace or to learn new skills when their jobs disappeared through technological change. High schools in the United States then, offered little to students who were interested in technical subjects (conceived as subjects that offer close harmony in the more or less simultaneous interplay of theory and practice).

Smith-Hughes through the Years

The policies and positions taken by the United States Congress in their enactment of Smith-Hughes have been extraordinarily powerful forces in determining the current status of vocational education. Remarkably, these central segregating and separating provisions have proven to be largely impervious to change in spite of the large-scale shifts in emphasis which have occurred since its original enactment. In fact, these provisions were later augmented and reinforced by subsequent actions. It will be useful to examine briefly how the emphasis on vocational-technical education has been altered through the years.

While the policy emphasis at the Federal level moved from the original focus on national defence to the severe unemployment problems in the 1930s, Federal influence in vocational programmes remained largely unchanged. However a significant change did occur in the 30's — the emphasis on vocational courses in what were then called "junior colleges" (which later evolved into community colleges).

In the next decade, the War Production Training Act, as implemented by the War Manpower Commission introduced the concept of "open-entry, open-exit" programmes. A collateral Federal effort was the Rural War Production Training Act which emphasized agriculture related programmes. By this time it had become abundantly clear that within vocational-technical education three restricted and restrictive programme tracks were in force: a general education effort, a vocational education programme, and various job training programmes.

During the 1940s and 50s, the programme of vocational education which had developed in the early 1900s from the need to "train boys and girls for work," envisioned as national defence strategy in the 20s, focused on unemployment in the 30s, now encountered both the need to assist with the war effort during the 40s, and the need to provide a transition to a peace-time economy. During this period and into the 1960s, States experienced first the burgeoning of industry related to the war effort, and later, growth in the junior college system and adult education.

Influences on vocational education during the 1950s were characterized by light industries springing from new technology, the emergence of the health occupations careers, and the inclusion of work experience as an appropriate part of public education. In addition, social policy at the Federal level led to two amendments to the George-Barden Act of 1946. The first amendment, Title II, Vocational Education in Practical Nursing, was a reflection of a Congressional interest in "the health of the people." Several years later, Title VIII sought to stimulate technical training programmes in the wake of the launching of Sputnik.

During the 1960s, vocational education experienced especially heavy enrollment growth. All the while, technological advances were producing increasing employment dislocation. The gap between the affluent and the disadvantaged widened; poverty in areas of economic depression could not be ignored. Congress responded by enacting the Manpower Development and Training Act of 1961 (MDTA), followed by the Vocational Education Act of 1963 (VEA). It is surprising to note that almost 50 years after the Smith–Hughes Act, in spite of all the intervening changes, the definition and purpose of vocational education as set out in the new VEA remained largely the same.

In sum, the essential nature of Federal vocational education remained constant from 1917 until 1963, though authorizations for Federal allocations were raised under both the George-Barden Act of 1946 and the National Defence Education Act of 1958. Measured in terms of funding and enrollment, this early form of categorical assistance was successful. In 1917, just before implementation of Smith-Hughes, there were 200,000 vocational students in the United States and something less than $3 million was spent annually on their training. Forty years later, enrollment had increased to 3.4 million students and expenditures stood at $176 million. Smith-Hughes required dollar for dollar matching of Federal money by the States, local governments, or some combination thereof. As the decade of the 1950s closed—the last decade for the Smith-Hughes version of categorical intervention—Federal funds were over-matched by both State and local funds, taken separately.

On the central, most traditional dimensions, the Smith-Hughes formulas had to be considered an enormous success by its strongest advocates. It had directly pumped hundreds of millions of dollars into the vocational education system. Its matching requirements had generated hundreds of millions of additional State and local funds all devoted to vocational education programmes. Even more impressively, vocational education enrollments had grown seventeenfold.

During this period of phenomenal growth, the whole arena of vocational education policy was left pretty much to the vocational education practitioners. There are several reasons for this phenomenon. Historically, vocational-technical education has not been a high priority area for the typical education reformer. Much more attention has been given over the years by education reformers and policy makers to concerns over the quality of preparation for postsecondary education. Several factors contributed to this "benign neglect." Most educators in positions to exercise authority at Federal, State or local levels have little or no experience with vocational education. Additionally, the academic research community has shown scant interest to the issues facing vocational education. Finally, until recently, there have been few pressures from the community to materially change the way vocational education is offered. As a result, policy influences affecting vocational education have been left, almost by default, to vocational educators. Because the Federal purposes in vocational education appeared to coincide so closely with the wishes of the vocational education community, i.e., to protect and expand practical training in secondary schools in the United States against the assumed opposition of the academic elite, the Federal acts were, practically speaking, self-enforcing.

5

Preparing Counsellors

Guidance helps people accomplish the following goals whether they are learners planning their education, training and careers, or adults planning their careers or further training, or preparing to become more employable.

- Identify own talents, strengths and weaknesses, family expectations and national requirements to sort out the personal relevance of the educational and vocational options available;
- Understand the available education and training options and the requirements for admission and success, and select an appropriate field of study;
- Understand the work options that are available, the qualifications required, the means of gaining entry, the life of the worker and the rewards of the jobs;
- Translate information about self, educational opportunities and the world of work into short-range and long-range career goals;
- Learn effective job-search procedures;
- Develop career adaptability to be able to take advantage of opportunities as they occur;
- Overcome self-defeating behaviours, gain self-confidence and learn life skills;
- Cope with the reactions to job loss of anger, depression, frustration and apathy, and learn to take continuing positive action to become employed again;
- Identify alternative occupations when current employment is in jeopardy.

Guidance is more than giving information. It is a blend of self-development and of the learning and assimilation of career, providing educational and labour market information. The development of self-confidence is often a prerequisite for taking action for one's career. The goals of guidance may be achieved via individual counselling, self-preparation, career development courses, computer-assisted guidance and Internet-based guidance systems.

Challenges of the Twenty-first Century

As the third millennium approaches, there is a growing recognition that guidance contributes to the personal, educational, economic and social development of individuals and nations.

State of the Economy

The first seven years of the 1990s were years of economic expansion in significant parts of Europe, North America and Asia, yet many countries worried about how well they could compete in the face of the globalization of trade. They examined their economic and educational policies and programmes to ensure that they would have competent, competitive and even entrepreneurial work forces. Typically, their recipes for future economic success included strengthening the career guidance services for learners and for workers in the labour force. As the international economy grew more worrisome and as economic management became a priority within an increasing range of countries, the development of competent labour forces was seen as increasingly important to the future economic well being of countries.

In the past a number of countries have followed policies that did not particularly welcome the private sector as an important part of society, but now as some governments downsize they look more and more to the private sector to provide growth in employment and to be good 'corporate citizens'. The years of neglect of the private sector is reflected in the lack of knowledge about basic labour market information (e.g., occupational descriptions, occupational classification system, job requirements, pay rates, hiring practices and job forecasts). The lack of this information and the lack of occupational structures for the gathering and classification of the information have presented problems to technical and vocational educators in deciding what programmes to offer. It also presents a problem to counsellors to provide vocational guidance when very little vocational information is available.

Innovations at the Turn of the Millennium

Guidance was first conducted through group talks and individual interviews with students, but increasingly it has been recognized that adults are in need of guidance as much as youth. It has also been accepted that career development is a cumulative learning often requiring more than an interview or two at significant transition points such as school leaving, preparation for higher education or at the time of job loss. Several current innovations are briefly described below.

Several countries are formulating career development guidelines to specify the characteristics of vocational maturity that people should be able to exhibit at each level of education and employment. These guidelines are then used as specifications for guidance programmes and for the evaluation of programmes. (Australian Education Council, 1992; National Occupational Information and Co-ordinating Committee; National Life Work Centre, 1998.)

Career and personal development courses typically address the following goals:

- Understand the importance of values, work, friends, family, income and self-fulfilment to personal and career development;
- Develop a sense of control over one's own life and work and explore one's own abilities, potential, needs, aspirations, self-monitoring, self-defeating behaviours, self-help skills and use of resources;
- Strengthen one's orientation to the future and identify steps to be taken, anticipate opportunities and barriers, timetable steps to the future, seek and identify opportunities, and take action;
- Examine a variety of occupations, learn about the education and training, licensing, certification or registration, working conditions and work-life style of the occupations;
- Learn decision-making and apply it to one's own career decisions including setting specific targets;
- Examine own self-awareness and tendency to analyse past experience, including what one has and has not accomplished and the reasons for successes and disappointments;
- Learn the job-search skills of preparing résumés, completing application forms, seeking interviews and being interviewed; and,

- Develop the transition skills of continuously developing one's competencies in the face of adversity and opportunity, obtain information on the transferability of one's skills to new opportunities, and of engage in continuous learning. Guidance courses are often taught by regular teachers with but a few days specialized training in the subject.

Career education, the infusion of career and labour market information into the regular subjects of the curriculum helps make the course material more relevant to everyday life and also instills the skills of research, thinking and questioning into education (rather than teaching them separately).

The past two decades have witnessed the growth of computer-assisted educational and career guidance systems that use: interest, aptitude and preference surveys; ed educational and occupational information; person-occupation matching systems; and educational and vocational planning systems. A requirement of such systems is a classification and description of occupations in a jurisdiction.

To make guidance available to adult populations, a number of governments established career centres providing a full range of guidance services including individual and group counselling, labour market information, and job search training. In addition, an increasing number of major employers have career centres for the use of their own staff. The companies actively encourage and assist their employees to acquire advanced skills to make them more promotable. Part of this service often includes personal career planning offered on a confidential basis.

Equity has become an increasingly important focus of career guidance and promises to continue to be more and more evident in career education and guidance. UNESCO is a major international influence in this movement (UNESCO, 1987; Bingham and Martin, 1989; Miller and Vetter, 1996) particularly as it relates to girls and women. Guidance programmes for persons with disabilities (Conger, 1997) and for aboriginals (Peavy, 1994, Charter et al., 1994) are becoming more and more important.

Peer helping is becoming very popular in some school systems because it has been demonstrated to be effective in creating a positive peer pressure in contrast to negative peer pressure. Peers help each other in learning, social activities and career planning.

Life-skills training to inculcate problem-solving abilities and their appropriate and responsible use in the management of one's life in such areas as personal, family, education, work and leisure is becoming a feature of many programmes for youth and adults. People who feel that they can influence their own lives, communicate better, have good relationships in the home and community, and exhibit social skills appropriate to the learning and workplaces are more employable and more likely to create opportunities for self-employment. (Allen et al., 1995.)

School guidance programmes in a number of countries now include the preparation by each student of a personal portfolio (National Occupational Information and Coordinating Committee that contains a record of achievement and action plans. These documents are drawn up by students as a basis for self-assessment and future planning. They also provide a medium for the recording of significant career information and relating it to one's plans.

Simulations of working life prompt the participants to obtain knowledge of themselves, occupations, education and training, pay and working conditions, living costs and other factors and integrate them into alternative career plans. Simulations are popular with learners and counsellors alike because they provide a realistic opportunity to test out expectations for the future (e.g. Barry, 1998).

Visits to work sites students in the ninth year are invited to spend the day in the workplace with either a parent, friend, relative or volunteer host. A true 'show and tell' experience for adults, in a multitude of different workplace settings including airports, police departments, civic centres, industrial enterprises, banks, restaurants, universities, radio stations, machine shops and hospitals. The initiative provides opportunities for students to see workers in different roles and responsibilities, and aims to enhance students' understanding of individual jobs in the context of the working community, while linking classroom and workplace experiences directly. The programme aims to create opportunities for students to see the realities of the workplace.

Internet

In an effort to make guidance available to all, and noting the increasing popularity of the Internet, a few affluent countries provide a full range of career, educational and labour-market information, and also career and personal planning courses, via the World Wide Web. In addition to information, some systems include inventories of interests and aptitudes, occupational choice systems, instructions on job search techniques, a resume generator, and even simulated job interviews. These countries like the idea of "self-serve" career guidance. The information provided by governments is often supplemented by information offered by educational institutions, employers, professional and trade associations, and other groups. In a few jurisdictions the Internet guidance programmes are supplemented with electronic mail communication with a counsellor and, in some cases, with other users through open discussion forums. Some experimentation is now underway to provide vocational counselling via interactive video conferencing on the Internet.

A by-product of Internet-based systems is that people in any country with access to the Internet can see the educational and occupational structures and opportunities in other countries and also use the guidance instruments (interest inventories, etc.) on-line. It is relevant to note that some of the users of Canadian Internet-based career systems access them from outside that country. A more planned effort to provide international guidance on the Internet is found in the European ESTIA project which provides information about education, work and the labour market in four countries, soon to expand to fourteen countries. Internet connections are far from being available to most people in most countries. However, the Internet delivery of career guidance will be increasingly common in the next century. On-line counseling has some distinct advantages: to reach people in rural and remote areas; to serve persons with disabilities that make it difficult for them to attend an office; and to accommodate people who are apprehensive about receiving counseling face to face.

Educational Reform

Some ministries of education are in the process of major educational reform because the emergence of a more 'learning-intensive' economy poses new challenges. Employment is becoming increasingly fluid, work is increasingly complex, occupational boundaries are changing or dissolving, and more jobs are temporary. For these reasons, continual learning is a more important part of work. Five main elements characterize an education system that is likely to prepare students effectively for this new environment:

- emphasis on science and technology;
- skill standards;
- close connection between vocational and academic education to meet the requirements of learning-intensive work;
- links between employers and school, and;
- workplace learning.

These changes present difficulties for the learners and many students (and their parents) are in need of a better understanding of the changes, the implications in terms of career prospects, the skills to adjust to a scientific mode of thinking and the cultures of new industrial working life. This situation calls for a special version of the guidance curriculum and programme generally to provide the orientation and to teach the learning skills.

School Dropouts

Students who prematurely discontinue their studies represent a major potential loss to themselves, the economy and the society. In some countries there is considerable pressure on students to quit school and help with the farm-work or otherwise bring supplemental income into their parents' household. Recently some countries have become increasingly active in attempting to lessen the number of dropouts - and this is quite feasible because dropping out is seldom done without prior notice on the part of the student's behaviour.

A number of mechanisms have been put in place: guidance curriculum; diagnostic surveys intended to help identify students likely to drop out so that remedial steps may be taken; remedial programmes for students falling behind in their studies; teaching of study skills; the implementation of peer helping programmes to make use of positive peer pressure and to combat negative peer pressure; combined work and study programmes; and changes in school management practices to give students the same rights of grievance and appeal that is common in the workplace. Guidance counsellors are often at the heart of these programmes.

School-to-work Transition

The articulation of school-based learning and work-based learning follows significantly different patterns from country to country. In some jurisdictions there is an almost seamless transition from the school to apprenticeship programmes. In other jurisdictions there is a complete separation between school and work. The role of guidance varies significantly according to the system. In the former it is the task of counsellors to assist students to select the appropriate types of work-based training programme and to prepare them for entry. In jurisdictions without this articulation, the school guidance programme has often been more geared to preparing the most academically inclined students for university than to help students who will go immediately into the labour force. Frequently in cultures that separate secondary education and apprenticeship programmes parents want their children to go to university and not to prepare for the trades even though the children have indicated a preference for a trade. Counsellors have a particular responsibility to explain to parents the many favourable aspects of a career in the trades.

Increasingly in jurisdictions that do not articulate school and work-based learning, schools integrate work experience assignments as an integral part of the curriculum and seek the co-operation of local employers, unions and professional associations. According to Stasz (1998) "the power of the work based learning is that authentic work experiences give learners opportunities to apply knowledge in useful contexts. They thereby can gain a deeper understanding of both their abilities and the opportunities they can create for themselves through experience and/or education. In the end, learning is a personal, developmental transformation, so it is crucial to pay attention to whether that transformation occurs, as well as to the context that will enable such a transformation. It is this context that teachers and counsellors, in and out of school, have the most ability to shape".

Guidance for Unemployed Workers

The following practices have been found (Bysshe, 1998 and others) to be helpful in preparing unemployed workers for new employment:

- Identify the "employability skills" that employers expect of workers and train workers in these skills;
- Use income-support programmes to train unemployed workers and to get them appropriate work experience to qualify for new employment;
- Teach job search techniques;
- Identify the information, assessment, guidance and training needs of individuals to help them become employed with-in a realistic time;
- Use an action plan, where the responsibilities of the client and the counsellor are clear;
- Provide ongoing help so that agreed plans are reviewed in the light of progress made and that necessary support can be given to deal with inevitable disappointments and failures;
- Address issues such as bolstering confidence and self-esteem, through appropriate measures;
- Develop and foster self-help to maximize the learning for the individual and ensure that all barriers to effective transition are being addressed; and,

- Act as the link between the individual, and learning and employment opportunities they wish to enter, including advocating on behalf of the individual.

Training of Counsellors

Although there are common elements in vocational guidance wherever practised, there are also important differences in terms of culture, education, employment practices and occupational structures from country to country. Consequently, guidance practitioners generally need to be trained in the country in which they will practise.

As has been already mentioned, when guidance is conducted by a course in career development, it is not unusual to have the course taught by regular classroom teachers who have had special preparation to teach the course. Whether it is to teach a career development curriculum or to conduct courses infused with career education the professional development of teachers should give them a basic framework for career planning and how to connect activities in the classroom to the events unfolding in the labour market.

When guidance is provided through individual counselling, however, the counsellor is expected to have specialized training in such areas as: counselling techniques; career, educational and labour market information; assessment techniques to measure skills, abilities, aptitudes, interests, values, and personality; needs assessment techniques; computer and Internet systems of guidance; organizing career development programmes; teaching job search techniques; establishing linkages with community-based organizations; and, public relations techniques to promote career development activities and services. Some training for counsellors is beginning to appear on the Internet and may be expected to become increasingly available through that means. Currently there are no internationally accepted standards for guidance counsellors but the International Association for Educational and Vocational Guidance (IAEVG) is in the process of establishing a committee to draft such a standard. International standards are increasingly important as on-line career counselling can be provided across national boundaries and therefore be immune from regulation by most, if not all, countries.

Guidance consultants in ministries usually have the same training as counsellors plus competencies in programme planning and adoption strategies; guidance curriculum development; differing cultural values and their relationship to work values; unique career planning needs of minorities, women, persons with disabilities, and older persons; and alternative approaches to career planning for learners with specific needs.

Many countries do not have "counsellors" although they do have psychologists, sociologists or others performing some of the functions of a counsellor. The unique training of educational and vocational counsellors typically is instruction in: the functioning of the labour market; the structure of the educational and training systems; how to use labour market information in the counselling interview; employability skills; and, job-search techniques. In some countries, training in these areas is needed by those who otherwise have relevant competencies.

Intelligence Quotient

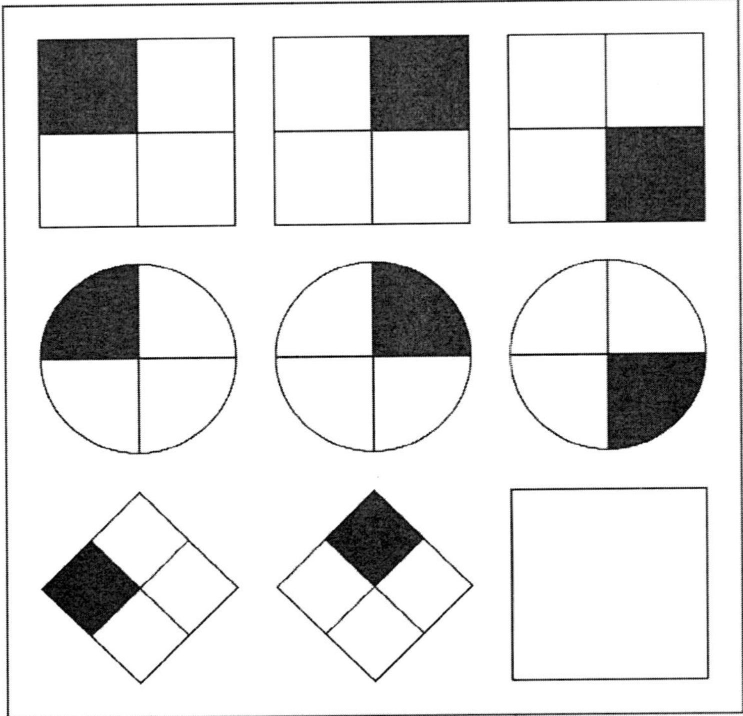

Figure: *An example of one kind of IQ test item, modelled after items in the Raven's Progressive Matrices test.*

An intelligence quotient, or IQ, is a score derived from one of several standardized tests designed to assess intelligence. The abbreviation "IQ" comes from the German term *Intelligenz-Quotient*, originally coined by psychologist William Stern. When current IQ tests are developed, the median raw score of the norming sample is defined as IQ 100 and scores each standard deviation (SD) up or down are defined as 15 IQ points greater or less, although this was not always so historically. By this definition, approximately 95 percent of the population scores an IQ between 70 and 130, which is within two standard deviations of the median.

IQ scores have been shown to be associated with such factors as morbidity and mortality, parental social status, and, to a substantial degree, biological parental IQ. While the heritability of IQ has been investigated for nearly a century, there is still debate about the significance of heritability estimates and the mechanisms of inheritance.

IQ scores are used as predictors of educational achievement, special needs, job performance and income. They are also used to study IQ distributions in populations and the correlations between IQ and other variables. Raw scores on IQ tests for many populations have been rising at an average rate that scales to three IQ points per decade since the early 20th century, a phenomenon called the Flynn effect. Investigation of differing patterns of increases in IQ battery subtest scores informs current research on human intelligence.

History

Early history:

Figure: *A Song Dynasty painting of candidates participating in the imperial examination, a rudimentary form of psychological testing.*

The first large-scale mental test may have been the imperial examination system in China. The test, an early form of psychological testing, assessed candidates based on their proficiency in topics such as civil law and fiscal policies. Modern mental testing began in France in the 19th century. It contributed to separating mental retardation from mental illness and reducing the neglect, torture, and ridicule heaped on both groups.

Englishman Francis Galton coined the term psychometrics, and developed a method for measuring intelligence based on nonverbal sensory-motor tests. It was initially popular, but was abandoned after the discovery that it had no relationship to outcomes such as college grades.

French psychologist Alfred Binet, together with psychologists Victor Henri and Théodore Simon, after about 15 years of development, published the Binet-Simon test in 1905, which focused on verbal abilities. It was intended to identify mental retardation in school children. The score on the Binet-Simon scale would reveal the child's mental age. For example, a six-year-old child who passed all the tasks usually passed by six-year-olds—but nothing beyond—would have a mental age that exactly matched his chronological age, 6.0. (Fancher, 1985). In Binet's view, there were limitations with the scale and he stressed what he saw as the remarkable diversity of intelligence and the subsequent need to study it using qualitative, as opposed to quantitative, measures (White, 2000). American psychologist Henry H. Goddard published a translation of it in 1910. The eugenics movement in the USA seized on it as a means to give them credibility in diagnosing mental retardation, and thousands of American women, most of them poor African Americans, were forcibly sterilized based on their scores on IQ tests, often without their consent or knowledge. American psychologist Lewis Terman at Stanford University revised the Binet-Simon scale, which resulted in the Stanford-Binet Intelligence Scales (1916). It became the most popular test in the United States for decades.

General Factor (g)

The many different kinds of IQ tests use a wide variety of methods. Some tests are visual, some are verbal, some tests only use abstract-reasoning problems, and some tests concentrate on arithmetic, spatial imagery, reading, vocabulary, memory or general knowledge. The psychologist Charles Spearman in 1904 made the first formal factor analysis of correlations between the tests. He found a single common factor explained the positive correlations among tests. This is an argument still accepted in principle by many psychometricians. Spearman named it *g* for "general factor" and labelled the smaller, specific factors or abilities for specific areas *s*. In any collection of IQ tests, by definition the test that best measures *g* is the one that has the highest correlations with all the others.

Most of these *g*-loaded tests typically involve some form of abstract reasoning. Therefore, Spearman and others have regarded *g* as the (perhaps genetically determined) real essence of intelligence. This is still a common but not universally accepted view. Other factor analyses of the data, with different results, are possible. Some psychometricians regard *g* as a statistical artifact. One of the most commonly used measures of *g* is Raven's Progressive Matrices, which is a test of visual reasoning.

The War Years in the United States

During World War I, a way was needed to evaluate and assign recruits. This led to the rapid development of several mental tests. The testing generated controversy and much public debate in the United States. Nonverbal or "performance" tests were developed for those who could not speak English or were suspected of malingering. After the war, positive publicity on army psychological testing helped to make psychology a respected field. Subsequently, there was an increase in jobs and funding in psychology in the United States. Group intelligence tests were developed and became widely used in schools and industry.

L.L. Thurstone argued for a model of intelligence that included seven unrelated factors (verbal comprehension, word fluency, number facility, spatial visualization, associative memory, perceptual speed, reasoning, and induction). While not widely used, it influenced later theories.

David Wechsler produced the first version of his test in 1939. It gradually became more popular and overtook the Binet in the 1960s. It has been revised several times, as is common for IQ tests, to incorporate new research. One explanation is that psychologists and educators wanted more information than the single score from the Binet. Wechsler's 10+ subtests provided this. Another is Binet focused on verbal abilities, while the Wechsler also included nonverbal abilities. The Binet has also been revised several times and is now similar to the Wechsler in several aspects, but the Wechsler continues to be the most popular test in the United States.

Cattell–Horn–Carroll Theory

Raymond Cattell (1941) proposed two types of cognitive abilities in a revision of Spearman's concept of general intelligence. Fluid intelligence (Gf) was hypothesized as the ability to solve novel problems by using reasoning, and crystallized intelligence (Gc) was hypothesized as a knowledge-based ability that was very dependent on education and experience. In addition, fluid intelligence was hypothesized to decline with age, while crystallized intelligence was largely resistant. The theory was almost forgotten, but was revived by his student John L. Horn (1966) who later argued Gf and Gc were only two among several factors, and he eventually identified 9 or 10 broad abilities. The theory continued to be called Gf-Gc theory.

John B. Carroll (1993), after a comprehensive reanalysis of earlier data, proposed the Three Stratum theory, which is a hierarchical model with three levels. The bottom stratum consists of narrow abilities that are highly specialized (e.g., induction, spelling ability). The second stratum consists of broad abilities. Carroll identified eight second-stratum abilities. Carroll accepted Spearman's concept of general intelligence, for the most part, as a representation of the uppermost, third stratum.

More recently (1999), a merging of the Gf-Gc theory of Cattell and Horn with Carroll's Three-Stratum theory has led to the Cattell–Horn–Carroll theory. It has greatly influenced many of the current broad IQ tests.

It is argued that this reflects much of what is known about intelligence from research. A hierarchy of factors is used; *g* is at the top. Under it are 10 broad abilities that in turn are subdivided into 70 narrow abilities. The broad abilities are:

- Fluid intelligence (Gf) includes the broad ability to reason, form concepts, and solve problems using unfamiliar information or novel procedures.
- Crystallized intelligence (Gc) includes the breadth and depth of a person's acquired knowledge, the ability to communicate one's knowledge, and the ability to reason using previously learned experiences or procedures.
- Quantitative reasoning (Gq) is the ability to comprehend quantitative concepts and relationships and to manipulate numerical symbols.
- Reading and writing ability (Grw) includes basic reading and writing skills.

- Short-term memory (Gsm) is the ability to apprehend and hold information in immediate awareness, and then use it within a few seconds.
- Long-term storage and retrieval (Glr) is the ability to store information and fluently retrieve it later in the process of thinking.
- Visual processing (Gv) is the ability to perceive, analyse, synthesize, and think with visual patterns, including the ability to store and recall visual representations.
- Auditory processing (Ga) is the ability to analyse, synthesize, and discriminate auditory stimuli, including the ability to process and discriminate speech sounds that may be presented under distorted conditions.
- Processing speed (Gs) is the ability to perform automatic cognitive tasks, particularly when measured under pressure to maintain focused attention.
- Decision/reaction time/speed (Gt)reflects the immediacy with which an individual can react to stimuli or a task (typically measured in seconds or fractions of seconds; it is not to be confused with Gs, which typically is measured in intervals of 2–3 minutes).

Modern tests do not necessarily measure all of these broad abilities. For example, Gq and Grw may be seen as measures of school achievement and not IQ. Gt may be difficult to measure without special equipment.

g was earlier often subdivided into only Gf and Gc, which were thought to correspond to the nonverbal or performance subtests and verbal subtests in earlier versions of the popular Wechsler IQ test. More recent research has shown the situation to be more complex.

Modern comprehensive IQ tests no longer give a single score. Although they still give an overall score, they now also give scores for many of these more restricted abilities, identifying particular strengths and weaknesses of an individual.

Other Theories

J.P. Guilford's Structure of Intellect (1967) model used three dimensions which when combined yielded a total of 120 types of intelligence. It was popular in the 1970s and early 1980s, but faded owing to both practical problems and theoretical criticisms.

Alexander Luria's earlier work on neuropsychological processes led to the PASS theory (1997). It argued that only looking at one general factor was inadequate for researchers and clinicians who worked with learning disabilities, attention disorders, mental retardation, and interventions for such disabilities.

The PASS model covers four kinds of processes (planning process, attention/arousal process, simultaneous processing, and successive processing).

The planning processes involve decision making, problem solving, and performing activities and requires goal setting and self-monitoring. The attention/arousal process involves selectively attending to a particular stimulus, ignoring distractions, and maintaining vigilance. Simultaneous processing involves the integration of stimuli into a group and requires the observation of relationships. Successive processing involves the integration of stimuli into serial order.

The planning and attention/arousal components comes from structures located in the frontal lobe, and the simultaneous and successive processes come from structures located in the posterior region of the cortex. It has influenced some recent IQ tests, and been seen as a complement to the Cattell-Horn-Carroll theory described above.

Modern tests

Well-known modern IQ tests include Raven's Progressive Matrices, Wechsler Adult Intelligence Scale, Wechsler Intelligence Scale for Children, Stanford-Binet, Woodcock-Johnson Tests of Cognitive Abilities, and Kaufman Assessment Battery for Children.

Approximately 95% of the population have scores within two standard deviations (SD) of the mean. If one SD is 15 points, as is common in almost all modern tests, then 95% of the population are within a range of 70 to 130, and 98% are below 131. Alternatively, two-thirds of the population have IQ scores within one SD of the mean; i.e. within the range 85-115.

IQ scales are ordinally scaled. While one standard deviation is 15 points, and two SDs are 30 points, and so on, this does not imply that mental ability is linearly related to IQ, such that IQ 50 means half the cognitive ability of IQ 100. In particular, IQ points are not percentage points.

The correlation between IQ test results and achievement test results is about 0.7.

Reliability and Validity

Psychometricians generally regard IQ tests as having high statistical reliability. A high reliability implies that—although test-takers may have varying scores when taking the same test on differing occasions, and they may have varying scores when taking different IQ tests at the same age—the scores generally agree with one another and across time. A test-taker's score on any one IQ test is surrounded by an error band that shows, to a specified degree of confidence, what the test-taker's true score is likely to be. For modern tests, the standard error of measurement is about three points, or in other words, the odds are about two out of three that a person's true IQ is in range from three points above to three points below the test IQ. Another description is there is a 95% chance the true IQ is in range from four to five points above to four to five points below the test IQ, depending on the test in question. Clinical psychologists generally regard them as having sufficient statistical validity for many clinical purposes.

IQ scores can differ to some degree for the same individual on different IQ tests. (IQ score table data and pupil pseudonyms adapted from description of KABC-II norming study cited in Kaufman 2009.)

Pupil	*KABC-II*	*WISC-III*	*WJ-III*
Asher	90	95	111
Brianna	125	110	105
Colin	100	93	101
Danica	116	127	118
Elpha	93	105	93
Fritz	106	105	105
Georgi	95	100	90
Hector	112	113	103
Imelda	104	96	97
Jose	101	99	86
Keoku	81	78	75
Leo	116	124	102

Flynn Effect

Since the early 20th century, raw scores on IQ tests have increased in most parts of the world. When a new version of an IQ test is normed, the standard scoring is set so performance at the population median results in a score of IQ 100. The phenomenon of rising raw score performance means if test-takers are scored by a constant standard scoring rule, IQ test scores have been rising at an average rate of around three IQ points per decade. This phenomenon was named the Flynn effect in the book *The Bell Curve* after James R. Flynn, the author who did the most to bring this phenomenon to the attention of psychologists.

Researchers have been exploring the issue of whether the Flynn effect is equally strong on performance of all kinds of IQ test items, whether the effect may have ended in some developed nations, whether there are social subgroup differences in the effect, and what possible causes of the effect might be.

Flynn's observations have prompted much new research in psychology and "demolish some long-cherished beliefs, and raise a number of other interesting issues along the way."

IQ and Age

IQ can change to some degree over the course of childhood. However, in one longitudinal study, the mean IQ scores of tests at ages 17 and 18 were correlated at r=.86 with the mean scores of tests at ages five, six, and seven and at r=.96 with the mean scores of tests at ages 11, 12, and 13. For decades practitioners' handbooks and textbooks on IQ testing have reported IQ declines with age after the beginning of adulthood.

However, later researchers pointed out this phenomenon is related to the Flynn effect and is in part a cohort effect rather than a true aging effect.

A variety of studies of IQ and aging have been conducted since the norming of the first Wechsler Intelligence Scale drew attention to IQ differences in different age groups of adults. Current consensus is that fluid intelligence generally declines with age after early adulthood, while crystallized intelligence remains intact. Both cohort effects (the birth year of the test-takers) and practice effects (test-takers taking the same form of IQ test more than once) must be controlled to gain accurate data. It is unclear whether any lifestyle intervention can preserve fluid intelligence into older ages.

The exact peak age of fluid intelligence or crystallized intelligence remains elusive. Cross-sectional studies usually show that especially fluid intelligence peaks at a relatively young age (often in the early adulthood) while longitudinal data mostly show that intelligence is stable until the mid adulthood or later. Subsequently, intelligence seems to decline slowly.

Genetics and Environment

Environmental and genetic factors play a role in determining IQ. Their relative importance has been the subject of much research and debate.

Heritability

Heritability is defined as the proportion of variance in a trait which is attributable to genotype within a defined population in a specific environment. A number of points must be considered when interpreting heritability. Heritability measures the proportion of 'variation' in a trait can be attributed to genes, and not the proportion of a trait caused by genes. The value of heritability can change if the impact of environment (or of genes) in the population is substantially altered. A high heritability of a trait does not mean environmental effects, such as learning, are not involved. Since heritability increases during childhood and adolescence, one should be cautious drawing conclusions regarding the role of genetics and environment from studies where the participants are not followed until they are adults.

Studies have found the heritability of IQ in adult twins to be 0.7 to 0.8 and in children twins 0.45 in the Western world. It may seem reasonable to expect genetic influences on traits like IQ should become less important as one gains experiences with age. However, the opposite occurs. Heritability measures in infancy are as low as 0.2, around 0.4 in middle childhood, and as high as 0.8 in adulthood. One proposed explanation is that people with different genes tend to reinforce the effects of those genes, for example by seeking out different environments. Debate is ongoing about whether these heritability estimates are too high, owing to inadequate consideration of various factors — such as the environment being relatively more important in families with low socioeconomic status, or the effect of the maternal (fetal) environment.

Recent research suggests that molecular genetics of psychology and social science requires approaches that go beyond the examination of candidate genes.

Shared Family Environment

Family members have aspects of environments in common (for example, characteristics of the home). This shared family environment accounts for 0.25–0.35 of the variation in IQ in childhood. By late adolescence, it is quite low (zero in some studies). The effect for several other psychological traits is similar. These studies have not looked at the effects of extreme environments, such as in abusive families.

Non-shared Family Environment and Environment Outside the Family

Although parents treat their children differently, such differential treatment explains only a small amount of nonshared environmental influence. One suggestion is that children react differently to the same environment because of different genes. More likely influences may be the impact of peers and other experiences outside the family.

Individual Genes

A very large proportion of the over 17,000 human genes are thought to have an effect on the development and functionality of the brain. While a number of individual genes have been reported to be associated with IQ, none have a strong effect. Deary and colleagues (2009) reported that no finding of a strong gene effect on IQ has been replicated. Most reported associations of genes with intelligence are false positive results. Recent findings of gene associations with normally varying intelligence differences in adults continue to show weak effects for any one gene; likewise in children.

Gene-environment Interaction

David Rowe reported an interaction of genetic effects with Socioeconomic Status, such that the heritability was high in high-SES families, but much lower in low-SES families. This has been replicated in infants, children and adolescents in the US, though not outside the US, for instance a reverse result was reported in the UK.

Dickens and Flynn (2001) have argued that genes for high IQ initiate environment-shaping feedback, as genetic effects cause bright children to seek out more stimulating environments that further increase IQ. In their model, environment effects decay over time (the model could be adapted to include possible factors, like nutrition in early childhood, that may cause permanent effects). The Flynn effect can be explained by a generally more stimulating environment for all people. The authors suggest that programmes aiming to increase IQ would be most likely to produce long-term IQ gains if they caused children to persist in seeking out cognitively demanding experiences.

Interventions

In general, educational interventions, as those described below, have shown short-term effects on IQ, but long-term follow-up is often missing. For example, in the US very large intervention programmes such as the Head Start Programme have not produced lasting gains in IQ scores. More intensive, but much smaller, projects Abecedarian Project have reported lasting effects, often on Socioeconomic status variables, rather than IQ.

A placebo controlled double-blind experiment found that vegetarians who took 5 grams of creatine per day for six weeks showed a significant improvement on two separate tests of fluid intelligence, Raven's Progressive Matrices, and the backward digit span test from the WAIS. The treatment group was able to repeat longer sequences of numbers from memory and had higher overall IQ scores than the control group. The researchers concluded that "supplementation with creatine significantly increased intelligence compared with placebo." A subsequent study found that creatine supplements improved cognitive ability in the elderly. However, a study on young adults (0.03 g/kg/day for six weeks, e.g., 2 g/day for 150-pound individual) failed to find any improvements.

Recent studies have shown that training in using one's working memory may increase IQ. A study on young adults published in April 2008 by a team from the Universities of Michigan and Bern supports the possibility of the transfer of fluid intelligence from specifically designed working memory training. Further research will be needed to determine nature, extent and duration of the proposed transfer. Among other questions, it remains to be seen whether the results extend to other kinds of fluid intelligence tests than the matrix test used in the study, and if so, whether, after training, fluid intelligence measures retain their correlation with educational and occupational achievement or if the value of fluid intelligence for predicting performance on other tasks changes. It is also unclear whether the training is durable of extended periods of time.

Music and IQ

Musical training in childhood has been found to correlate with higher than average IQ. In a 2004 study indicated that 6 year-old children who received musical training (voice or piano lessons) had an average increase in IQ of 7.0 points while children who received alternative training (e.g. drama) or no training had an average increase in IQ of only 4.3 points (which may be consequence of the children entering grade school) as indicated by full scale IQ. Children were tested using Wechsler Intelligence Scale for Children–Third Edition, Kaufman Test of Educational Achievement and Parent Rating Scale of the Behavioural Assessment System for Children.

Listening to classical music was reported to increase IQ; specifically spatial ability. In 1994 Frances Rauscher and Gorden Shaw reported that college students who listened to 10 minutes of Mozart's Sonata for Two Pianos, showed an increase in IQ of 8 to 9 points on the spatial subtest on the Standford-Binet Intelligence Scale. The phenomenon was coined the Mozart effect.

Multiple attempted replications (e.g.) have shown that this is at best a short-term effect (lasting no longer than 10 to 15 minutes), and is not related to IQ-increase.

Music Lessons

In 2004, Schellenberg devised an experiment to test his hypothesis that music lessons can enhance the IQ of children. He had 144 samples of 6 year old children which were put into 4 groups; keyboard lessons, vocal lessons, drama lessons or no lessons at all, for 36 weeks. The samples' IQ was measured both before and after the lessons had taken place using the Wechsler Intelligence Scale for Children–Third Edition, Kaufman Test of Educational Achievement and Parent Rating Scale of the Behavioural Assessment System for Children. All four groups had increases in IQ, most likely resulted by the entrance of grade school. The notable difference with the two music groups compared to the two controlled groups was a slightly higher increase in IQ. The children in the control groups on average had an increase in IQ of 4.3 points, while the increase in IQ of the music groups was 7.0 points. Though the increases in IQ were not dramatic, one can still conclude that musical lessons do have a positive effect for children, if taken at a young age. It is hypothesized that improvements in IQ occur after musical lessons because the music lessons encourage multiple experiences which generates progression in a wide range of abilities for the children. Testing this hypothesis however, has proven difficult.

Another test also performed by Schellenberg tested the effects of musical training in adulthood. He had two groups of adults, one group whom were musically trained and another group who were not. He administered tests of intelligence quotient and emotional intelligence to the trained and non-trained groups and found that the trained participants had an advantage in IQ over the untrained subjects even with gender, age, environmental issues (e.g. income, parent's education) held constant. The two groups, however, score similarly in the emotional intelligence test. The test results (like the previous results) show that there is a positive correlation between musical training and IQ, but it is not evident that musical training has a positive effect on emotional intelligence.

IQ and Brain Anatomy

Several neurophysiological factors have been correlated with intelligence in humans, including the ratio of brain weight to body weight and the size, shape and activity level of different parts of the brain. Specific features that may affect IQ include the size and shape of the frontal lobes, the amount of blood and chemical activity in the frontal lobes, the total amount of gray matter in the brain, the overall thickness of the cortex and the glucose metabolic rate.

Health and IQ

Health is important in understanding differences in IQ test scores and other measures of cognitive ability. Several factors can lead to significant cognitive impairment, particularly if they occur during pregnancy and childhood when the brain is growing and the blood–brain barrier is less effective. Such impairment may sometimes be permanent, sometimes be partially or wholly compensated for by later growth.

Since about 2010 researchers such as Eppig, Hassel and MacKenzie have found a very close and consistent link between IQ scores and infectious diseases, especially in the infant and preschool populations and the mothers of these children. They have postulated that fighting infectious diseases strains the child's metabolism and prevents full brain development. Hassel postulated that it is by far the most important factor in determining population IQ. However they also found that subsequent factors such as good nutrition, regular quality schooling can offset early negative effects to some extent.

Developed nations have implemented several health policies regarding nutrients and toxins known to influence cognitive function. These include laws requiring fortification of certain food products and laws establishing safe levels of pollutants (e.g. lead, mercury, and organochlorides). Improvements in nutrition, and in public policy in general, have been implicated in worldwide IQ increases.

Cognitive epidemiology is a field of research that examines the associations between intelligence test scores and health. Researchers in the field argue that intelligence measured at an early age is an important predictor of later health and mortality differences.

Social Outcomes

Intelligence is a better predictor of educational and work success than any other single score.

Some measures of educational aptitude are essentially IQ tests; For instance Frey and Detterman (2004) reported a correlation of 0.82 between *g* (general intelligence factor) and SAT scores another has found correlation of 0.81 between *g* and GCSE scores.

Correlations between IQ scores (general cognitive ability) and achievement test scores are reported to be 0.81 by Deary and colleagues, with the explained variance ranging "from 58.6% in Mathematics and 48% in English to 18.1% in Art and Design".

School Performance

The American Psychological Association's report "Intelligence: Knowns and Unknowns" states that wherever it has been studied, children with high scores on tests of intelligence tend to learn more of what is taught in school than their lower-scoring peers. The correlation between IQ scores and grades is about .50. This means that the explained variance is 25%. Achieving good grades depends on many factors other than IQ, such as "persistence, interest in school, and willingness to study" (p. 81).

It has been found IQ correlation with school performance depends on the IQ measurement used. For undergraduate students, the Verbal IQ as measured by WAIS-R has been found to correlate significantly (0.53) with the GPA of the last 60 hours. In contrast, Performance IQ correlation with the same GPA was only 0.22 in the same study.

Job Performance

According to Schmidt and Hunter, "for hiring employees without previous experience in the job the most valid predictor of future performance is general mental ability." The validity of IQ as a predictor of job performance is above zero for all work studied to date, but varies with the type of job and across different studies, ranging from 0.2 to 0.6. The correlations were higher when the unreliability of measurement methods was controlled for.

While IQ is more strongly correlated with reasoning and less so with motor function, IQ-test scores predict performance ratings in all occupations. That said, for highly qualified activities (research, management) low IQ scores are more likely to be a barrier to adequate performance, whereas for minimally-skilled activities, athletic strength (manual strength, speed, stamina, and coordination) are more likely to influence performance.

It is largely through the quicker acquisition of job-relevant knowledge that higher IQ mediates job performance.

In establishing a causal direction to the link between IQ and work performance, longitudinal studies by Watkins and others suggest that IQ exerts a causal influence on future academic achievement, whereas academic achievement does not substantially influence future IQ scores. Treena Eileen Rohde and Lee Anne Thompson write that general cognitive ability, but not specific ability scores, predict academic achievement, with the exception that processing speed and spatial ability predict performance on the SAT math beyond the effect of general cognitive ability.

The US military has minimum enlistment standards at about the IQ 85 level. There have been two experiments with lowering this to 80 but in both cases these men could not master soldiering well enough to justify their costs.

In 2000 the New London, CT police department turned away a recruit for having an IQ above 125, under the argument that those with overly-high IQs will become bored and exhibit high turnover in the job. This policy has been challenged as discriminatory, but was upheld by the 2nd U.S. Circuit Court of Appeals in New York.

The American Psychological Association's report "Intelligence: Knowns and Unknowns" states that since the explained variance is 29%, other individual characteristics such as interpersonal skills, aspects of personality etc. are probably of equal or greater importance, but at this point there are no equally reliable instruments to measure them.

Income

While it has been suggested that "in economic terms it appears that the IQ score measures something with decreasing marginal value. It is important to have enough of it, but having lots and lots does not buy you that much.", large scale longitudinal studies indicate an increase in IQ translates into an increase in performance at all levels of IQ: i.e., that ability and job performance are monotonically linked at all IQ levels. Charles Murray, coauthor of *The Bell Curve,* found that IQ has a substantial effect on income independently of family background.

The link from IQ to wealth is much less strong than that from IQ to job performance. Some studies indicate that IQ is unrelated to net worth.

The American Psychological Association's 1995 report *Intelligence: Knowns and Unknowns* stated that IQ scores accounted for (explained variance) about a quarter of the social status variance and one-sixth of the income variance. Statistical controls for parental SES eliminate about a quarter of this predictive power. Psychometric intelligence appears as only one of a great many factors that influence social outcomes.

Some studies claim that IQ only accounts for (explains) a sixth of the variation in income because many studies are based on young adults, many of whom have not yet reached their peak earning capacity, or even their education. On pg 568 of *The g Factor*, Arthur Jensen claims that although the correlation between IQ and income averages a moderate 0.4 (one sixth or 16% of the variance), the relationship increases with age, and peaks at middle age when people have reached their maximum career potential. In the book, *A Question of Intelligence*, Daniel Seligman cites an IQ income correlation of 0.5 (25% of the variance).

A 2002 study further examined the impact of non-IQ factors on income and concluded that an individual's location, inherited wealth, race, and schooling are more important as factors in determining income than IQ.

IQ and Crime

The American Psychological Association's 1995 report *Intelligence: Knowns and Unknowns* stated that the correlation between IQ and crime was -0.2. It was -0.19 between IQ scores and number of juvenile offences in a large Danish sample; with social class controlled, the correlation dropped to -0.17. A correlation of 0.20 means that the explained variance is less than 4%.

It is important to realize that the causal links between psychometric ability and social outcomes may be indirect. Children with poor scholastic performance may feel alienated. Consequently, they may be more likely to engage in delinquent behaviour, compared to other children who do well.

In his book *The g Factor* (1998), Arthur Jensen cited data which showed that, regardless of race, people with IQs between 70 and 90 have higher crime rates than people with IQs below or above this range, with the peak range being between 80 and 90.

The 2009 *Handbook of Crime Correlates* stated that reviews have found that around eight IQ points, or 0.5 SD, separate criminals from the general population, especially for persistent serious offenders. It has been suggested that this simply reflects that "only dumb ones get caught" but there is similarly a negative relation between IQ and self-reported offending.

That children with conduct disorder have lower IQ than their peers "strongly argues" for the theory.

A study of the relationship between US county-level IQ and US county-level crime rates found that higher average IQs were associated with lower levels of property crime, burglary, larceny rate, motor vehicle theft, violent crime, robbery, and aggravated assault.

These results were not "confounded by a measure of concentrated disadvantage that captures the effects of race, poverty, and other social disadvantages of the county."

Other Correlations with IQ

In addition, IQ and its correlation to health, violent crime, gross state product, and government effectiveness are the subject of a 2006 paper in the publication *Intelligence.*

The paper breaks down IQ averages by U.S. states using the federal government's National Assessment of Educational Progress math and reading test scores as a source.

The American Psychological Association's 1995 report *Intelligence: Knowns and Unknowns* stated that the correlations for most "negative outcome" variables are typically smaller than 0.20, which means that the explained variance is less than 4%.

Tambs *et al.* found that occupational status, educational attainment, and IQ are individually heritable; and further found that "genetic variance influencing educational attainment ... contributed approximately one-fourth of the genetic variance for occupational status and nearly half the genetic variance for IQ."

In a sample of U.S. siblings, Rowe *et al.* report that the inequality in education and income was predominantly due to genes, with shared environmental factors playing a subordinate role.

A recent USA study connecting political views and intelligence has shown that the mean adolescent intelligence of young adults who identify themselves as "very liberal" is 106.4, while that of those who identify themselves as "very conservative" is 94.8. Two other studies conducted in the UK reached similar conclusions.

There are also other correlations such as those between religiosity and intelligence and fertility and intelligence.

Real-life Accomplishments

Table: *Average adult combined IQs associated with real-life accomplishments by various tests*

Accomplishment	*IQ*	*Test/study*	*Year*
MDs, JDs, or PhDs	125+	WAIS-R	1987
College graduates	112	KAIT	2000
		K-BIT	1992
	115	WAIS-R	
1–3 years of college	104	KAIT	
		K-BIT	
	105–110	WAIS-R	
Clerical and sales workers	100–105		
High school graduates, skilled workers (e.g., electricians, cabinetmakers)	100	KAIT	
		WAIS-R	
	97	K-BIT	
1–3 years of high school (completed 9–11 years of school)	94	KAIT	
	90	K-BIT	
	95	WAIS-R	
Semi-skilled workers (e.g. truck drivers, factory workers)	90–95		
Elementary school graduates (completed eighth grade)	90		
Elementary school dropouts (completed 0–7 years of school)	80–85		
Have 50/50 chance of reaching high school	75		

Average IQ of various occupational groups:

Accomplishment	*IQ*	*Test/study*	*Year*
Professional and technical	112		
Managers and administrators	104		
Clerical workers, sales workers, skilled workers, craftsmen, and foremen	101		

Contd...

Accomplishment	***IQ***	***Test/study***	***Year***
Semi-skilled workers (operatives, service workers, including private household)	92		
Unskilled workers	87		

Type of work that can be accomplished:

Accomplishment	***IQ***	***Test/study***	***Year***
Adults can harvest vegetables, repair furniture	60		
Adults can do domestic work	50		

There is considerable variation within and overlap between these categories. People with high IQs are found at all levels of education and occupational categories. The biggest difference occurs for low IQs with only an occasional college graduate or professional scoring below 90.

Group Differences

Among the most controversial issues related to the study of intelligence is the observation that intelligence measures such as IQ scores vary between ethnic and racial groups and sexes. While there is little scholarly debate about the *existence* of some of these differences, their *causes* remain highly controversial both within academia and in the public sphere.

Sex

Most IQ tests are constructed so that there are no overall score differences between females and males. Popular IQ batteries such as the WAIS and the WISC-R are also constructed in order to eliminate sex differences. In a paper presented at the International Society for Intelligence Research in 2002, it was pointed out that because test constructors and the Educational Testing Service (which developed the SAT) often eliminate items showing marked sex differences in order to reduce the perception of bias, the "true sex" difference is masked. Items like the MRT and RT tests that show a male advantage in IQ are often removed.

Race

The 1996 Task Force investigation on Intelligence sponsored by the American Psychological Association concluded that there are significant variations in IQ across races. The problem of determining the causes underlying this variation relates to the question of the contributions of "nature and nurture" to IQ. Psychologists such as Alan S. Kaufman and Nathan Brody and statisticians such as Bernie Devlin argue that there are insufficient data to conclude that this is because of genetic influences. One of the most notable researchers arguing for a strong genetic influence on these average score differences was Arthur Jensen. In contrast, other researchers such as Richard Nisbett argue that environmental factors can explain all of the average group differences.

Public Policy

In the United States, certain public policies and laws regarding military service, education, public benefits, capital punishment, and employment incorporate an individual's IQ into their decisions. However, in the case of Griggs v. Duke Power Co. in 1971, for the purpose of minimizing employment practices that disparately impacted racial minorities, the U.S. Supreme Court banned the use of IQ tests in employment, except when linked to job performance via a Job analysis. Internationally, certain public policies, such as improving nutrition and prohibiting neurotoxins, have as one of their goals raising, or preventing a decline in, intelligence.

A diagnosis of mental retardation is in part based on the results of IQ testing. Borderline intellectual functioning is a categorization where a person has below average cognitive ability (an IQ of 71–85), but the deficit is not as severe as mental retardation (70 or below).

In the United Kingdom, the eleven plus exam which incorporated an intelligence test has been used from 1945 to decide, at eleven years old, which type of school a child should go to. They have been much less used since the widespread introduction of comprehensive schools.

Criticism and Views

Relation between IQ and intelligence: IQ is the most researched attempt at measuring intelligence and by far the most widely used in practical setting. However, although IQ attempts to measure some notion of intelligence, it may fail to act as an accurate measure of "intelligence" in its broadest sense. IQ tests only examine particular areas embodied by the broadest notion of "intelligence", failing to account for certain areas which are also associated with "intelligence" such as creativity or emotional intelligence.

There are critics such as Keith Stanovich who do not dispute the stability of IQ test scores or the fact that they predict certain forms of achievement rather effectively. They do argue, however, that to base a concept of intelligence on IQ test scores alone is to ignore many important aspects of mental ability.

Criticism of *g*

Some scientists dispute IQ entirely. In *The Mismeasure of Man* (1996), paleontologist Stephen Jay Gould criticized IQ tests and argued that that they were used for scientific racism. He argued that *g* was a mathematical artifact and criticized: ...the abstraction of intelligence as a single entity, its location within the brain, its quantification as one number for each individual, and the use of these numbers to rank people in a single series of worthiness, invariably to find that oppressed and disadvantaged groups—races, classes, or sexes—are innately inferior and deserve their status.(pp. 24–25)

Psychometrician Arthur Jensen responded as follows:...what Gould has mistaken for "reification" is neither more nor less than the common practice in every science of hypothesizing explanatory models to account for the observed relationships within a given domain. Well known examples include the heliocentric theory of planetary motion, the Bohr atom, the electromagnetic field, the kinetic theory of gases, gravitation, quarks, Mendelian genes, mass, velocity, etc. None of these constructs exists as a palpable entity occupying physical space.

Psychologist Peter Schönemann was also a persistent critic of IQ, calling it "the IQ myth". He argued that g is a flawed theory and that the high heritability estimates of IQ are based on false assumptions.

Jensen has rejected the criticism by Gould and also argued that even if *g* was replaced by a model with several intelligences this would change the situation less than expected. All tests of cognitive ability would continue to be highly correlated with one another and there would still be a black-white gap on cognitive tests.

Test Bias

The American Psychological Association's report *Intelligence: Knowns and Unknowns* stated that in the United States IQ tests as predictors of social achievement are not biased against African Americans since they predict future performance, such as school achievement, similarly to the way they predict future performance for Caucasians.

However, IQ tests may well be biased when used in other situations. A 2005 study stated that "differential validity in prediction suggests that the WAIS-R test may contain cultural influences that reduce the validity of the WAIS-R as a measure of cognitive ability for Mexican

American students," indicating a weaker positive correlation relative to sampled white students. Other recent studies have questioned the culture-fairness of IQ tests when used in South Africa. Standard intelligence tests, such as the Stanford-Binet, are often inappropriate for children with autism; the alternative of using developmental or adaptive skills measures are relatively poor measures of intelligence in autistic children, and may have resulted in incorrect claims that a majority of children with autism are mentally retarded.

Outdated Methodology

A 2006 article stated that contemporary psychologic research often did not reflect substantial recent developments in psychometrics and "bears an uncanny resemblance to the psychometric state of the art as it existed in the 1950s."

"Intelligence: Knowns and Unknowns"

In response to the controversy surrounding *The Bell Curve*, the American Psychological Association's Board of Scientific Affairs established a task force in 1995 to write a report on the state of intelligence research which could be used by all sides as a basis for discussion, "Intelligence: Knowns and Unknowns". The full text of the report is available through several websites.

In this paper the representatives of the association regret that IQ-related works are frequently written with a view to their political consequences: "research findings were often assessed not so much on their merits or their scientific standing as on their supposed political implications".

The task force concluded that IQ scores do have high predictive validity for individual differences in school achievement. They confirm the predictive validity of IQ for adult occupational status, even when variables such as education and family background have been statistically controlled. They stated that individual differences in intelligence are substantially influenced by both genetics and environment.

The report stated that a number of biological factors, including malnutrition, exposure to toxic substances, and various prenatal and perinatal stressors, result in lowered psychometric intelligence under at least some conditions. The task force agrees that large differences do exist between the average IQ scores of blacks and whites, saying:

The cause of that differential is not known; it is apparently not due to any simple form of bias in the content or administration of the tests themselves. The Flynn effect shows that environmental factors can produce differences of at least this magnitude, but that effect is mysterious in its own right. Several culturally based explanations of the Black/ White IQ differential have been proposed; some are plausible, but so far none has been conclusively supported. There is even less empirical support for a genetic interpretation. In short, no adequate explanation of the differential between the IQ means of Blacks and Whites is presently available.

The APA journal that published the statement, *American Psychologist,* subsequently published eleven critical responses in January 1997, several of them arguing that the report failed to examine adequately the evidence for partly genetic explanations.

Dynamic Assessment

Notable and increasingly influential alternative to the wide range of standard IQ tests originated in the writings of psychologist Lev Vygotsky (1896-1934) of his most mature and highly productive period of 1932-1934. The notion of the zone of proximal development that he introduced in 1933, roughly a year before his death, served as the banner for his proposal to diagnose development as the level of actual development that can be measured by the child's independent problem solving and, at the same time, the level of proximal, or potential development that is measured in the situation of moderately assisted problem solving by the child. The maximum level of complexity and difficulty of the problem that the child is capable to solve under some guidance indicates the level of potential development. Then, the difference between the higher level of potential and the lower level of actual development indicates the zone of proximal development. Combination of the two indexes—the level of actual and the zone of the proximal development—according to Vygotsky, provides a significantly more informative indicator of psychological development than the assessment of the level of actual development alone.

The ideas on the zone of development were later developed in a number of psychological and educational theories and practices. Most notably, they were developed under the banner of dynamic assessment that focuses on the testing of learning and developmental potential (for instance, in the work of Reuven Feuerstein and his associates, who has criticized standard IQ testing for its putative assumption or acceptance of "fixed and immutable" characteristics of intelligence or cognitive functioning). Grounded in developmental theories of Vygotsky and Feuerstein, who recognized that human beings are not static entities but are always in states of transition and transactional relationships with the world, dynamic assessment received also considerable support in the recent revisions of cognitive developmental theory by Joseph Campione, Ann Brown, and John D. Bransford and in theories of multiple intelligences by Howard Gardner and Robert Sternberg.

IQ Classification

IQ classification is the practice by IQ test publishers of designating IQ score ranges as various categories with labels such as "superior" or "average." IQ classification was preceded historically by attempts to classify human beings by general ability based on other forms of behavioural observation. Those other forms of behavioural observation are still important for validating classifications based on IQ tests.

High IQ Societies

There are social organizations, some international, which limit membership to people who have scores as high as or higher than the 98th percentile on some IQ test or equivalent. Mensa International is perhaps the best known of these. There are other groups requiring a score above the 99th percentile.

Educational Quotient

An educational quotient, or EQ, is a score designed to assess a subject's level of general education. Though related to intelligence quotient, there is no direct correlation between the two. A person of high IQ, may have a low EQ, and vice-versa. A person's EQ is generally found by dividing the results of their Wide Range Achievement Test by their IQ and multiplying by 100, or by dividing their Education Age by their Chronological Age and multiplying by 100.

Emotional Intelligence

Emotional intelligence (EI) is the ability to identify, assess, and control the emotions of oneself, of others, and of groups. It can be divided into *ability EI* and *trait EI.*

Criticisms have centred on whether EI is a real intelligence and whether it has incremental validity over IQ and the Big Five personality traits. The earliest roots of emotional intelligence can be traced to Charles Darwin's work on the importance of emotional expression for survival and adaptation. In the 1900s, even though traditional definitions of intelligence emphasized cognitive aspects such as memory and problem-solving, several influential researchers in the intelligence field of study had begun to recognize the importance of the non-cognitive aspects. For instance, as early as 1920, E.L. Thorndike used the term social intelligence to describe the skill of understanding and managing other people.

When orders are reasonable, fair, simple, clear and consistent, there is a reciprocal satisfaction between the leader and the group. Art of War of Sun Tzu

Similarly, in 1940 David Wechsler described the influence of non-intellective factors on intelligent behaviour, and further argued that our models of intelligence would not be complete until we could adequately describe these factors. In 1983, Howard Gardner's *Frames of Mind: The Theory of Multiple Intelligences* introduced the idea of multiple intelligences which included both *interpersonal intelligence* (the capacity to understand the intentions, motivations and desires of other people) and *intrapersonal intelligence* (the capacity to understand oneself, to appreciate one's feelings, fears and motivations). In Gardner's view, traditional types of intelligence, such as IQ, fail to fully explain cognitive ability.

Thus, even though the names given to the concept varied, there was a common belief that traditional definitions of intelligence were lacking in ability to fully explain performance outcomes.

The first use of the term "emotional intelligence" is usually attributed to Wayne Payne's doctoral thesis, *A Study of Emotion: Developing Emotional Intelligence* from 1985. However, prior to this, the term "emotional intelligence" had appeared in Leuner (1966). Stanley Greenspan (1989) also put forward an EI model, followed by Peter Salovey and Mayer (1990), and Daniel Goleman (1995). The distinction between trait emotional intelligence and ability emotional intelligence was introduced in 2000.

Definitions

Substantial disagreement exists regarding the definition of EI, with respect to both terminology and operationalizations. Currently, there are three main models of EI:

1. Ability model
2. Mixed model (usually subsumed under trait EI)
3. Trait model

Different models of EI have led to the development of various instruments for the assessment of the construct. While some of these measures may overlap, most researchers agree that they tap different constructs.

Ability Model

Salovey and Mayer's conception of EI strives to define EI within the confines of the standard criteria for a new intelligence. Following their continuing research, their initial definition of EI was revised to "The ability to perceive emotion, integrate emotion to facilitate thought, understand emotions and to regulate emotions to promote personal growth."

The ability-based model views emotions as useful sources of information that help one to make sense of and navigate the social environment. The model proposes that individuals vary in their ability to process information of an emotional nature and in their ability to relate emotional processing to a wider cognition. This ability is seen to manifest itself in certain adaptive behaviours. The model claims that EI includes four types of abilities:

1. Perceiving emotions – the ability to detect and decipher emotions in faces, pictures, voices, and cultural artifacts—including the ability to identify one's own emotions. Perceiving emotions represents a basic aspect of emotional intelligence, as it makes all other processing of emotional information possible.
2. Using emotions – the ability to harness emotions to facilitate various cognitive activities, such as thinking and problem solving. The emotionally intelligent person can capitalize fully upon his or her changing moods in order to best fit the task at hand.
3. Understanding emotions – the ability to comprehend emotion language and to appreciate complicated relationships among emotions. For example, understanding emotions encompasses the ability to be sensitive to slight variations between emotions, and the ability to recognize and describe how emotions evolve over time.
4. Managing emotions – the ability to regulate emotions in both ourselves and in others. Therefore, the emotionally intelligent person can harness emotions, even negative ones, and manage them to achieve intended goals.

The ability EI model has been criticized in the research for lacking face and predictive validity in the workplace.

Measurement

The current measure of Mayer and Salovey's model of EI, the Mayer-Salovey-Caruso Emotional Intelligence Test (MSCEIT) is based on a series of emotion-based problem-solving items. Consistent with the model's claim of EI as a type of intelligence, the test is modelled on ability-based IQ tests. By testing a person's abilities on each of the four branches of emotional intelligence, it generates scores for each of the branches as well as a total score.

Central to the four-branch model is the idea that EI requires attunement to social norms. Therefore, the MSCEIT is scored in a consensus fashion, with higher scores indicating higher overlap between an individual's answers and those provided by a worldwide sample of respondents. The MSCEIT can also be expert-scored, so that the amount of overlap is calculated between an individual's answers and those provided by a group of 21 emotion researchers.

Although promoted as an ability test, the MSCEIT is unlike standard IQ tests in that its items do not have objectively correct responses. Among other challenges, the consensus scoring criterion means that it is impossible to create items (questions) that only a minority of respondents can solve, because, by definition, responses are deemed emotionally "intelligent" only if the majority of the sample has endorsed them. This and other similar problems have led some cognitive ability experts to question the definition of EI as a genuine intelligence.

In a study by Føllesdal, the MSCEIT test results of 111 business leaders were compared with how their employees described their leader. It was found that there were no correlations between a leader's test results and how he or she was rated by the employees, with regard to empathy, ability to motivate, and leader effectiveness. Føllesdal also criticized the Canadian company Multi-Health Systems, which administers the MSCEIT test. The test contains 141 questions but it was found after publishing the test that 19 of these did not give the expected answers. This has led Multi-Health Systems to remove answers to these 19 questions before scoring, but without stating this officially.

Mixed Model

The model introduced by Daniel Goleman focuses on EI as a wide array of competencies and skills that drive leadership performance. Goleman's model outlines five main EI constructs:

1. Self-awareness – the ability to know one's emotions, strengths, weaknesses, drives, values and goals and recognize their impact on others while using gut feelings to guide decisions.
2. Self-regulation – involves controlling or redirecting one's disruptive emotions and impulses and adapting to changing circumstances.
3. Social skill – managing relationships to move people in the desired direction
4. Empathy - considering other people's feelings especially when making decisions and
5. Motivation - being driven to achieve for the sake of achievement.

Goleman includes a set of emotional competencies within each construct of EI. Emotional competencies are not innate talents, but rather learned capabilities that must be worked on and can be developed to achieve outstanding performance. Goleman posits that individuals are born with a general emotional intelligence that determines their potential for learning emotional competencies. Goleman's model of EI has been criticized in the research literature as mere "pop psychology" (Mayer, Roberts, & Barsade, 2008).

Measurement

Two measurement tools are based on the Goleman model:

1. The Emotional Competency Inventory (ECI), which was created in 1999, and the Emotional and Social Competency Inventory (ESCI), which was created in 2007.
2. The Emotional Intelligence Appraisal, which was created in 2001 and which can be taken as a self-report or 360-degree assessment.

Trait Model

Soviet-born British psychologist Konstantin Vasily Petrides ("K. V. Petrides") proposed a conceptual distinction between the ability based model and a trait based model of EI and has been developing the latter over many years in numerous scientific publications. Trait EI is "a constellation of emotional self-perceptions located at the lower levels of personality." In lay terms, trait EI refers to an individual's self-perceptions of their emotional abilities. This definition of EI encompasses behavioural dispositions and self perceived abilities and is measured by self report, as opposed to the ability based model which refers to actual abilities, which have proven highly resistant to scientific measurement. Trait EI should be investigated within a personality framework. An alternative label for the same construct is trait emotional self-efficacy.

The trait EI model is general and subsumes the Goleman and Bar-On models discussed above. The conceptualization of EI as a personality trait leads to a construct that lies outside the taxonomy of human cognitive ability. This is an important distinction in as much as it bears directly on the operationalization of the construct and the theories and hypotheses that are formulated about it.

Measurement

There are many self-report measures of EI, including the EQ-i, the Swinburne University Emotional Intelligence Test (SUEIT), and the Schutte EI model. None of these assess intelligence, abilities, or skills (as their authors often claim), but rather, they are limited measures of trait emotional intelligence. One of the more comprehensive and widely researched measures of this construct is the Trait Emotional Intelligence Questionnaire (TEIQue), which was specifically designed to measure the construct comprehensively and is available in many languages.

The TEIQue provides an operationalization for the model of Petrides and colleagues, that conceptualizes EI in terms of personality. The test encompasses 15 subscales organized under four factors: Well-Being, Self-Control, Emotionality, and Sociability. The psychometric properties of the TEIQue were investigated in a study on a French-speaking population, where it was reported that TEIQue scores were globally normally distributed and reliable.

The researchers also found TEIQue scores were unrelated to nonverbal reasoning (Raven's matrices), which they interpreted as support for the personality trait view of EI (as opposed to a form of intelligence). As expected, TEIQue scores were positively related to some of the Big Five personality traits (extraversion, agreeableness, openness, conscientiousness) as well as inversely related to others (alexithymia, neuroticism). A number of quantitative genetic studies have been carried out within the trait EI model, which have revealed significant genetic effects and heritabilities for all trait EI scores. Two recent studies (one a meta-analysis) involving direct comparisons of multiple EI tests yielded very favourable results for the TEIQue.

Bar-On Model of Emotional-social Intelligence (ESI)

Bar-On defines emotional intelligence as being concerned with effectively understanding oneself and others, relating well to people, and adapting to and coping with the immediate surroundings to be more successful in dealing with environmental demands. Bar-On posits that EI develops over time and that it can be improved through training, programming, and therapy. Bar-On hypothesizes that those individuals with higher than average EQs are in general more successful in meeting environmental demands and pressures. He also notes that a deficiency in EI can mean a lack of success and the existence of emotional problems.

Problems in coping with one's environment are thought, by Bar-On, to be especially common among those individuals lacking in the subscales of reality testing, problem solving, stress tolerance, and impulse control. In general, Bar-On considers emotional intelligence and cognitive intelligence to contribute equally to a person's general intelligence, which then offers an indication of one's potential to succeed in life. However, doubts have been expressed about this model in the research literature (in particular about the validity of self-report as an index of emotional intelligence) and in scientific settings it is being replaced by the trait emotional intelligence (trait EI) model discussed below.

Measurement

The Bar-On Emotional Quotient Inventory (EQ-i), is a self-report measure of EI developed as a measure of emotionally and socially competent behaviour that provides an estimate of one's emotional and social intelligence. The EQ-i is not meant to measure personality traits or cognitive capacity, but rather the mental ability to be successful in dealing with environmental demands and pressures. One hundred and thirty three items (questions or factors) are used to obtain a Total EQ (Total Emotional Quotient) and to produce five composite scale scores, corresponding to the five main components of the Bar-On model. A limitation of this model is that it claims to measure some kind of ability through self-report items.

Alexithymia

Alexithymia from the Greek words *lexis* and *thumos* (literally "lack of words for emotions") is a term coined by Peter Sifneos in 1973 to describe people who appeared to have deficiencies in understanding, processing, or describing their emotions. Viewed as a spectrum between high and low EI, the alexithymia construct is strongly inversely related to EI, representing its lower range. The individual's level of alexithymia can be measured with self-scored questionnaires such as the Toronto Alexithymia Scale (TAS-20) or the Bermond-Vorst Alexithymia

Questionnaire (BVAQ) or by observer rated measures such as the Observer Alexithymia Scale (OAS).

Criticisms of Theoretical Foundation

Cannot be recognized as form of intelligence: Goleman's early work has been criticized for assuming from the beginning that EI is a type of intelligence. Eysenck (2000) writes that Goleman's description of EI contains unsubstantiated assumptions about intelligence in general, and that it even runs contrary to what researchers have come to expect when studying types of intelligence:

"[Goleman] exemplifies more clearly than most the fundamental absurdity of the tendency to class almost any type of behaviour as an 'intelligence'... If these five 'abilities' define 'emotional intelligence', we would expect some evidence that they are highly correlated; Goleman admits that they might be quite uncorrelated, and in any case if we cannot measure them, how do we know they are related? So the whole theory is built on quicksand: there is no sound scientific basis."

Similarly, Locke (2005) claims that the concept of EI is in itself a misinterpretation of the intelligence construct, and he offers an alternative interpretation: it is not another form or type of intelligence, but intelligence—the ability to grasp abstractions—applied to a particular life domain: emotions. He suggests the concept should be re-labelled and referred to as a skill.

The essence of this criticism is that scientific enquiry depends on valid and consistent construct utilization, and that before the introduction of the term EI, psychologists had established theoretical distinctions between factors such as abilities and achievements, skills and habits, attitudes and values, and personality traits and emotional states. Thus, some scholars believe that the term *EI* merges and conflates such accepted concepts and definitions.

Has Little Predictive Value

Landy (2005) claimed that the few incremental validity studies conducted on EI have shown that it adds little or nothing to the explanation or prediction of some common outcomes (most notably academic and work success). Landy suggested that the reason why some studies have found a small increase in predictive validity is a methodological fallacy, namely, that alternative explanations have not been completely considered:

> *"EI is compared and contrasted with a measure of abstract intelligence but not with a personality measure,*

or with a personality measure but not with a measure of academic intelligence." *Landy (2005)*

Similarly, other researchers have raised concerns about the extent to which self-report EI measures correlate with established personality dimensions. Generally, self-report EI measures and personality measures have been said to converge because they both purport to measure personality traits. Specifically, there appear to be two dimensions of the Big Five that stand out as most related to self-report EI – neuroticism and extroversion. In particular, neuroticism has been said to relate to negative emotionality and anxiety. Intuitively, individuals scoring high on neuroticism are likely to score low on self-report EI measures.

The interpretations of the correlations between EI questionnaires and personality have been varied. The prominent view in the scientific literature is the Trait EI view, which re-interprets EI as a collection of personality traits.

Criticisms of Measurement Issues

Ability model measures measure conformity, not ability: One criticism of the works of Mayer and Salovey comes from a study by Roberts et al. (2001), which suggests that the EI, as measured by the MSCEIT, may only be measuring conformity. This argument is rooted in the MSCEIT's use of consensus-based assessment, and in the fact that scores on the MSCEIT are negatively distributed (meaning that its scores differentiate between people with low EI better than people with high EI).

Ability Model Measures Measure Knowledge (not actual ability)

Further criticism has been leveled by Brody (2004), who claimed that unlike tests of cognitive ability, the MSCEIT "tests knowledge of emotions but not necessarily the ability to perform tasks that are related to the knowledge that is assessed". The main argument is that even though someone knows how he should behave in an emotionally laden situation, it doesn't necessarily follow that the person could actually carry out the reported behaviour.

Ability Model Measures Measure Personality and General Intelligence

New research is surfacing that suggests that ability EI measures might be measuring personality in addition to general intelligence. These studies examined the multivariate effects of personality and intelligence on EI and also corrected estimates for measurement error (which is often not done in some validation studies). For example, a study by Schulte, Ree, Carretta (2004), showed that general intelligence (measured with the Wonderlic Personnel Test), agreeableness (measured by the NEO-PI), as well as gender had a multiple R of .81 with the MSCEIT. This result has been replicated by Fiori and Antonakis (2011),; they found a multiple R of .76 using Cattell's "Culture Fair" intelligence test and the Big Five Inventory (BFI); significant covariates were intelligence (standardized beta = .39), agreeableness (standardized beta = .54), and openness (standardized beta = .46). Antonakis and Dietz (2011a), who investigated the Ability Emotional Intelligence Measure found similar results (Multiple R = .69), with significant predictors being intelligence, standardized beta = .69 (using the Swaps Test and a Wechsler scales subtest, the 40-item General Knowledge Task) and empathy, standardized beta = .26.

Self-report Measures are Susceptible to Faking

More formally termed socially desirable responding (SDR), faking good is defined as a response pattern in which test-takers systematically represent themselves with an excessive positive bias (Paulhus, 2002). This bias has long been known to contaminate responses on personality inventories (Holtgraves, 2004; McFarland & Ryan, 2000; Peebles & Moore, 1998; Nichols & Greene, 1997; Zerbe & Paulhus, 1987), acting as a mediator of the relationships between self-report measures (Nichols & Greene, 1997; Ganster et al., 1983).

It has been suggested that responding in a desirable way is a response set, which is a situational and temporary response pattern (Pauls & Crost, 2004; Paulhus, 1991). This is contrasted with a response style, which is a more long-term trait-like quality. Considering the contexts some self-report EI inventories are used in (e.g., employment settings), the problems of response sets in high-stakes scenarios become clear (Paulhus & Reid, 2001).

There are a few methods to prevent socially desirable responding on behaviour inventories. Some researchers believe it is necessary to warn test-takers not to fake good before taking a personality test (e.g., McFarland, 2003). Some inventories use validity scales in order to determine the likelihood or consistency of the responses across all items.

Claims for Predictive Power are Too Extreme

Landy distinguishes between the "commercial wing" and "the academic wing" of the EI movement, basing this distinction on the alleged predictive power of EI as seen by the two currents. According to Landy, the former makes expansive claims on the applied value of EI, while the latter is trying to warn users against these claims. As an example, Goleman (1998) asserts that "the most effective leaders are alike in one crucial way: they all have a high degree of what has come to be known as emotional intelligence. ...emotional intelligence is the sine qua non of leadership".

In contrast, Mayer (1999) cautions "the popular literature's implication—that highly emotionally intelligent people possess an unqualified advantage in life—appears overly enthusiastic at present and unsubstantiated by reasonable scientific standards." Landy further reinforces this argument by noting that the data upon which these claims are based are held in "proprietary databases", which means they are unavailable to independent researchers for reanalysis, replication, or verification. Thus, the credibility of the findings cannot be substantiated in a scientific way, unless those datasets are made public and available for independent analysis.

In an academic exchange, Antonakis and Ashkanasy/Dasborough mostly agreed that researchers testing whether EI matters for leadership have not done so using robust research designs; therefore, currently there is no strong evidence showing that EI predicts leadership outcomes when accounting for personality and IQ. Antonakis argued that EI might not be needed for leadership effectiveness (he referred to this as the "curse of emotion" phenomenon, because leaders who are too sensitive to their and others' emotional states might have difficulty making decisions that would result in emotional labour for the leader or followers). A recently-published meta-analysis seems to support the Antonakis position:

In fact, Harms and Credé found that overall (and using data free from problems of common source and common methods), EI measures correlated only $\rho = 0.11$ with measures of transformational leadership. Interestingly, ability-measures of EI fared worst (i.e., $\rho = 0.04$); the WLEIS (Wong-Law measure) did a bit better ($\rho = 0.08$), and the Bar-On measure better still ($\rho = 0.18$).

However, the validity of these estimates does not include the effects of IQ or the big five personality, which correlate both with EI measures and leadership. In a subsequent paper analysing the impact of EI on both job performance and leadership, Harms and Credé found that the meta-analytic validity estimates for EI dropped to zero when Big Five traits and IQ were controlled for. Joseph and Newman meta-analytically showed the same result for Ability EI, but further demonstrated that self-reported and Trait EI measures retain a small amount of predictive validity for job performance after controlling Big Five traits and IQ. Newman, Joseph, and MacCann contend that the greater predictive validity of Trait EI measures is due to their inclusion of content related to achievement motivation, self efficacy, and self-rated performance.

NICHD Pushes for Consensus

The National Institute of Child Health and Human Development has recognized the divide on the topic of emotional intelligence explains the need for the mental health community to agree on some guidelines to describe good mental health and positive mental living conditions. In their section, "Positive Psychology and the Concept of Health," they explain. "Currently there are six competing models of positive health, which are based on concepts such as being above normal, character strengths and core virtues, developmental maturity, social-emotional intelligence, subjective well-being, and resilience. But these concepts define health in philosophical rather than empirical terms. Dr. [Lawrence] Becker suggested the need for a consensus on the concept of positive psychological health..."

EI and Job Performance

Research of EI and job performance shows mixed results: a positive relation has been found in some of the studies, in others there was no relation or an inconsistent one. This led researchers Cote and Miners (2006) to offer a compensatory model between EI and IQ, that posits that the association between EI and job performance becomes more positive as cognitive intelligence decreases, an idea first proposed in the context of academic performance (Petrides, Frederickson, & Furnham, 2004). The results of the former study supported the compensatory model: employees with low IQ get higher task performance and organizational citizenship behaviour directed at the organization, the higher their EI.

A meta-analytic review by Joseph and Newman also revealed that both Ability EI and Trait EI tend to predict job performance much better in jobs that require a high degree of emotional labour (where 'emotional labour' was defined as jobs that require the effective display of positive emotion). In contrast, EI shows little relationship to job performance in jobs that do not require emotional labour. In other words, emotional intelligence tends to predict job performance for emotional jobs only.

A more recent study suggests that EI is not necessarily a universally positive trait. They found a negative correlation between EI and managerial work demands; while under low levels of managerial work demands, they found a negative relationship between EI and teamwork effectiveness. An explanation for this may suggest gender differences in EI, as women tend to score higher levels than men. This furthers the idea that job context plays a role in the relationships between EI, teamwork effectiveness, and job performance.

Another interesting find was discussed in a study that assessed a possible link between EI and entrepreneurial behaviours and success. In accordance with much of the other findings regarding EI and job performance, they found that levels of EI only predicted a small amount of entrepreneurial behaviour.

Self-esteem and Drug use

A 2012 study cross examined emotional intelligence, self-esteem, and marijuana dependence. Out of a sample of 200, 100 of which were dependent on cannabis and the other 100 emotionally healthy, the dependent group scored exceptionally low on EI when compared to the control group. They also found that the dependent group also scored low on self-esteem when compared to the control.

Another study in 2010 examined whether or not low levels of EI had a relationship with the degree of drug and alcohol addiction. In the assessment of 103 residents in a drug rehabilitation centre, they examined their EI along with other psychosocial factors in a 1 month interval of treatment. They found that participants' EI scores improved as their levels of addiction lessened as part of their treatment.

Personality Test

A personality test is a questionnaire or other standardized instrument designed to reveal aspects of an individual's character or psychological makeup. The first personality tests were developed in 1920s and were intended to ease the process of personnel selection, particularly in the armed forces. Since these early efforts of these test, a wide variety of personality tests have been developed, notably the Myers Briggs Type Indicator (MBTI), the MMPI, and a number of tests based on the Five Factor Model of personality.

Today, personality tests have become a $400 million-a-year industry and are used in a range of contexts, including individual and relationship counseling, career planning, employee selection and development, and customer interaction management.

Figure: *The four temperaments as illustrated by Johann Kaspar Lavater*

The origins of personality testing date back to the 18th and 19th centuries, when personality was assessed through phrenology, the measurement of the human skull, and physiognomy, which assessed personality based on a person's outer appearances. These early pseudoscientific techniques were eventually replaced with more empirical methods in the 20th century. One of the earliest modern personality tests was the Woolworth Personality Data Sheet, a self-report inventory developed for World War I and used for the psychiatric screening of new draftees.

Overview

There are many different types of personality tests. The most common type is the self-report inventory, also commonly referred to as objective personality tests. Self-report inventory tests involve the administration of many questions/items to test-takers who respond by rating the degree to which each item reflects their behaviour and can be scored objectively. The term 'item' is used because many test questions are not actually questions; they are typically statements on questionnaires that allow respondents to indicate level of agreement (using a Likert scale or, more accurately, a Likert-type scale).

A sample item on a personality test, for example, might ask test-takers to rate the degree to which they agree with the statement "I talk to a lot of different people at parties" by using a scale of 1 ("strongly disagree") to 5 ("strongly agree"). The most widely used objective tests of personality is the Minnesota Multiphasic Personality Inventory (MMPI) which was originally designed to distinguish individuals with different psychological problems. Since then, it has become popular as a means of attempting to identify personality characteristics of people in many every-day settings. In addition to self-report inventories, there are many other methods for assessing personality, including observational measures, peer-report studies, and projective tests (e.g. the TAT and Ink Blots).

Personality Test Topics

Norms: The meaning of *personality test* scores are difficult to interpret in a direct sense. For this reason substantial effort is made by producers of personality tests to produce norms to provide a comparative basis for interpreting a respondent's test scores. Common formats for these norms include percentile ranks, z scores, sten scores, and other forms of standardised scores.

Test Development

A substantial amount of research and thinking has gone into the topic of *personality test* development. Development of personality tests tends to be an iterative process whereby a test is progressively refined. Test development can proceed on theoretical or statistical grounds. There are three commonly used general strategies: Inductive, Deductive, and Empirical. Scales created today will often incorporate elements of all three methods.

Deductive or Theoretical strategies can involve taking a previously established psychological or other theory to define the content domain and then developing test items that should in principle measure the domain of interest. This can then be accompanied by assessment by experts of the developed items to the defined construct. Test items are then selected or eliminated based upon which will result in the strongest internal validity for the scale. Advantages of this method include clearly defined and face valid questions for each measure. Measures are also more likely to apply across populations. Additionally, it requires less statistical methodology for initial development, and will often outperform other methods while requiring fewer items. However, the construct of interest must be well understood to create a thorough measure, and it may be difficult to prevent or determine if individuals are faking on the measure.

Statistical strategies are varied. Common strategies involve the use of exploratory factor analysis and confirmatory factor analysis to verify that items that are proposed to group together into factors actually do group together empirically. Reliability analysis and Item Response Theory are additional complimentary approaches. Inductive approaches are reliant on statistical strategies. Inductive strategies begin by constructing a wide group of items with no theoretical connection and administering it to a large group of participants. This allows researchers to analyse natural relationships among the questions and label components of the scale based upon how the questions group together.

The Five Factor Model of personality was developed using this method. Advantages statistical methods include the opportunity to discover previously unidentified or unexpected relationships between items or constructs. It also may allow for the development of subtle items that prevent test takers from knowing what is being measured and may represent the actual structure of a construct better than a pre-developed theory. Criticisms include a vulnerability to finding item relationships that do not apply to a broader population, difficulty identifying what may be measured in each component because of confusing item relationships, or constructs that were not fully addressed by the originally created questions.

Empirical strategies are similarly reliant on statistical methods. Empirical test construction attempts to create a measure that differentiates between different established groups. For example, this may include depressed and non-depressed individuals, or individuals high or low in levels of aggression. The goal of item creation is to find items that will be answered differently by the groups of interest. The Minnesota Multiphasic Personality Inventory was initially developed using this method.

Test Evaluation

There are several criteria for evaluating a *personality test.* Fundamentally, a *personality test* is expected to demonstrate reliability and validity.

Analysis

A respondent's response is used to compute the analysis. Analysis of data is a long process. Two major theories are used here; Classical test theory (CTT)- used for the observed score, and item response theory (IRT)- "a family of models for persons' responses to items". The two theories focus upon different 'levels' of responses and researchers are implored to use both in order to fully appreciate their results.

Non-response

Firstly, item non-response needs to be addressed. Non-response can either be 'unit'- where a person gave no response for any of the n items, or 'item'- i.e., individual question. Unit non-response is generally dealt with exclusion. Item non-response should be handled by imputation- the method used can vary between test and questionnaire items. Literature about the most appropriate method to use and when can be found here.

Scoring

The conventional method of scoring items is to assign '0' for an incorrect answer '1' for a correct answer. When tests have more response options (e.g. ordinal-polytomous items)- '0' when incorrect, '1' for being partly correct and '2' for being correct. Personality tests can also be scored using a dimensional (normative) or a typological (ipsative) approach. Dimensional approaches such as the Big 5 describe personality as a set of continuous dimensions on which individuals differ. From the item scores, a 'observed' score is computed. This is generally found by summing the un-weighted item scores.

Criticism and Controversy

Biased test taker interpretation: One problem of a personality test is that the users of the test could only find it accurate because of the subjective validation involved. This is where the person only acknowledges the information that applies to him/her.

Application to Non-clinical Samples

Critics have raised issues about the ethics of administering personality tests, especially for non-clinical uses. By the 1960s, tests like the MMPI were being given by companies to employees and applicants as often as to psychiatric patients. Sociologist William H. Whyte was among those who saw the tests as helping to create and perpetuate the oppressive groupthink of "The Organization Man" mid-20th century corporate capitalistic mentality.

Personality versus Social Factors

In the 60s and 70s some psychologists dismissed the whole idea of personality, considering much behaviour to be context-specific. This idea was supported by the fact that personality often does not predict behaviour in specific contexts. However, more extensive research has shown that when behaviour is aggregated across contexts, that personality can be a modest to good predictor of behaviour. Almost all psychologists now acknowledge that both social and individual difference factors (i.e., personality) influence behaviour. The debate is currently more around the relative importance of each of these factors and how these factors interact.

Respondent Faking

One problem with self-report measures of personality is that respondents are often able to distort their responses. Emotive tests in particular could in theory become prey to unreliable results due to people striving to pick the answer they feel the best fitting of an ideal character and therefore not their true response. This is particularly problematic in employment contexts and other contexts where important decisions are being made and there is an incentive to present oneself in a favourable manner.

Work in experimental settings has also shown that when student samples have been asked to deliberately fake on a personality test, they clearly demonstrated that they are capable of doing so. Hogan, Barett and Hogan (2007) analysed data of 5,266 applicants who did a personality test based on the big five. At the first application the applicants were rejected. After six months the applicants reapplied and completed the same personality test. The answers on the personality tests were compared and there was no significant difference between the answers.

So in practice, most people do not significantly distort. Nevertheless, a researcher has to be prepared for such possibilities. Also, sometimes participants think that tests results are more valid than they really are because they like the results that they get. People want to believe that the positive traits that the test results say they possess are in fact present in their personality. This leads to distorted results of people's sentiments on the validity of such tests.

Several strategies have been adopted for reducing respondent faking. One strategy involves providing a warning on the test that methods exist for detecting faking and that detection will result in negative consequences for the respondent (e.g., not being considered for the job). Forced choice item formats (ipsative testing) have been adopted which require respondents to choose between alternatives of equal social desirability. Social desirability and lie scales are often included which detect certain patterns of responses, although these are often confounded by true variability in social desirability.

More recently, Item Response Theory approaches have been adopted with some success in identifying item response profiles that flag fakers. Other researchers are looking at the timing of responses on electronically administered tests to assess faking. While people can fake in practice they seldom do so to any significant level. To successfully fake means knowing what the ideal answer would be. Even with something as simple as assertiveness people who are unassertive and try to appear assertive often endorse the wrong items. This is because unassertive people confuse assertion with aggression, anger, oppositional behaviour, etc.

Psychological Research

Personality testing is frequently used in psychological research to test various theories of personality. Research published by David Dunning of Cornell University, Chip Heath of Stanford University and Jerry M. Suls of the University of Iowa reveals that observers who are not involved in any type of relationship with an individual are better judges of the individual's relationships and abilities. These workers have studied a large body of investigations into self-evaluation, indicating that individuals may have flawed views about themselves and their social relationships, sometimes leading to decisions that can impact negatively on other persons' lives and/or their own.

Additional Applications

A study by American Management Association reveals that 39 percent of companies surveyed use personality testing as part of their hiring process. However, ipsative personality tests are often misused in recruitment and selection, where they are mistakenly treated as if they were normative measures.

More people are using personality testing to evaluate their business partners, their dates and their spouses. Salespeople are using personality testing to better understand the needs of their customers and to gain a competitive edge in the closing of deals. College students have started to use personality testing to evaluate their roommates. Lawyers are beginning to use personality testing for criminal behaviour analysis, litigation profiling, witness examination and jury selection.

Dangers

Personality tests have been around for a long time, but it wasn't until it became illegal for employers to use polygraphs that we began to see the widespread use of personality tests. The idea behind these personality tests is that employers can reduce their turnover rates and prevent economic losses in the form of people prone to thievery, drug abuse, emotional disorders or violence in the workplace.

Employers also see employment tests as more of an accurate assessment for someone's behavioural characteristics versus an employment reference who may respond neutrally or favourably in fear of a defamation lawsuit. But the problem with using personality tests as a hiring tool is the notion a person's job performance in one environment will be the same in every environment. However, the reality is that one's environment plays a crucial role in determining job performance, and not all environments are created equally. One danger of using personality tests is the results may be skewed based on a person's mood so good candidates may potentially be screened out because of unfavourable responses that reflect that mood.

Another danger of personality tests is that they can create false-negative results (i.e. honest people being labelled as dishonest) especially in cases when stress on the applicant's part is involved. There is also the issue of privacy to be of concern forcing applicants to reveal private thoughts and feelings through his or her responses that seem to become a condition for employment. Another danger of personality tests is the illegal discrimination of certain groups under the guise of a personality test.

Complacentment

It is easy for personality test participants to become complacent about their own personal uniqueness and instead become dependent on the description associated with them. This can be potentially dangerous with persons who are already suffering from a form of identity disorder or may be a catalyst to instigate particular behaviours in a person who was previously believed to be of sound mental health. The severity of the damage that individuals can sustain to their personal identity was made clear during the case Wilson v Johnson&Johnson in which the plaintiff (Wilson) sued his former employer (Johnson&Johnson) for irreparable damages that resulted from the over abundance of personality tests being administered in the workplace. Wilson argued that repeated questioning and scrutiny of his personality was a cause of strain and eventually breakdown.

In this historic case, Wilson was awarded $4.7 million after jurors agreed that excessive testing caused strain and led to unnecessary scrutiny resulting in personal grief. Similar cases have been tried since and won, but none with such magnitude as this first monumental case that won mental health rights for employees.

Examples of Personality Tests

- The first modern personality test was the Woodworth Personal data sheet, which was first used in 1919. It was designed to help the United States Army screen out recruits who might be susceptible to shell shock.
- The Rorschach inkblot test was introduced in 1921 as a way to determine personality by the interpretation of abstract inkblots.
- The Thematic Apperception Test was commissioned by the Office of Strategic Services (O.S.S.) in the 1930s to identify personalities that might be susceptible to being turned by enemy intelligence.
- The Minnesota Multiphasic Personality Inventory was published in 1942 as a way to aid in assessing psychopathology in a clinical setting. It can also be used to assess the Personality Psychopathology Five (PSY-5), which are similar to the Five Factor Model (FFM; or Big Five personality traits). These five scales on the MMPI-2 include aggressiveness, psychoticism, disconstraint, negative emotionality/neuroticism, and introversion/low positive emotionality.
- Myers-Briggs Type Indicator (MBTI) is a psychometric questionnaire designed to measure psychological preferences in how people perceive the world and make decisions. This 16-type indicator test is based on Carl Jung's *Psychological Types*, developed during World War II by Isabel Myers and Katherine Briggs. The 16-type indicator includes a combination of Extroversion-Introversion, Sensing-Intuition, Thinking-Feeling and Judging-Perceiving.The MBTI utilizes 2 opposing behavioural divisions on 4 scales that yields a "personality type".
- Keirsey Temperament Sorter developed by David Keirsey is influenced by Isabel Myers sixteen types and Ernst Kretschmer's four types.
- The True Colours (personality) Test developed by Don Lowry in 1978 is based on the work of David Keirsey in his book,

"Please Understand Me" as well as the Myers-Briggs Type Indicator and provides a model for understanding personality types using the colours blue, gold, orange and green to represent four basic personality temperaments.

- The 16PF Questionnaire (16PF) was developed by Raymond Cattell and his colleagues in the 1940s and 1950s in a search to try to discover the basic traits of human personality using scientific methodology. The test was first published in 1949, and is now in its 5th edition, published in 1994. It is used in a wide variety of settings for individual and marital counseling, career counseling and employee development, in educational settings, and for basic research.
- The EQSQ Test developed by Professor Simon Baron-Cohen, Sally Wheelwright, and their team at the University of Cambridge, England, centres on the empathizing-systemizing theory of the male versus the female brain types.
- The Personal Style Indicator (PSI) classifies four aspects of innate behaviour by testing a person's preferences in word associations.
- The Personality and Preference Inventory (PAPI), originally designed by Dr Max Kostick, Proféssor of Industrial Psychology at Boston State College, in Massachusetts, USA, in the early 1960s evaluates the behaviour and preferred work styles of individuals.
- The Strength Deployment Inventory, developed by Elias Porter, Ph.D. in 1971 and is based on his theory of Relationship Awareness. Porter was the first known psychometrician to use colours (Red, Green and Blue) as shortcuts to communicate the results of a personality test.
- The Newcastle Personality Assessor (NPA), created by Daniel Nettle, is a short questionnaire designed to quantify personality on five dimensions: Extraversion, Neuroticism, Conscientious, Agreeableness, and Openness.
- The DISC assessment is based on the research of William Moulton Marston and later work by John Grier, and identifies four personality types: Dominance; Influence; Steadiness and Conscientiousness. It is used widely in Fortune 500 companies, for-profit and non-profit organizations.
- The Winslow Personality Profile measures 24 traits on a decile scale. It was mentioned in the Disney movie *Miracle* due to its use to help select the members of the team. It has been used

in the National Football League, the National Basketball Association, the National Hockey League and every draft choice for Major League Baseball for the last 30 years and can be taken online for personal development.

- Other personality tests include Forté Profile, Millon Clinical Multiaxial Inventory, Eysenck Personality Questionnaire, Swedish Universities Scales of Personality, and Enneagram of Personality.
- The HEXACO Personality Inventory – Revised (HEXACO PI-R) is based on the HEXACO model of personality structure, which consists of six domains, the five domains of the Big Five model, as well as the domain of Honesty-Humility.
- The Pro Development assessment is a professional development instrument for leaders that measures convergence of an individual's Missions – (motivations and interests that excite an individual to action), Competencies – (abilities and aptitudes that enable action) and Styles – (personality and behaviours that make an individual unique). PRO-D also produces an astonishingly accurate perspective of how the different dimensions of mission, style and competency interact for the Person – Role – Organization. It was developed in Princeton under the advisement of George Gallup and Win Manning (ETS).
- The Personality Inventory for DSM-5 (PID-5) was developed in September 2012 by the DSM-5 Personality and Personality Disorders Workgroup with regard to a personality trait model proposed for DSM-5. The PID-5 includes 25 maladaptive personality traits as determined by Krueger, Derringer, Markon, Watson, and Skodol.
- The "Clifton Strengths Finder" is the internet-based personality test at the heart of the popular book "Now, Discover Your Strengths".
- The "Process Communication Model" (PCM) is a non-clinical personality assessment, communication and management methodology developed by Taibi Kahler, Ph.D. Originally developed in collaboration with NASA for astronaut selection, the model has now been applied to corporate management, interpersonal communications, and a variety of other purposes, including analysis of call centre interactions.
- The Birkman Method (TBM) was developed by Roger W. Birkman, Ph.D in the late 1940s. The instrument consists of ten scales describing "occupational preferences" (Interests), 11

scales describing "effective behaviours" (Usual behaviour) and 11 scales describing interpersonal and environmental expectations (Needs). A corresponding set of 11 scale values was derived to describe "less than effective behaviours" (Stress behaviour). TBM was created empirically. The psychological model is most closely associated with the work of Kurt Lewin. Occupational profiling consists of 22 job families with over 200 associated job titles connected to O*Net.

Personality Tests of the Five Factor Model

Different types of the Big Five personality traits:

- The NEO PI-R, or the Revised NEO Personality Inventory, is one of the most significant measures of the Five Factor Model (FFM). The measure was created by Costa and McCrae and contains 240 items in the forms of sentences. Costa and McCrae had divided each of the five domains into six facets each, 30 facets total, and changed the way the FFM is measured.
- The Five-Factor Model Rating Form (FFMRF) was developed by Lynam and Widiger in 2001 as a shorter alternative to the NEO PI-R. The form consists of 30 facets, 6 facets for each of the Big Five factors. The form can be obtained at http://samppl.psych.purdue.edu/~dbsamuel/research.html.
- The Five Factor Personality Inventory — Children (FFPI-C) was developed to measure personality traits in children based upon the Five Factor Model (FFM).
- The Big Five Inventory (BFI), developed by John, Donahue, and Kentle, is a 44-item self-report questionnaire consisting of adjectives that assess the domains of the Five Factor Model (FFM). The 10-Item Big Five Inventory is a simplified version of the well-established BFI. It is developed to provide a personality inventory under time constraints. The BFI-10 assesses the 5 dimensions of BFI using only two items each to cut down on length of BFI.
- The Semi-structured Interview for the Assessment of the Five-Factor Model (SIFFM) is the only semi-structured interview intended to measure a personality model or personality disorder. The interview assesses the five domains and 30 facets as presented by the NEO PI-R, and it additional assesses both normal and abnormal extremities of each facet.

6

Employment Testing

Employment testing is the practice of administering written, oral, or other tests as a means of determining the suitability or desirability of a job applicant. The premise is that if scores on a test correlate with job performance, then it is economically useful for the employer to select employees based on scores from that test.

Legal Context (United States)

The United States Supreme Court has decided several cases clarifying the place of employment testing in the context of discrimination law. In particular, these cases have addressed the discriminatory use of tests when promoting employees by requiring tests beyond the education required for the job. A central finding in Griggs v. Duke Power Co. was that the employer must demonstrate (or be prepared to demonstrate) that its selection process is related to the job being filled.

Employers considering the use of employment tests, particularly knowledge and aptitude-based tests, should perform due diligence to assure that questions are reasonably related to the job. This is often accomplished with advice from counsel. For example, applicants for an engineering position may be required to complete a math test, as math is a skill commonly required for engineers. To comply with the decision in Griggs, the employer must assure that the test is a reasonable measure of job performance. Therefore, if the math questions were engineering-related and documents could prove that employees with insufficient knowledge of math would not succeed as engineers, then the examination would meet the Griggs test. Conversely, employers that require a receptionist to take a math test may be considered unreasonable, because math is unrelated to a receptionist's job duties. For all employment tests, common sense and reasonableness must apply.

Test Types Used

Different types of assessments may be used for employment testing, including personality tests, intelligence tests, work samples, and assessment centres. Some correlate better with job performance than with others; employers often use more than one to maximize predictive power.

Performance Assessment Tests

Performance-based assessment testing is a process to find out if applicants can do the job for which they are applying. It is done through tests, which are directly administered and judged by Hiring Managers who will be supervising the potential hire. Performance assessments can be used as a pre-screening tool to test applied knowledge, skills-job match and commitment of the applicant towards the job position.

The tests are peer-to-peer and reflect real business tasks that candidates have to perform, should they be selected for the role. The tests are open ended, time bound, business related questions which applicants need to submit their responses for in order to prove their abilities. The most important question that performance testing, seeks to answer is: How would you solve this problem? Web tools like, HireVue, GapJumpers and CodeEval allow candidate responses to be judged directly by Hiring Managers of the respective departments to select the ones most suited for the role, thus making the process efficient for the company.

Personality Tests

Personality tests may potentially be useful in personnel selection. Of the well-known Big Five personality traits, only conscientiousness correlates substantially with traditional measures of job performance, and that correlation is strong enough to be predictive. However, other factors of personality can correlate substantially with non-traditional aspects of job performance, such as leadership and effectiveness in a team environment. The Myers-Briggs Type Indicator (MBTI) is also used.

The Minnesota Multiphasic Personality Inventory (MMPI) is a highly validated psychopathology test that is generally used in a clinical psychology setting and may reveal potential mental health disorders. However, this can be considered by the Equal Employment Opportunity Commission as the employer having knowledge of a medical condition prior to an offer of employment. This is an illegal basis for a hiring decision in the United States. Employers considering personality tests should focus on tests designed for job purposes and do not provide any information regarding an applicant's mental health or stability.

Notable situations in which the MMPI may be used are in final selection for police officers, fire fighters, and other security and emergency personnel, especially when the employees are required to carry weapons. An assessment of mental stability and fitness can be reasonably related and necessary in the performance of the job.

Cognitive Ability Tests

Tests of cognitive ability can assess general intelligence and correlate very highly with overall job performance. Individuals with higher levels of cognitive ability tend to perform better on their jobs. This is especially true for jobs that are particularly intellectually demanding.

Job-knowledge Tests

Employers administer job-knowledge tests when applicants must already possess a body of knowledge before being hired. Job-knowledge tests are particularly useful when applicants must have specialized or technical knowledge that can only be acquired through extensive experience or training. Job-knowledge tests are commonly used in fields such as computer programming, law, and financial management.

Licensing exams and certification programmes are also types of job-knowledge tests. Passing such exams indicates competence in the exam's subject area. Tests must be representative of the tested field, otherwise litigation can be brought against the test-giver.

Situational Judgement Tests

Situational judgement tests are commonly used as employee-selection and employee-screening tools and have been developed to predict employment success. These tests present realistic hypothetical scenarios in a multiple-choice format. Applicants are asked to state what they would do in a difficult job-related situation. Responses are scored according to the level of effectiveness, rather than as right or wrong.

Situational judgement tests measure the suitability of job applicants by assessing attributes such as problem solving, service orientation, and striving for achievement. These tests screen for candidates with key attributes and assess their capabilities to perform and respond to job-related situations.

Therefore, results from situational judgement tests provide more indicative and job-specific information concerning an applicant's competencies, which may not be initially apparent in their resume or during an interview. Situational judgement tests are becoming increasingly popular for selection for customer-facing positions in fields such as sales, retail and hospitality.

Aptitude Testing

An aptitude is a component of a competency to do a certain kind of work at a certain level, which can also be considered "talent". Aptitudes may be physical or mental. Aptitude is not knowledge, understanding, learned or acquired abilities (skills) or attitude. The innate nature of aptitude is in contrast to achievement, which represents knowledge or ability that is gained.

Intelligence

Aptitude and intelligence quotient are related, and in some ways opposite views of human mental ability. Whereas intelligence quotient sees intelligence as being a single measurable characteristic affecting all mental ability, aptitude refers to one of many different characteristics which can be independent of each other, such as aptitude for military flight, air traffic control, or computer programming. This is more similar to the theory of multiple intelligences.

Concerning a single measurable characteristic affecting all mental ability, analysis of any group of intelligence test scores will nearly always show them to be highly correlated. The U.S. Department of Labour's General Learning Ability, for instance, is determined by combining Verbal, Numerical and Spatial aptitude subtests. In a given person some are low and others high.

In the context of an aptitude test the "high" and "low" scores are usually not far apart, because all ability test scores tend to be correlated. Aptitude is better applied intra-individually to determine what tasks a given individual is more skilled at performing. Inter-individual aptitude differences are typically not very significant due to IQ differences.

Of course this assumes individuals have not already been pre-screened for aptitude through some other process such as SAT scores, GRE scores, or finishing medical school.

Combined Aptitude and Knowledge Tests

Tests that assess learned skills or knowledge are frequently called achievement tests. However, certain tests can assess both types of constructs. An example that leans both ways is the Armed Services Vocational Aptitude Battery (ASVAB), which is given to recruits entering the armed forces of the United States. Another is the SAT, which is designed as a test of aptitude for college in the United States, but has achievement elements. For example, it tests mathematical reasoning, which depends both on innate mathematical ability and education received in mathematics.

Aptitude tests can typically be grouped according to the type of cognitive ability they measure:

1. Fluid intelligence: the ability to think and reason abstractly, effectively solve problems and think strategically. It's more commonly known as 'street smarts' or the ability to 'quickly think on your feet'. Examples of what employers can learn from your fluid intelligence about your suitability for the role for which you are applying
2. Crystallised intelligence: the ability to learn from past experiences and relevant learning, and to apply this learning to work-related situation. Work situations that require crystallised intelligence include producing and analysing written reports, comprehending work instructions, using numbers as a tool to make effective decisions, etc

Attitude Testing

An attitude is an expression of favour or disfavour towards a person, place, thing, or event (the attitude object). Prominent psychologist Gordon Allport once described attitudes "the most distinctive and indispensable concept in contemporary social psychology.". Attitude can be formed from a person's past and present. Attitude is also measurable and changeable as well as influencing the person's emotion and behaviour.

In lay language, attitude may refer to the distinct concept of mood, or be especially synonymous with teenage rebellion.

Definitions of Attitude

An attitude can be defined as a positive or negative evaluation of people, objects, event, activities, ideas, or just about anything in your environment, but there is debate about precise definitions. Eagly and Chaiken, for example, define an attitude "a psychological tendency that is expressed by evaluating a particular entity with some degree of favour or disfavour." Though it is sometimes common to define an attitude as affect towards an object, affect (i.e., discrete emotions or overall arousal) is generally understood to be distinct from attitude as a measure of favourability.

This definition of attitude allows for one's evaluation of an attitude object to vary from extremely negative to extremely positive, but also admits that people can also be conflicted or ambivalent towards an object meaning that they might at different times express both positive and negative attitude towards the same object. This has led to some discussion of whether individual can hold multiple attitudes towards the same object.

Whether attitudes are explicit (i.e., deliberately formed) versus implicit (i.e., subconscious) has been a topic of considerable research. Research on implicit attitudes, which are generally unacknowledged or outside of awareness, uses sophisticated methods involving people's response times to stimuli to show that implicit attitudes exist (perhaps in tandem with explicit attitudes of the same object). Implicit and explicit attitudes seem to affect people's behaviour, though in different ways. They tend not to be strongly associated with each other, although in some cases they are. The relationship between them is poorly understood.

Jung's Definition

Attitude is one of Jung's 57 definitions in Chapter XI of *Psychological Types*. Jung's definition of attitude is a "readiness of the psyche to act or react in a certain way" (Jung, [1921] 1971:par. 687). Attitudes very often come in pairs, one conscious and the other unconscious. Within this broad definition Jung defines several attitudes.

The main (but not only) attitude dualities that Jung defines are the following.

- Consciousness and the unconscious. The "presence of two attitudes is extremely frequent, one conscious and the other unconscious. This means that consciousness has a constellation of contents different from that of the unconscious, a duality particularly evident in neurosis" (Jung, [1921] 1971: par. 687).
- Extraversion and introversion. This pair is so elementary to Jung's theory of types that he labelled them the "attitude-types".

- Rational and irrational attitudes. "I conceive reason as an attitude" (Jung, [1921] 1971: par. 785).
- The rational attitude subdivides into the thinking and feeling psychological functions, each with its attitude.
- The irrational attitude subdivides into the sensing and intuition psychological functions, each with its attitude. "There is thus a typical thinking, feeling, sensation, and intuitive attitude" (Jung, [1921] 1971: par. 691).
- Individual and social attitudes. Many of the latter are "isms".

In addition, Jung discusses the abstract attitude. "When I take an abstract attitude..." (Jung, [1921] 1971: par. 679). Abstraction is contrasted with creationism. "CREATIONISM. By this I mean a peculiarity of thinking and feeling which is the antithesis of abstraction" (Jung, [1921] 1971: par. 696). For example: "I hate his attitude for being Sarcastic."

Measuring Attitudes

Many measurements and scales are used to examine attitudes. Attitudes can be difficult to measure because measurement is arbitrary, meaning people have to give attitudes a scale to measure it against, and attitudes are ultimately a hypothetical construct that cannot be observed directly.

Following the explicit-implicit dichotomy, attitudes can be examined through direct and indirect measures.

Explicit Measurements Explicit measures tend to rely on self-reports or easily observed behaviours. These tend to involve bipolar scales (e.g., good-bad, favourable-unfavourable, support-oppose, etc.). Explicit measures can also be used by measuring the straightforward attribution of characteristics to nominate groups, such as "I feel that baptists are....?" or "I think that men are...?" Likert scales and other self-reports are also commonly used.

Implicit Measurements Implicit measures are not consciously directed and are assumed to be automatic, which may make implicit measures more valid and reliable than explicit measures (such as self-reports). For example, people can be motivated such that they find it socially desirable to appear to have certain attitudes. An example of this is that people can hold implicit prejudicial attitudes, but express explicit attitudes that report little prejudice. Implicit measures help account for these situations and look at attitudes that a person may not be aware of or want to show. Implicit measures therefore usually rely on an indirect measure of attitude. For example, the Implicit Association Test (IAT) examines the strength between the target concept and an attribute element by considering the latency in which a person can examine two response keys when each has two meanings. With little time to carefully examine what the participant is doing they respond according to internal keys. This priming can show attitudes the person has about a particular object.

Attitude Structure

The classic, tripartite view offered by William J. McGuire is that an attitude contains cognitive, affective, and behavioural components. Empirical research, however, fails to support clear distinctions between thoughts, emotions, and behavioural intentions associated with a particular attitude. A criticism of the tripartite view of attitudes is that it requires cognitive, affective, and behavioural associations of an attitude to be consistent, but this may be implausible. Thus some views of attitude structure see the cognitive and behavioural components as derivative of affect or affect and behaviour as derivative of underlying beliefs.

Despite debate about the particular structure of attitudes, there is considerable evidence that attitudes reflect more than evaluations of a particular object that vary from positive to negative. Attitudes also have other characteristics, such as importance, certainty, or accessibility (measures of attitude strength) and associated knowledge.

There is also considerable interest in inter-attitudinal structure, which connects different attitudes to one another and to more underlying psychological structures, such as values or ideology.

Attitude Function

Another classic view of attitudes is that attitudes serve particular functions for individuals. That is, researchers have tried to understand why individuals hold particular attitudes or why they hold attitudes in general by considering how attitudes affect the individuals who hold them. Daniel Katz, for example, writes that attitudes can serve "instrumental, adjustive or utilitarian," "ego-defensive," "value-expressive," or "knowledge" functions. The functional view of attitudes suggests that in order for attitudes to change (e.g., via persuasion), appeals must be made to the function(s) that a particular attitude serves for the individual. As an example, the "ego-defensive" function might be used to influence the racially prejudicial attitudes of an individual who sees themselves as open-minded and tolerant. By appealing to that individual's image of themselves as tolerant and open-minded, it may be possible to change their prejudicial attitudes to be more consistent with their self-concept. Similarly, a persuasive message that threatens self-image is much more likely to be rejected.

Daniel Katz classified attitudes into four different groups based on their functions

1. Utilitarian: provides us with general approach or avoidance tendencies
2. Knowledge: help people organize and interpret new information
3. Ego-defensive: attitudes can help people protect their self-esteem
4. Value-expressive: used to express central values or beliefs

Utilitarian People adopt attitudes that are rewarding and that help them avoid punishment. In other words any attitude that is adopted in a person's own self-interest is considered to serve a utilitarian function. Consider you have a condo, people with condos pay property taxes, and as a result you don't want to pay more taxes. If those factors lead to your attitude that " Increases in property taxes are bad" you attitude is serving a utilitarian function.

Knowledge People need to maintain an organized, meaningful, and stable view of the world. That being said important values and general principles can provide a framework for our knowledge. Attitudes achieve this goal by making things fit together and make sense. Example:

- I believe that I am a good person.
- I believe that good things happen to good people.
- Something bad happens to Bob.
- So I believe Bob must not be a good person.

Ego-Defensive This function involves psychoanalytic principles where people use defence mechanisms to protect themselves from psychological harm. Mechanisms include:

- Denial
- Repression
- Projection
- Rationalization

The ego-defensive notion correlates nicely with Downward Comparison Theory which holds the view that derogating a less fortunate other increases our own subjective well-being. We are more likely to use the ego-defensive function when we suffer a frustration or misfortune.

Value-Expressive

- Serves to express one's central values and self-concept.
- Central values tend to establish our identity and gain us social approval thereby showing us who we are, and what we stand for.

An example would concern attitudes towards a controversial political issue.

Attitude Formation

According to Doob (1947), learning can account for most of the attitudes we hold. The study of attitude formation is the study of how people form evaluations of persons, places or things. Theories of classical conditioning, instrumental conditioning and social learning are mainly responsible for formation of attitude. Unlike personality, attitudes are expected to change as a function of experience. In addition, exposure to the 'attitude' objects may have an effect on how a person forms his or her attitude. This concept was seen as the "Mere-Exposure Effect". Robert Zajonc showed that people were more likely to have a positive attitude on 'attitude objects' when they were exposed to it frequently than if they were not. Mere repeated exposure of the individual to a stimulus is a sufficient condition for the enhancement of his atitude towards it. Tesser (1993) has argued that hereditary variables may affect attitudes - but believes that they may do so indirectly. For example, consistency theories, which imply that we must be consistent in our beliefs and values. As with any type of heritability, to determine if a particular trait has a basis in our genes, twin studies are used. The most famous example of such a theory is Dissonance-reduction theory, associated with Leon Festinger, which explains that when the components of an attitude (including belief and behaviour) are at odds an individual may adjust one to match the other (for example, adjusting a belief to match a behaviour). Other theories include balance theory, originally proposed by Heider (1958), and the self-perception theory, originally proposed by Daryl Bem.

Attitude Change

Attitudes can be changed through persuasion and an important domain of research on attitude change focuses on responses to communication. Experimental research into the factors that can affect the persuasiveness of a message include:

1. Target Characteristics: These are characteristics that refer to the person who receives and processes a message. One such trait is intelligence - it seems that more intelligent people are less easily persuaded by one-sided messages. Another variable that has been studied in this category is self-esteem. Although it is sometimes thought that those higher in self-esteem are less easily persuaded, there is some evidence that the relationship between self-esteem and persuasibility is actually curvilinear, with people of moderate self-esteem being more easily persuaded than both those of high and low self-esteem levels (Rhodes & Woods, 1992). The mind frame and mood of the target also plays a role in this process.
2. Source Characteristics: The major source characteristics are expertise, trustworthiness and interpersonal attraction or attractiveness. The credibility of a perceived message has been found to be a key variable here; if one reads a report about health and believes it came from a professional medical journal, one may be more easily persuaded than if one believes it is from a popular newspaper. Some psychologists have debated whether this is a long-lasting effect and Hovland and Weiss (1951) found the effect of telling people that a message came from a credible source disappeared after several weeks (the so-called "sleeper effect"). Whether there is a sleeper effect is controversial. Perceived wisdom is that if people are informed of the source of a message before hearing it, there is less likelihood of a sleeper effect than if they are told a message and then told its source.
3. Message Characteristics: The nature of the message plays a role in persuasion. Sometimes presenting both sides of a story is useful to help change attitudes. When people are not motivated to process the message, simply the number of arguments presented in a persuasive message will influence attitude change, such that a greater number of arguments will produce greater attitude change.
4. Cognitive Routes: A message can appeal to an individual's cognitive evaluation to help change an attitude. In the *central route* to persuasion the individual is presented with the data and motivated to evaluate the data and arrive at an attitude changing conclusion. In the *peripheral route* to attitude change, the individual is encouraged to not look at the content but at the source. This is commonly seen in modern advertisements

that feature celebrities. In some cases, physician, doctors or experts are used. In other cases film stars are used for their attractiveness.

Emotion and Attitude Change

Emotion is a common component in persuasion, social influence, and attitude change. Much of attitude research emphasized the importance of affective or emotion components. Emotion works hand-in-hand with the cognitive process, or the way we think, about an issue or situation. Emotional appeals are commonly found in advertising, health campaigns and political messages. Recent examples include no-smoking health campaigns and political campaign advertising emphasizing the fear of terrorism. Attitudes and attitude objects are functions of cognitive, affective and conative components. Attitudes are part of the brain's associative networks, the spider-like structures residing in long term memory that consist of affective and cognitive nodes.

By activating an affective or emotion node, attitude change may be possible, though affective and cognitive components tend to be intertwined. In primarily affective networks, it is more difficult to produce cognitive counterarguments in the resistance to persuasion and attitude change. Affective forecasting, otherwise known as intuition or the prediction of emotion, also impacts attitude change. Research suggests that predicting emotions is an important component of decision making, in addition to the cognitive processes. How we feel about an outcome may override purely cognitive rationales.

In terms of research methodology, the challenge for researchers is measuring emotion and subsequent impacts on attitude. Since we cannot see into the brain, various models and measurement tools have been constructed to obtain emotion and attitude information. Measures may include the use of physiological cues like facial expressions, vocal changes, and other body rate measures. For instance, fear is associated with raised eyebrows, increased heart rate and increase body tension (Dillard, 1994). Other methods include concept or network mapping, and using primes or word cues in the era .

Components of Emotion Appeals

Any discrete emotion can be used in a persuasive appeal; this may include jealousy, disgust, indignation, fear, blue, disturbed, haunted,and anger. Fear is one of the most studied emotional appeals in communication and social influence research.

Important consequences of fear appeals and other emotion appeals include the possibility of reactance which may lead to either message rejections or source rejection and the absence of attitude change. As the EPPM suggests, there is an optimal emotion level in motivating attitude change. If there is not enough motivation, an attitude will not change; if the emotional appeal is overdone, the motivation can be paralyzed thereby preventing attitude change.

Emotions perceived as negative or containing threat are often studied more than perceived positive emotions like humor. Though the inner-workings of humor are not agreed upon, humor appeals may work by creating incongruities in the mind. Recent research has looked at the impact of humor on the processing of political messages. While evidence is inconclusive, there appears to be potential for targeted attitude change is receivers with low political message involvement.

Important factors that influence the impact of emotion appeals include self efficacy, attitude accessibility, issue involvement, and message/source features. Self efficacy is a perception of one's own human agency; in other words, it is the perception of our own ability to deal with a situation. It is an important variable in emotion appeal messages because it dictates a person's ability to deal with both the emotion and the situation. For example, if a person is not self-efficacious about their ability to impact the global environment, they are not likely to change their attitude or behaviour about global warming.

Dillard (1994) suggests that message features such as source non-verbal communication, message content, and receiver differences can impact the emotion impact of fear appeals. The characteristics of a message are important because one message can elicit different levels of emotion for different people. Thus, in terms of emotion appeals messages, one size does not fit all.

Attitude accessibility refers to the activation of an attitude from memory in other words, how readily available is an attitude about an object, issue, or situation. Issue involvement is the relevance and salience of an issue or situation to an individual. Issue involvement has been correlated with both attitude access and attitude strength. Past studies conclude accessible attitudes are more resistant to change.

Attitude-behaviour Relationship

The effects of attitudes on behaviours represents a significant research enterprise within psychology. Two theoretical approaches have dominated this research: the theory of reasoned action and, its theoretical descendant, the theory of planned behaviour, both of which are associated with Icek Ajzen. Both of these theories describe the link between attitude and behaviour as a deliberative process, with an individual actively choosing to engage in an attitude-related behaviour. An alternative model, called MODE for "Motivation and Opportunity as DEterminants" was proposed by Russell H. Fazio, which focuses on motivations and opportunities for deliberative attitude-related behaviour to occur. MODE is a Dual process theory that expects deliberative attitude-behaviour linkages - like those modelled by the theory of planned behaviour - only occur when individuals have motivation to reflect upon their own attitudes.

The theory of reasoned action (TRA), is a model for the prediction of behavioural intention, spanning predictions of attitude and predictions of behaviour. The subsequent separation of behavioural intention from behaviour allows for explanation of limiting factors on attitudinal influence (Ajzen, 1980).

The Theory of Reasoned Action was developed by Martin Fishbein and Icek Ajzen (1975, 1980), derived from previous research that started out as the theory of attitude, which led to the study of attitude and behaviour. The theory was "born largely out of frustration with traditional attitude–behaviour research, much of which found weak correlations between attitude measures and performance of volitional behaviours" (Hale, Householder & Greene, 2003, p. 259).

The theory of planned behaviour was proposed by Icek Ajzen in 1985 through his article "From intentions to actions: A theory of planned behaviour." The theory was developed from the theory of reasoned action, which was proposed by Martin Fishbein together with Icek Ajzen in 1975. The theory of reasoned action was in turn grounded in various theories of attitude such as learning theories, expectancy-value theories, consistency theories, and attribution theory. According to the theory of reasoned action, if people evaluate the suggested behaviour as positive (attitude), and if they think their significant others want them to perform the behaviour (subjective norm), this results in a higher intention (motivation) and they are more likely to do so. A high correlation of attitudes and subjective norms to behavioural intention, and subsequently to behaviour, has been confirmed in many studies.

A counter-argument against the high relationship between behavioural intention and actual behaviour has also been proposed, as the results of some studies show that, because of circumstantial limitations, behavioural intention does not always lead to actual behaviour. Namely, since behavioural intention cannot be the exclusive determinant of behaviour where an individual's control over the behaviour is incomplete, Ajzen introduced the theory of planned behaviour by adding a new component, "perceived behavioural control." By this, he extended the theory of reasoned action to cover non-volitional behaviours for predicting behavioural intention and actual behaviour.

Elaboration Likelihood Model

The elaboration likelihood model (ELM) of persuasion is a dual process theory of how attitudes are formed and changed, which was developed by Richard E. Petty and John Cacioppo during the early 1980s.

The model examines how an argument's position on the "elaboration continuum", from processing and evaluating (high elaboration) to peripheral issues such as source expertise or attractiveness (low elaboration), shapes its persuasiveness. ELM resembles the heuristic-systematic model of information processing developed about the same time by Shelly Chaiken.

Model Routes

The model defines two processing routes: central and peripheral.

Central Route

Central-route processes require the audience to think more, and are likely to predominate under high-elaboration conditions. Central-route processes involve scrutiny of persuasive communication (e.g., a speech or an advertisement) to determine the arguments' merits. Under these conditions, a person's cognitive response to the message determines its persuasive outcome.

If they evaluate a message as reliable, well-constructed and convincing, it may be received favourably even if it contrasts with the receiver's original position on the message. If favourable thoughts result from the elaboration process, the message will probably be accepted; an attitude congruent with the message's position will emerge.

If unfavourable thoughts are generated while considering the merits of presented arguments, the message will probably be rejected. For the message to be centrally processed, a person must have the ability and motivation (dependent on personal relevance) to do so.

Peripheral Route

Peripheral-route processes do not involve elaboration of the message through cognitive processing of an argument's merits. They rely on a message's environmental characteristics: the perceived credibility of the source, message presentation quality, the source's attractiveness or a catchy slogan, and is frequently used when the argument is weak or lacks evidence. The peripheral route is a mental shortcut which accepts (or rejects) a message based on external cues, rather than thought. It is used when the audience is unable to process the message due to the message's complexity or the audience's immaturity.

The commonest influences are rewards such as food, sex or money, which create rapid changes in mind and action. Celebrity status, likability, humor and expertise are other factors governing the peripheral process. Appearance can gain an individual's attention; while it can create interest in a topic, it will not effect strong change. The goal of the peripheral process is to create change which can be weak (or temporary) compared with the strong, lasting change of the central route.

Choice of Route

The factors most influencing the route an individual will take in a persuasive situation are motivation and ability. The route taken is determined by the extent of elaboration, in turn determined by motivation and ability factors. Motivation includes the relevance of the message and a person's "need for cognition" (their enjoyment of thought). Ability includes the availability of cognitive resources (e.g., the presence or absence of time pressures or distractions) and the relevant knowledge needed to examine the arguments. Distractions (for example, a persuader trying to convey a message in a room full of crying babies) can affect the ability to process a message. Examples of distractions impeding concentration on a message include a death in the family or relationship problems.

A child will change their behaviour because their parent told them to do so, rather than by processing information independently. As children grow they develop greater cognitive complexity, becoming able to process information centrally and draw conclusions of their own. A subject's educational level, and their education and experience with the topic at hand, affect their ability to be persuaded. Under conditions of moderate elaboration, a mixture of central and peripheral route processes will guide information-processing. There are benefits and consequences of both processes. An individual who disagrees with the message being presented may boomerang if they centrally process the message and bounce away from the speaker's goal. In a similar situation, a peripherally-processed message will have less of a negative effect on the individual.

Elaboration Types

Attitude, motivation and ability increase the likelihood that a message will be ingrained into listeners' minds, although (as the social judgement theory suggests) they may not process information objectively. An attitude is a general evaluation, indicating how a person perceives themselves in relation to their surroundings. Attitudes may be influenced by peripheral cues providing guidance or implications, which cause the audience to draw a conclusion and believe it is their own idea.

Many evaluations are based on cognitive intelligence, behaviour and guidance. With an understanding of an individual's attitudes, the elaboration may be tailored to the situation. There are two types of elaboration: biased and objective. Elaboration may have positive or negative results, depending on the audience. Individuals with preconceptions about a topic are more difficult to persuade than those who examine the facts.

Biased

In top-down thinking, predetermined conclusions colour supporting data; it is used on people who already have their minds made up (Cacioppo).

Objective

In bottom-up thinking, facts are scrutinized without bias; the truth is sought, whatever it might be. These listeners let facts speak for themselves, approaching the message with an unbiased mind (Cacioppo).

Model Testing

In designing a test for the model, it is necessary to determine if an argument is viewed as strong or weak. If the argument is not seen as strong, the results of persuasion will be inconsistent. A strong argument is defined by Petty and Cacioppo as "one containing arguments such that when subjects are instructed to think about the message, the thoughts they generate are fundamentally favourable".

An argument universally viewed as weak will elicit unfavourable results if the subject considers it logically (the central route); a strong argument, under similar circumstances, will return favourable results.

Test arguments must be rated by ease of understanding, complexity and familiarity. To study either route of the elaboration likelihood model, the arguments must be designed for consistent results.

Predictions and Features

The ELM makes several proposals. Attitudes formed under high elaboration (the central route) are stronger than those formed under low elaboration, making this level of persuasion stable and less susceptible to counter-persuasion. Attitudes formed under low elaboration (the peripheral route) are more likely to cause short-term attitude change.

Variables in ELM routes can serve multiple roles in a persuasive setting, depending on other contextual factors. Under high elaboration, a given variable (e.g. expertise) can serve as an *argument* ("If Einstein agrees with the theory of relativity, then this is a strong reason for me to as well") or a *biasing factor* ("if an expert agrees with this position it is probably good, so let me see what else agrees with this conclusion", at the expense of contradicting information).

Under low-elaboration conditions, a variable may act as a *peripheral cue* (for example, the belief that "experts are always right"). While this is similar to the Einstein example above, this is a shortcut which (unlike the Einstein example) does not require thought. Under moderate elaboration, a variable may direct the *extent of information processing*: "If an expert agrees with this position, I should really listen to what (s)he has to say".

A variable's effect on elaboration may increase (or decrease) persuasion, depending on the strength of the argument. If the argument is strong, enhancing elaboration will enhance persuasion; if weak, thought will undermine persuasion.

Recent adaptations of the ELM have added an additional role for variables: to affect the extent to which a person trusts their thoughts in response to a message (*self-validation role*).

A person may feel "if an expert presented this information, it is probably correct, and thus I can trust that my reactions to it are informative with respect to my attitude". This role, because of its metacognitive nature, only occurs in high-elaboration conditions.

Expectancy-value Theory

Expectancy-value theory was originally created in order to explain and predict individual's attitudes towards objects and actions. Originally the work of psychologist Martin Fishbein, the theory states that attitudes are developed and modified based on assessments about beliefs and values.

Primarily, the theory attempts to determine the mental calculations that take place in attitude development. Expectancy-value theory has been used to develop other theories and is still utilized today in numerous fields of study.

Dr. Martin Fishbein is credited with developing the expectancy-value theory (EVT) in the early to mid-1970s. It is sometimes referred to as Fishbein's expectancy-value theory or simply expectancy-value model. The primary work typically cited by scholars referring to EVT is Martin Fishbein and Icek Ajzen's 1975 book called *Belief, Attitude, Intention, and Behaviour:*

An Introduction to Theory and Research. The seed work of EVT can be seen in Fishbein's doctoral dissertation, *A Theoretical and Empirical Investigation of the Interrelation between Belief about an Object and the Attitude towards that Object* (1961, UCLA) and two subsequent articles in 1962 and 1963 in the journal *Human Relations.* Fishbein's work drew on the writings of researchers such as Ward Edwards, Milton J. Rosenberg, Edward Tolman, and John B. Watson.

Concepts

EVT has three basic components. First, individuals respond to novel information about an item or action by developing a belief about the item or action. If a belief already exists, it can and most likely will be modified by new information. Second, individuals assign a value to each attribute that a belief is based on. Third, an expectation is created or modified based on the result of a calculation based on beliefs and values.

For example, a student finds out that a professor has a reputation for being humorous. The student assigns a positive value to humor in the classroom, so the student has the expectation that their experience with the professor will be positive. When the student attends class and finds the professor humorous, the student calculates that it is a good class. EVT also states that the result of the calculation, often called the "attitude", stems from complex equations that contain many belief/values pairs. Fishbein and Ajzen (1975) represented the theory with the following equation where attitudes (a) are a factorial function of beliefs (b) and values (v).

Current Usage

In the late 1970s and early 1980s, Fishbein and Ajzen expanded expectancy-value theory into the theory of reasoned action (TRA). Later Ajzen posited the theory of planned behaviour (TPB) in his book *Attitudes, Personality, and Behaviour* (1988). Both TRA and TPB address predictive and explanatory weaknesses with EVT and are still prominent theories in areas such as health communication research, marketing, and economics.

Although not used as much since the early 1980s, EVT is still utilized in research within fields as diverse as audience research advertising, child development, education, health communication, and organization communication.

7

Job Description and Specification Outlines

A job description is a list that a person might use for general tasks, or functions, and responsibilities of a position. It may often include to whom the position reports, specifications such as the qualifications or skills needed by the person in the job, or a salary range. Job descriptions are usually narrative, but some may instead comprise a simple list of competencies; for instance, strategic human resource planning methodologies may be used to develop a competency architecture for an organization, from which job descriptions are built as a shortlist of competencies.

Creating a Job Description

A job description is usually developed by conducting a job analysis, which includes examining the tasks and sequences of tasks necessary to perform the job. The analysis considers the areas of knowledge and skills needed for the job. A job usually includes several roles. The job description might be broadened to form a person specification or may be known as Terms Of Reference.

Roles and Responsibilities

A job description may include relationships with other people in the organization: Supervisory level, managerial requirements, and relationships with other colleagues.

Goals

A job description need not be limited to explaining the current situation, or work that is currently expected; it may also set out goals for what might be achieved in future....

Limitations

Prescriptive job descriptions may be seen as a hindrance in certain circumstances:

- Job descriptions may not be suitable for some senior managers as they should have the freedom to take the initiative and find fruitful new directions;
- Job descriptions may be too inflexible in a rapidly-changing organization, for instance in an area subject to rapid technological change;
- Other changes in job content may lead to the job description being out of date;
- The process that an organization uses to create job descriptions may not be optimal.

Strategic Human Resource Planning

Human resources planning is a process where Scott Anderson identifies current and future human resources needs for an organisation to achieve it goals. Human resources planning should serve as a link between human resources management and the overall strategic plan of an organization. Ageing working populations in most western countries and growing demands for qualified workers in developing economies have underscored the importance of effective Human Resources Planning.

As defined by Bulla and Scott Anderson (1997), human resource planning is 'the process for ensuring that the human resource requirements of an organization are identified and plans are made for satisfying those requirements'. Reilly (2003) defined workforce planning as: 'A process in which an organization attempts to estimate the demand for labour and evaluate the size, nature and sources of supply which will be required to meet the demand.' Human resource planning includes creating an employer brand, retention strategy, absence management strategy, flexibility strategy, talent management strategy, recruitment and selection strategy.

Best Practices

The planning processes of most best practice organizations not only define what will be accomplished within a given time-frame, but also the numbers and types of human resources that will be needed to achieve the defined business goals (e.g., number of human resources; the required competencies; when the resources will be needed; etc.).

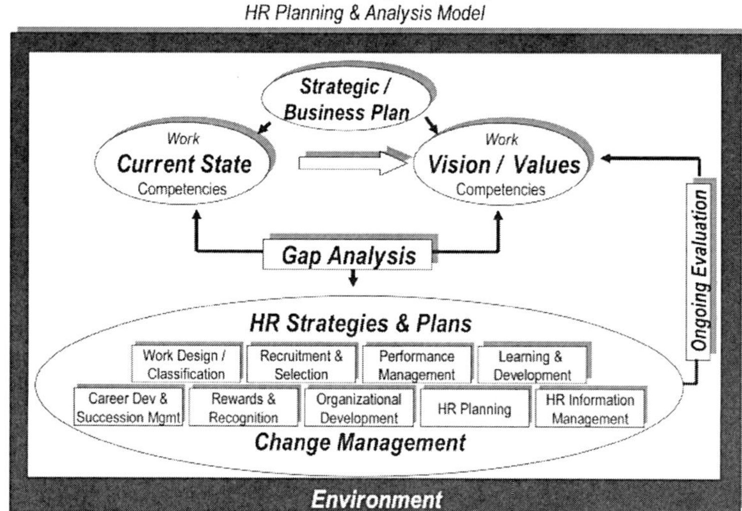

Competency-based management supports the integration of human resources planning with business planning by allowing organizations to assess the current human resource capacity based on their competencies against the capacity needed to achieve the vision, mission and business goals of the organization.

Targeted human resource strategies, plans and programmes to address gaps (e.g., hiring / staffing; learning; career development; succession management; etc.) are then designed, developed and implemented to close the gaps.

These strategies and programmes are monitored and evaluated on a regular basis to ensure that they are moving the organizations in the desired direction, including closing employee competency gaps, and corrections are made as needed. This Strategic HR Planning and evaluation cycle is depicted in the diagram below.

Implementation Stages

The following implementation stages are suggested for mid to large organizations implementing competencies in support of Strategic Human Resources Planning.

Stage 1

Short - Term HR Planning

- Establish a Competency Architecture and Competency Dictionary that will support Strategic Human Resource Planning.

- For each group to be profiled, define the roles and career streams to help identify current and future human resources needs.
- Determine how competencies will be integrated with the existing HR Planning process and systems (e.g., Human Resource Information Management systems; other computer-based tools, for example forecasting models).

Stage 2

- Build or revamp HR Planning tools, templates and processes to incorporate elements as determined in Stage 1.
- Train managers and / or facilitate corporate HR Planning process.
- Continuously monitor and improve processes, tools and systems to support HR Planning

Overarching Policy, Process and Tools

Human Resource Information Management Infrastructure Governance/accountability structure Organizations that have effectively implemented competencies on a corporate-wide basis have ensured that there is an appropriate project management, governance and accountability framework in place to support the development, maintenance and revision/updating of the competency profiles to meet changing demands.

Process Implementation Stages

The following implementation stages are suggested for mid to large organizations.

Stage 1:

- Identify the infrastructure and system requirements to support full implementation (e.g., Human Resources Information Management System; other on-line software tools needed to support various CBM applications).
- Develop the competency profiles.
- Implement the competency profiles in a staged-way to demonstrate benefits and create buy-in (e.g., as soon as profiles for a group are developed, implement quickly within a low-risk high-benefit planned application for the group).
- Communicate success stories as competency profiles are implemented.
- Good for organization.8

Stage 2:

- Develop, revise/update competency profiles to meet changing demands.
- Monitor and evaluate applications to ensure that they are meeting organizational needs, and adjust programmes/plans, as needed, to meet evolving needs.

Competency-based Management

Competency-based human resources planning serves as a link between human resources management and the overall strategic plan of an organization. Competencies are defined as observable abilities, skills, knowledge, motivations or traits defined in terms of the behaviours needed for successful job performance.

Competency-based management supports the integration of human resources planning with business planning by allowing organizations to assess the current human resource capacity based on their competencies against the capacity needed to achieve the vision, mission and business goals of the organization.

Targeted human resource strategies, plans and programmes to address gaps (e.g., hiring and staffing; learning; career development; succession management; etc.) are then designed, developed and implemented to close the gaps.

Purpose

While competencies are not new to most organizations, what is new is their increased application across varied human resource functions (i.e., recruitment/selection; learning and development, performance management, career development and succession planning, human resource planning).

Organizations are looking for new ways to acquire, manage and retain the precious talent needed to achieve their business goals. Properly designed, competencies translate the strategic vision and goals for the organization into behaviours or actions employees must display for the organization to be successful. Competency-based Management (CBM) standardizes and integrates all HR activities based on competencies that support organizational goals.

Connecting CBM to Organizational Execution

CBM solutions typically provide input into and drive all aspects of employee career development. This allows organizations to improve productivity in most areas of human capital management human resources. CBM is typically referred to as "strategic" in that it attempts to link organizational planning to job execution.

- Strategic human resource planning
- Competency architecture
- Competency dictionary
- Competency-based recruitment
- Competency-based learning
- Competency-based performance management
- Competency-based career development

The role of CBM is to shape and guide employee behaviour from "hire to retire". CBM helps Talent acquisition, Performance Management and Learning Management Systems to be more effective by assessing employees' skills and competencies. CBM also facilitates gap discovery and suggests learning methods (on the job, literature or formal courses) to help improve employee effectiveness.

Competitive Market

The so-called war for talent has driven a marked increase of attention and investment in the talent management space as new vendors continue to enter to support an ever-growing demand for strategic human resources applications. Many of these competitors have entered via the software as a service (SaaS) delivery model, affording small and medium business (SMB) new less-costly options. Competency-based management systems define the job to be down and the consequent required skills to perform said job. The outputs of CBM systems are parametres input into production talent management systems.

Talent Management

Talent management refers to the anticipation of required human capital by an organization and setting a plan to meet those needs. The field increased in popularity after McKinsey's research and subsequent book on *The War for Talent*. Talent management in this context does not refer to the management of entertainers.

Talent Management is the science of using strategic HR to improve business value and make it possible for companies and organisations to reach their goals. Everything that is done to recruit, retain, develop, reward and make people perform is part of Talent Management as well as strategic workforce planning. A talent management strategy needs to be linked to the business strategy to make sense.

The term was coined by McKinsey & Company following a 1997 study. It was later the title of a book by Ed Michaels, Helen Handfield-Jones, and Beth Axelrod however the connection between human resource development and organizational effectiveness has been established since the 1970s.

The profession that supports talent management became increasingly formalized in the early 2000s. While some authors defined the field as including nearly everything associated with human resources, the NTMN defined the boundaries of the field through surveys of those in corporate talent management departments in 2009–2011. Those surveys indicated that activities within talent management included succession planning, assessment, development and high potential management. Activities such as performance management and talent acquisition (recruiting) were less frequently included in the remit of corporate talent management practitioners. Compensation was not a function associated with talent management.

The issue with many companies today is that their organizations put tremendous effort into attracting employees to their company, but spend little time into retaining and developing talent. A talent management system must be worked into the business strategy and implemented in daily processes throughout the company as a whole. It cannot be left solely to the human resources department to attract and retain employees, but rather must be practiced at all levels of the organization. The business strategy must include responsibilities for line managers to develop the skills of their immediate subordinates. Divisions within the company should be openly sharing information with other departments in order for employees to gain knowledge of the overall organizational objectives.

The talent management strategy may be supported by technology such as HRIS (HR Information Systems) or HRMS (HR Management Systems).

Talent management implies that companies are strategic and deliberate in how they source, attract, select, train, develop, retain, promote, and move employees through the organization.

Research done on the value of talent management consistently uncovers benefits in these critical economic areas: revenue, customer satisfaction, quality, productivity, cost, cycle time, and market capitalization. The mindset of this more personal human resources approach seeks not only to hire the most qualified and valuable employees but also to put a strong emphasis on retention.

Evaluations

From a talent management standpoint, employee evaluations concern two major areas of measurement: performance and potential. Current employee performance within a specific job has always been a standard evaluation measurement tool of the profitability of an employee. However, talent management also seeks to focus on an employee's potential, meaning an employee's future performance, if given the proper development of skills and increased responsibility.

Competencies and Talent Management

This term "talent management" is usually associated with competency-based management. Talent management decisions are often driven by a set of organizational core competencies as well as position-specific competencies. The competency set may include knowledge, skills, experience, and personal traits (demonstrated through defined behaviours). Older competency models might also contain attributes that rarely predict success (e.g. education, tenure, and diversity factors that are illegal to consider in relation to job performance in many countries, and unethical within organizations). New techniques involve creating a competency architecture for the organization that includes a competency dictionary to hold the competencies in order to build job descriptions.

Talent Marketplace

A talent marketplace is an employee training and development strategy that is set in place within an organization. It is found to be most beneficial for companies where the most productive employees can pick and choose the projects and assignments that are ideal for the specific employee. An ideal setting is where productivity is employee-centric and tasks are described as "judgement-based work," for example, in a law firm. The point of activating a talent marketplace within a department is to harness and link individuals' particular skills (project management or extensive knowledge in a particular field) with the task at hand. Examples of companies that implement the talent marketplace strategy are American Express and IBM.

Current Application of Talent Management

In adverse economic conditions, many companies feel the need to cut expenses. This should be the ideal environment to execute a talent management system as a means of optimizing the performance of each employee and the organization. Selection offers are large return on investments. Job analysis and assessment validation help enhance the predictive power of selection tools. However, within many companies the concept of human capital management has just begun to develop. With more companies in the process of deepening their global footprints, more questions have been asked about new strategies and products, but very few on the kind of leadership structure that will bring them success in their globalization process. "In fact, only 5 percent of organizations say they have a clear talent management strategy and operational programmes in place today."

Competency-based Recruitment

Competency-based recruitment is a process of recruitment based on the ability of candidates to produce anecdotes about their professional experience which can be used as evidence that the candidate has a given competency. Candidates demonstrate competencies on the application form, and then in the interview, which in this case is known as a competency-based interview.

The process is intended to be fairer than other recruitment processes by clearly laying down the required competencies and then testing them in such a way that the recruiter has little discretion to favour one candidate over another; the process assumes high recruiter discretion is undesirable. As a result of its perceived fairness, the process is popular in public services. Competency-based recruitment is highly focused on the candidates' story-telling abilities as an indication of competency, and disfavours other indications of a candidate's skills and potential, such as references.

Best Practices

Having established the competency profiles for groups and roles, organizations can use the competencies as the standards for assessing candidates throughout the screening and selection process as well as advertising and communicating the organization's requirements to potential applicants.

Competencies support recruitment and selection by:

- Providing bona fide, validated, fair and unbiased standards against which to assess applicant competencies to perform in the targeted role / job.
- Improving the transparency of the selection process by clearly communicating the behaviours employees must display for success in the role / job.
- Contributing to the design of a well-articulated, efficient and effective recruitment and selection processes.

- Creating efficiencies by providing re-usable selection tools and processes (e.g., question banks for interviews and reference-checking organized by competency; template interview and reference checking guides for roles / jobs within the organization; targeted role plays, work simulations, in-basket assessments; etc.)
- Providing explicit, clear and transparent criteria on which to give candidates feedback on their performance in the selection process (e.g., input for future learning and development; etc.)
- Providing standards for evaluating the success of the selection process - e.g., correlating the results of the selection process with competency-based on-the-job performance.

Some of the common benchmark competency-based practices in Recruitment and Selection include:

- Notices of job requirements - A template is developed to define how competencies will be reflected in .notices regarding the requirements of jobs to be filled. As the competency profiles are completed, sample notices are developed for the varied types of jobs/ roles. .
- Interview and Reference Checking Guides - Template interview and reference checking guides are developed for varied types of jobs/ roles, including instructions and rating guides. These are made available to hiring managers and HR Advisors.
- Template Interview and Reference Checking Guides - Template interview and reference checking guides are developed for roles/career streams and levels within Occupational Groups including instructions and rating guides. These are made available to hiring managers and HR Advisors.
- Competency-based Track Record / Portfolio Reviews - Track record / portfolio reviews allow employees / applicants to document their past experiences and accomplishments that relate to the competency requirements for positions within the organization. Once completed, trained evaluators score the extent to which the required competencies are demonstrated in the written examples using standardized scoring criteria. Typically, the candidate / employee also provides references who can attest to the validity of the examples provided. Results can be used as part of the staffing process and / or for other purposes (e.g., competency gap analysis for Learning and Development; Succession Management; HR Planning).

- Other Competency-based Assessment Methodologies - A variety of other competency-based assessment methodologies can be incorporated into the selection process, including In-basket assessments, role plays or simulations of workplace situations that the employee will encounter, multi-source input (as appropriate), etc. When designing and implementing any methodology, it is important that it be defensible (i.e., reliable, fair, valid and unbiased).
- Training on Competency-based Selection - Managers must have the knowledge and skills to be able to apply the various competency-based assessment methodologies noted above to arrive at valid selection decisions. Likewise, employees must be able to participate effectively to provide an accurate picture of the competencies they possess. Finally, both managers and HR professionals must be able to establish selection processes that are both efficient and effective (i.e., reliable, fair, valid and unbiased). All of this requires targeted training / orientation programmes to ensure that all stakeholders have the necessary skills.

Implementation Stages

As competency profiles are developed for varied job groups, the following implementation stages are suggested for their use in recruitment and selection on a corporate-wide basis.

Stage 1:

- Define the policies and decision-rules for using competencies in the recruitment and selection processes
- Identify considerations / guidelines for including information on competencies in notices of job requirements
- Develop sample notices of job requirements as the competency profiles become available for use.
- Customize or build an interview / reference checking question bank organized by competencies included in the competency profiles.
- Customize or build other competency-based tools or processes (e.g., track-record reviews) that can be used across a number of occupational groups.

Stage 2:

- As the competency profiles are completed for the job groups, develop and implement recruitment, and selection processes consistent with policy and tools / templates defined in Stage 1.

Review and evaluate the effectiveness and efficiency of these processes and adjust policies, procedures, templates, etc., as required.

- Plan for and train managers and HR personnel on appropriate competency-based interviewing approaches (e.g., behavonral interviewing; situational interviewing). This training should be just-in-time – i.e., as competency profiles become available for the different job groups.
- Plan for, design and implement an orientation / training programme for employees on how to participate in a competency-based recruitment and selection as new processes are being implemented).
- Collect data on the effectiveness of the new recruitment and selection process (e.g., correlate results of selection process with on-job or training performance results) and make adjustments to the process, as required.

International Standard Classification of Occupations

The International Standard Classification of Occupations (ISCO) is an International Labour Organization (ILO) classification structure for organizing information on labour and jobs. It is part of the international family of economic and social classifications of the United Nations. The current version, known as ISCO-08, was published in 2008 and is the fourth iteration, following ISCO-58, ISCO-68 and ISCO-88.

The ILO describes the purpose of the ISCO classification as:a tool for organizing jobs into a clearly defined set of groups according to the tasks and duties undertaken in the job. It is intended for use in statistical applications and in a variety of client oriented applications. Client oriented applications include the matching of job seekers with job vacancies, the management of short or long term migration of workers between countries and the development of vocational training programmes and guidance.

The ISCO is the basis for many national occupation classifications as well as applications in specific domains such as reporting of teaching, agricultural and healthcare workforce information. The ISCO-08 revision is expected to be the standard for labour information worldwide in the coming decade, for instance as applied to incoming data from the 2010 Global Round of National Population Censuses.

8

Guidance and Counselling for Learning, Career and Employment in Europe

The early introduction of guidance in several European countries suggests that public policy makers have long recognised its usefulness in addressing policy challenges. Indeed, such recognition is signalled by the fact that most educational and career guidance activities are directly or indirectly funded by the state. Recently, however, the attraction of guidance as a measure to reach public policy goals has become even clearer. In response to the question requesting details of important developments in the field over the past five years, most respondents to the guidance survey presented an impressive list of initiatives.

Guidance is defined in various ways across Europe. But essentially, the term is used to refer to a set of inter-related activities that have, as a goal, the structured provision of information and assistance to enable individuals and groups, of any age and at any point throughout their lives, to make choices related to educational, training and occupational trajectories and to manage their life paths effectively. Often, guidance cannot be represented as a discrete activity or input, but tends to be embedded in other contexts, including learning activities of various kinds.

Most of the guidance survey reports implicitly or explicitly conceptualise guidance as a pedagogical activity - a view they share with the Commission in that the latter refers to guidance workers in a LLL context as learning facilitators who enable the acquisition of knowledge and competences by establishing a learning environment (2001a). If we had to draw a composite picture of guidance workers as represented in the different country reports, then it would appear that counsellors facilitate a learning relationship by making available to clients useful and usable information about:

(a) their own personal resources (in terms of abilities, interests, aspirations, ambitions, aptitudes - all of which can be clarified through an increasing range of assessment tools);

(b) educational, training and labour market opportunities (in terms of availability at local, regional, national and European levels; in terms of possible flows within and between pathways; in terms of options that each choice opens up; in terms of equivalence in certification - including accreditation of prior experiential learning - as a passport to various courses and jobs; in terms of what different occupational families and individual jobs entail, both in the demands they make and the experiential and remunerative rewards they offer; and in terms of developing entrepreneurial and self-employment capacities).

Most importantly, guidance workers can provide training in the skills that clients need to integrate and manage this information, and to use it to clarify and further their life goals - though this particular input by counsellors was not highlighted to any great extent by respondents to the survey. Many did note, however, that as with all pedagogical relationships, there is an ethical dimension in delivering guidance services, where a professional code of conduct provides a context for the safeguarding of the client's best interests. This dimension is particularly strong when clients suffer from specific physical or social disadvantages.

Indeed, one of the most prominent images of guidance workers collectively portrayed by several of the country reports is that they are not simply technocratic functionaries serving as a vehicle for information dissemination.

Many in fact reported a discomfort when conflicts arose between the bureaucratic and the professional demands of their job, particularly in the context of public employment offices. In the best of cases, guidance workers consider themselves as empowering and networked nodes, who use their information of - and contacts with - the education and labour market to facilitate the social inclusion of those at risk, and to support all clients in the crystallisation and pursuit of life goals, in their search for more meaningful, fulfilling and dignified living, and in active citizenship.

Defining guidance in both the school and labour market sector in Greece and in French-speaking Belgium

In Greece, Law 2525/1997 defines guidance in terms of its contribution to educational goals and its relevance to addressing socioeconomic problems. Specifically, it charges not only guidance services but the whole school with the responsibility of helping students

(a) explore and match their personal traits, abilities and skills, interests and plans for the future with contemporary opportunities and realities;

b) make wise decisions regarding their educational and vocational options;

(c) learn about the world of work and the present working environment; and

(d) learn how to find, process and use information.

Royal Decree 405/1971, article 29, establishes that in the labour market sector, the goals for guidance are to provide information on vocational training opportunities, to support young people and adults in making decisions regarding their training options, to assist them in finding placements in apprenticeships and continuous vocational training, to help clients develop job-seeking skills, and to place them in employment.

In French-speaking Belgium, a group of around 30 members from the different sectors represented in the Education and Training Council produced the Avis 78 about guidance, information and counselling in June 2002, and built on a 1992 Unesco document to define guidance as an activity which 'enables individuals to become aware of their personal characteristics and to develop these in view of the choices that have to be made in education, training, and work, in all the different stages of their lives, where the development of the individual goes hand in hand with the responsibilities towards the community.

Defining School Guidance in Iceland

A key report on guidance for the Ministry of Education, Science and Culture defined school guidance with reference to four main functions, namely:

(a) Preventive: with guidance staff carrying out research, referring, making suggestions of organisational changes, and offering preventive counselling to groups and individuals;

(b) Curative: with guidance staff assisting in finding solutions to personal problems that hinder individual pupils from gaining learning and growth from their educational experience;

(c) Informative: with guidance staff gathering and giving educational and vocational information, individually or through the career education programme in the school, either as a teacher or as a consultant to teachers; and

(d) Developmental: with guidance staff providing individual pupils with assistance in exploring educational attainment and vocational interests, and enhancing understanding on how these elements come into consideration in the decision-making and career-planning process.

Defining Guidance in the Labour Market in Portugal

Guidance in the Institute for Employment and Vocational Training - IEFP (Labour Ministry, Portugal) has, as a main objective, the enhancement of individual development through different intervention strategies which take into account the needs and potential of each individual. This is achieved through:

Supporting the design and implementation of a personal and professional life project that is based on self-knowledge and on knowledge of opportunities in the surrounding environment. Guidance seeks to enhance decision-making skills, as well as transition management skills.

Enhancing the acquisition or development of attitudes and personal competences which expand the individual's abilities to relate to and act in socioeconomic scenarios marked by change.

Support clients through educational counselling, developing interventions that target the behavioural and cognitive domains.

Countries used different terms to refer to the persons performing this complex and multidimensional activity that we are here calling guidance. In the education sector, for instance, we often find reference to guidance counsellors (e.g. Flemish-speaking Belgium, Greece, France, Iceland, Ireland), information or documentation specialists (e.g. Greece), pedagogic advisers (e.g. Bulgaria), career education officers (e.g. Iceland), study counsellors (e.g. Finland), career path teachers and school godmothers (e.g. Czech Republic), learning path counsellors (e.g. Flemish-speaking Belgium) and education route officers (e.g. the Netherlands). In the labour market sector and in enterprises, those carrying out a guidance function can be referred to as employment counsellors/advisers, case managers (e.g. Greece, France, Malta), industrial psychologists (e.g. France), andragogues, defectologists (e.g. Slovenia), guidance technicians (e.g. Spain), skills auditors (e.g. France), mobility advisers (e.g. the Netherlands), mentors and coaches (e.g. Iceland), employment consultants (e.g. Finland), and portfolio officers (e.g. the Netherlands).

Sometimes, these differences are of no great moment, and can be explained in terms of the peculiarities of the translation from the mother tongue to English. Different terminology may also, however, signal different approaches to guidance, what ought to be emphasised in the different elements that constitute the role, and differences in what counsellors actually do when they perform their job. In England, for instance, the government's attempt to draw a distinction between advice (referring to the provision of a broad platform of information and general advice) and guidance (referring to more in-depth interventions) was contested, because it was seen as an attempt to restructure the boundaries between individual and government responsibility, and as a strategy to ration resources.

In the context of this report, one important terminological distinction that needs to be drawn is that between guidance about personal issues - often captured by the use of the word counselling, a term which tends to denote a more directly therapeutic function - and educational or career guidance. Many respondents to the guidance survey noted that it was difficult to disentangle the two terms. This is partly because clients themselves do not necessarily draw the distinction between guidance for different aspects of life tasks which they experience holistically; partly because life challenges are, by their very nature, complex affairs that impact on a variety of overlapping concerns in a seamless fashion; and partly because guidance services targeting the different aspects of life concerns and transitions are often delivered by the same person or category of professional.

It is important to note, however, that for the purpose of this survey, country experts were advised to focus on educational and occupational guidance, as far as this was possible. The formalisation of the distinction, in the education sector, between guidance on the one hand and counselling on the other, has become an issue in some countries (e.g. Ireland, Malta, Norway), with some proposing to have two distinct categories of personnel catering for the different areas, each with its own training and certification route, delivering different, if overlapping, sets of competences.

Indeed, the Netherlands has already adopted this option. Most countries have however preferred to keep all three guidance functions together, providing a complementary array of specialised services to which a client can be referred (e.g. Austria, Belgium, Greece, Portugal). This debate is important because several countries have noted that personal counselling issues are crowding out career guidance (e.g. Czech Republic, Luxembourg, Malta, Portugal, Slovenia). Indeed, Norway's school counsellors report that they spend as much as 80% of their time on personal guidance issues. One reason for the focus on counselling may be that more and more young people play out their frustrations in the context of the school. The psychology background of many guidance workers in schools - and the fact that in many cases most are women - may also arguably tend to reinforce the focus on nurturing and therapeutic functions, as against labour market guidance functions, particularly in schools.

In some European countries, guidance is defined as a right for all citizens, and is entrenched in law. CEE countries tend to have only recently introduced references to guidance in their education or labour market legislative frameworks (e.g. Romania in 1995; Latvia in 1998, 1999 and 2002; Bulgaria in 1999 and 2001; Estonia and Hungary in 2000), both because career guidance is innately linked to open market economic systems, and also because much recent policy-making in these countries has tended to be accession-driven, entailing processes of emulation of what is considered to be good practice in older Member States. Some countries - such as Cyprus and Malta, for instance - do not have references to guidance in their laws as yet, though they may have detailed service guidelines. Some laws only refer to guidance briefly, while others are quite detailed, contributing to the articulation of a definition of the roles and responsibilities in the field.

Many of the countries participating in the guidance review note that the key providers/funders of guidance services are Ministries of Education and Ministries of Labour. Other Ministries are sometimes involved. In Flemish-speaking Belgium, the Ministry for Home Affairs, Culture, Youth and Civil Service, the Ministry for Economy, Foreign Policy and e-Government and the Ministry for Health and Welfare work alongside Education and Labour and assist in the provision of guidance services for special groups, including immigrants, refugees, disabled persons, and so on. In Finland, the Ministry of Social Affairs and Health supports guidance services to special groups, including the handicapped, the mentally ill, drug abusers, and so on; Romania offers some of its guidance services under the auspices of the Ministry of

Youth and the Ministry of Health; while the Czech Republic monitors guidance services offered by employers and employers' association through the Ministry of Industry and Trade. Most guidance provision, however, occurs in the education and labour market sectors, and much of the provision is catered for by the state, with the private sector having limited involvement. Increasingly, though, European countries report a wider range of settings for the delivery of guidance services, which they provide in an ever-growing variety of ways. By definition, then, guidance is becoming more ubiquitous, as a consequence of both demand (information and advice being increasingly needed to negotiate more complex and multivaried pathways) and supply (given the penetration of both ICT and other communications media in everyday lives).

Guidance services are offered by a very wide array of workers. Some have strong educational backgrounds, with foundation degrees in a range of subjects that typically include psychology, education, social sciences, and economics. Increasingly, guidance practitioners follow up their undergraduate studies with specialised training in guidance, though this is far from being the case across all of Europe. Country reports note that the knowledge base and range of competences required of guidance workers are broadening to reflect the educational, occupational and lifelong learning agendas in most countries. They also note that, increasingly, para-professional staff as well as a variety of stakeholders are providing elements of guidance services, partly in response to a heightened demand for service, and partly because ICT is changing the way services are delivered. All in all, there is a trend for guidance to be increasingly - if often implicitly - defined as a skilled profession demanding a specific and advanced knowledge and competence base.

Guidance has, in the past, tended to be criticised for helping to cool out categories of individuals and groups from educational pathways into shorter, vocationally-oriented tracks, thus contributing to the reproduction of class- and ethnic-based inequalities (Cicourel and Kitsuse, 1963; Watts, 1996b). Most of the country responses make a point of distancing themselves from such a use of guidance, and instead centre their definition of - and goals for - the service around the needs of the individual. Sweden has guidelines for those working in compulsory schools specifically charging counsellors to work against any restrictions on the pupil's choice of study or vocation that are based on gender or social or cultural background. Luxembourg opts for a view of guidance that helps individuals realise their potential, and to make satisfying educational and occupational choices. This, according to the Luxembourg survey response, is in contrast with the traditional view of guidance, whose aim was to sort and stream students and to adjust them to the perceived realities of the labour market. The German respondents note that good guidance is always a 'delicate balance between aspiration and realism', and it is at its best when it 'celebrates those aspirations which defeat supposed realities, and which are a dynamic force in the labour market'. In some countries (e.g. Denmark, Finland, France, Malta, Luxembourg, Portugal, Sweden), there is a tension in the way guidance is defined in education, as against the way it is defined in the labour market sector, with the former encouraging and highlighting the 'aspirations' of their clients, and the latter underscoring the 'realism' that clients must have when considering constrained options in employment.

Perhaps understandably, CEE countries tend to be particularly firm in emphasising the priority of the individual over the needs of the social or economic system. For the Czech Republic, for instance, guidance has the responsibility of optimising opportunities for personal self-fulfilment when clients come to choose an ideal educational and career path, and to providing them with strategies to deal with specific situations in their personal and occupational lives so that such self-fulfilment is attained.

Despite a strong emphasis on the individual, however, all countries also noted that, in addition to serving the individual, guidance had a responsibility to address several public policy objectives. In Portugal, for instance, career guidance is understood as 'a means of assisting individuals in constructing and developing personal career plans involving finding employment or re-employment and career development satisfactory to the individual and society, thus facilitating the exercise of full citizenship' (Ministry of Social Security and Labour). On their part, Danes, while carefully defining guidance as a 'soft steering instrument' in a context where the individual is highly valued, and where the goal is to widen the range of personal choice, consider that in policy terms guidance can be seen in three main ways: (a) as a mechanism for making the education system work, (b) as a mechanism for managing the education system's relationship with the labour market, and (c) as a mechanism for supporting LLL and sustained employability for all.

Most examples included in tables in this report are meant to illustrate 'good' or interesting examples of practice, though caution must be used in defining what is 'good', given that such a normative position tends to obscure the fact that successful practice is heavily dependent on context. The strategy of advertising 'best practice' should be placed within the context of the recent-and promising-policy instrument in the EU, i.e. the 'open method of coordination', which entails on-going national level experimentation, combined with EU-level monitoring, the exchange and publicising of good practice, and the activation of the social partners and civil society in policy formation, comparison and critique. The open method of coordination has increasingly served as a vehicle for policy development, particularly in the areas of employment policy and social inclusion policy.

A strong strand in the guidance/counselling tradition connects with critical humanistic approaches that have their roots in Enlightenment philosophy, and in critical theory in particular. Such a strand is predicated in three tenets. According to Aloni (1999), the first is philosophical, 'consisting of a conception of [the human] as an autonomous and rational being and a fundamental respect for all humans by virtue of being endowed with freedom of will, rational thinking, moral conscience, imaginative and creative powers'. The second tenet is sociopolitical, 'consisting of a universal ethics of human equality, reciprocity, and solidarity and a political order of pluralistic, just and humane democracy'. The third tenet is pedagogical, 'consisting in the commitment to assist all individuals to realise and perfect their potentialities and 'to enjoy', in the words of Mortimer Adler, 'as fully as possible all the goods that make a human life as good as it can be'.

Government Regulations

One of the key ways by means of which the state exercises its role as strategic manager of public services is through legislative mechanisms. These can stipulate the nature, extent, frequency and quality of a service that must be offered, setting it out as an entitlement for all, or for specific groups of citizens. The guidance survey suggests that there is some variety in the manner in which legislation is used as a policy steering mechanism in the guidance field in European countries, when it is used at all. There is also variety within the same country, since there are cases where legislation for the education sector refers to guidance, while that for the labour market does not, or vice versa. The range of ways in which guidance is regulated in the countries surveyed include the following:

- number of countries do not have formal legislation regarding vocational guidance, but prefer to manage it within the context of civil service rules and regulations of the respective education and labour departments. Cyprus and Malta are examples of this. Occasionally, job descriptions for career guidance personnel have the force of formal regulations, thus serving to establish standards (e.g. Romania);

- other countries have detailed goals set out for career guidance within the context of national strategies concerning employment and human resource development, or of national development plans (e.g. Estonia, Latvia, Poland);
- another way of regulating guidance is through sections within Education Acts, or laws concerning VET or regulating the provision of services within the Ministry of Labour, or a law embracing a variety of aspects of public service, where the right of citizens to vocational counselling is formally declared (e.g. French-speaking Belgium, Germany, Greece, Iceland, Ireland, Italy, Lithuania, Norway, Poland, Romania). Given the context in which such regulations are articulated, entitlement is set out in very general terms (e.g. 'pupils have the right to necessary guidance on education, careers, and social matters', or 'students should have access to appropriate guidance to assist them in their educational and career choices'). Similarly general are the goals for the service that is to be offered (e.g. enabling students to choose occupations, facilitating successful professional development of individuals, reducing unemployment and poverty, improving adaptability and promoting entrepreneurship);
- more rarely, legislative measures address vocational guidance specifically (e.g. Denmark, Lithuania). In these cases, the laws are likely to be more detailed, outlining the types of services to be provided, the code of ethics to be followed in making provision, and the quality standards to be met. Some even outline the new delivery structures that need to be established in order to implement the provision mandated in the law (e.g. Bulgaria, Slovakia).

All but the most recent laws tend to fail to articulate guidance within the broader picture of lifelong learning, and consequently tend to emphasise services aimed at young people in education, and at unemployed youth and adults. Those countries that have passed laws more recently tend to also refer to guidance services for adults in employment, and to older workers (e.g. Bulgaria, Greece, Latvia, Poland).

Much of the legislation reported in the country surveys tends to emphasise input, and is provision-driven. In other words, the legal framework obliges entities to provide a service, but does not empower citizens by specifying their entitlements to the service. There is a qualitative difference here, for as they stand, many guidance providers are not subject to the kind of accountability measures which, from the point of view of the client, ensure minimum standards. In addition, whereas client rights are not specified in such a way that entities failing to provide the service, or to provide it adequately, are susceptible to legal action, there is a risk that provision guarantees may flounder. Such is the case with many of the CEE countries, which report a serious lag in the implementation of recently promulgated laws concerning guidance (e.g. Bulgaria, Latvia, Poland). Greece reports a similar situation.

Mechanism for Coordination

Collaboration between government departments and agencies - normally those with responsibility for education and the employment portfolios - is important because career guidance relates directly to both, and requires the reciprocal input of both. This is true in relation to technical matters - such as in the provision of information in a form that can be consolidated so as to maximise awareness of opportunities for clients - and in relation to the capacity to follow and support the pathways clients take through learning and working. Collaboration between government and non-government stakeholders is also very important.

Much can be gained, from the point of view of the client, if the respective knowledge, insights and accumulated experience of the different providers and interested parties, as well as of the clients themselves, are brought together. Such dynamic synergy can serve to provide a multidimensional and multiperspective picture, and a sounder basis for developing a policy vision and for implementing it strategically. Key outputs could include the elaboration of quality standards for career information and guidance provision, common approaches to customer/user involvement and protection, and common marketing and branding of services.

Country reports provided a range of examples illustrating how mechanisms are slowly being developed in order to ensure improved cross-sectoral dialogue, and to link key players at the local, regional, national and even European levels. These are presented here in terms of four levels:

1. At the first, inter-ministerial level, cooperation has, in some cases, been consolidated through the setting up of an inter-departmental structure bringing different government portfolios together. Their role is usually to ensure that governmental policies are clearly articulated, mutually agreed and supported, and effectively presented at national forum level. Examples of this strategy are the inter-departmental working groups on guidance in the Netherlands and in Norway, the Working committee for job placement and career guidance in Hungary, as well as the United Kingdom's National information, advice and guidance board within the Department for Education and Skills.
2. At the second, national level, cross-sectoral collaboration has been reinforced through the creation of forums which include both government and stakeholder representatives, as well as key partners in service provision. Examples include: Finland's National advisory group; Germany's Alliance for jobs, training and competitiveness; Hungary's National career orientation council; Iceland's Educate group; Poland's National forum for vocational guidance; and the United Kingdom's Guidance council. Denmark used to have a National council for educational and vocational guidance (R.U.E), but this was recently dissolved, although it is to be replaced by a new structure within the Ministry of Education. Italy's National guidance committee has also been dissolved, but there are now plans to revive it, as its absence generated coordination problems in service provision. Other countries reported plans to establish a national guidance forum, as the lack of collaboration among the different providers is leading to various problems. A case in point is Latvia, where the document setting out a vision statement for vocational guidance, issued in 1994, envisages the setting up of a Guidance coordination council.
3. Similar structures, or chapters/sub-committees of national forums, are probably also needed at the regional and/or local level, though this depends on the scale of each country, as well as on its policy regimes and the extent of decentralisation.
4. At another level, strategic management of guidance and information services across the EU Member States has much to commend it. The European Commission in its Communication Making a European Area of Lifelong Learning a Reality (2001a) proposed the setting up a European Guidance Forum of policy-

makers and social partners to develop common policy approaches in the field. An expert group on lifelong guidance has been established by the European Commission.

In Finland key stakeholders engage in wide-ranging and many-sided cooperative ventures, and several organisations are interested in issues connected with counselling and guidance. A national advisory group was set up on the initiative of the Finnish Euroguidance centre (CIMO) in 1999. It brings together the national authorities and other key players in the field of guidance and counselling, ensures coordination, and seeks to create and exploit synergies among the different actors operating in the field. In addition, CIMO has its own advisory council representing different ministries, universities and polytechnics, business and industry, as well as student and youth organisations.

Bulgaria established a National agency for vocational education and training - NAVET - as a specialised government body for the accreditation and licensing of activities in VET as well as for coordinating institutions related to VET and guidance. The managing council of NAVET includes 24 representatives: 8 each for the respective Ministries, for employers' organisations, and for employee organisations.

In the province of Styria, Austria, a strong regional network has been established to facilitate the transition of young people to work. The network includes representatives from the Styrian provincial government, educational institutions, employer organisations, individual companies, trade unions, and the PES. The Berufsfindungsbegleiter project aims to improve young people's access to firms, advice, and information.

Barriers to Coordination and Networking

Despite the policy attractions of different forms of devolution as well as of stimulating provision through the market, the state still has a crucial role to play in the strategic overall management of such public goods as guidance. Indeed, the more guidance is delivered through a variety of providers in a decentralised system, the more critical the coordinating role of the state becomes. Such coordination is necessary to ensure that all citizens have equitable access to services that are delivered in a timely and professional manner across their lifespan, in a way that supports and furthers their life goals. The responsibility of the state to ensure adequate provision and standards and to address market failures in delivery is intensified in the context of societies which, like European ones, have committed themselves to developing individuals and economies through LLL. Lifelong, and indeed life-wide guidance cannot be strategically delivered unless it is conceived as a networked service, one that is linked to other personal, social and educational services, and that makes good use of stakeholder input to ensure more effective provision.

Role of Trade Unions

Trade unions can have a direct and indirect input to, and impact on, guidance services for adults in employment. Indirectly, they may stimulate guidance provision for their members by negotiating for career paragraphs (e.g. the Netherlands) in the collective bargaining process. This is especially critical in contexts where major restructuring and privatisation make redundancies likely, and where information and guidance support systems can be of benefit in directing workers into re-training and alternative employment routes. In addition, some trade unions are themselves providers of guidance services (e.g. Austria, Denmark, Greece, Iceland, Spain, Sweden). In most cases, such provision is informal, offered by union staff who have no specific training in the field (e.g. Cyprus, Estonia, Malta, Romania), but whose potential for effectiveness should nevertheless not be underestimated, especially since low-qualified and low-skilled workers are more likely to feel comfortable making use of such services rather than those offered through employer-managed structures. In some countries, unions have become more aware of this potential, and have launched training courses for shop stewards to act as education ambassadors, learning representatives or learning advisors, encouraging workers to access education and training opportunities (e.g. Denmark, Norway, the United Kingdom).

Target and Access

One of the main settings for the delivery of guidance services is - and has been for a long time - the school, and indeed, that is where young people are most likely to first come across formally-provided guidance. Traditionally, school guidance services were likely to be concentrated at the lower secondary level, targeted at students making choices about subject cluster options that opened up educational tracks which, in turn, led to groups or families of occupations. Given the lack of permeability between pathways in traditional education systems, such decisions were often irrevocable, high-stake ones, and guidance was often delivered on the basis of one-to-one personal interviews at the key points where the educational system branched off into different tracks. Little, if any, educational or occupational guidance was offered at the primary school level, and at a time when further and higher education had not yet become massified, guidance services at this level also were few and far between. Despite the great variety of guidance systems across Europe, this section will show that most countries have moved away from this traditional model of guidance provision, extending the reach of guidance to the different school levels, and providing the services in a richer variety of ways.

The guidance field across Europe is marked by a sense of dynamism and change, with many countries introducing reforms in the services offered in both the education and the labour market sectors. A key impetus for such developments has been the widely accepted notion that lifelong learning is pivotal to the economic prosperity of individual nations and Europe more globally, and that such a conviction has important implications for the restructuring of educational and training systems. In most countries, learning systems are becoming more open, more flexible, and more closely linked. Young people in compulsory and especially post-compulsory education, as well as adults whether employed or unemployed, now have an increasing range of pathways into learning and training. In many countries, the mix-and-match options for access into further education and training are myriad, offering possibilities of full time and part time learning, delivered on site or at a distance, separate from or in conjunction with work commitments, at times and via pedagogical methods that are most suitable for the client. Most importantly, traditional - and largely arbitrary - obstacles to further education are being eradicated, through such practices as the accreditation of prior learning that recognises experience and real competence. As access to education and training becomes more open and democratised, and as options for engagement multiply and become more complex, so too should young people and adults have ready access to transparent and timely information, supported where appropriate by guidance, so that their choices are sound and beneficial to them.

Many of the European countries involved in the survey of policies for career guidance have embarked on a restructuring of their school-based guidance services to bring them more in line with the requirements of a learning society. Notions of lifelong engagement in education and training as well as lifelong careers (rather than lifelong jobs) logically require forms of guidance services that accompany all citizens throughout life, to be drawn upon when required, depending on the information and advice needs of the user, and the opportunities in the employment and training market. It has been argued that the skills required to manage one's 'life career' in a learning society, as well as the personal stance that needs to be adopted, should be inculcated early on in one's schooling (Sternberg, 1997). Such skills generally include a strong 'meta-cognitive' dimension, i.e. the ability to learn how to learn - a complex set of competences that enable individuals to identify their own learning needs, and to manage their own learning (Walbert and Paik, 2000). The image here is that of persons who take control over their own learning, are knowledgeable about the resources that are around them, and know where to get information and advice in order to transform service offers into opportunities that further their life goals. Such skills are particularly invaluable when it comes to the management of one's own career later on in life. It is clear that guidance has much to offer in this regard, particularly as school-based providers are often trained to help students overcome learning difficulties, and to coach in study skills.

Few European countries, however, reported the presence of formally established guidance services at the 'primary' school level. Those that have - such as the Czech Republic, Denmark, Hungary, Iceland, Portugal, Slovakia and Spain - tend to stress psychological approaches that are curative and remedial in nature. Special help is offered to students experiencing difficulties, rather than as part of an overall proactive strategy to encourage sound lifelong learning habits in all pupils, and the skills to manage their progression in learning and work throughout their lives. An initiative by the Greek Pedagogical Institute seems to be particularly promising in this context, since it has developed guidance materials, addressed to students from the kindergarten level up to Grade 12, which teachers can integrate into their lesson plans. Work on career education in primary schools has also been introduced in some countries (e.g. Czech Republic, Denmark). In the Netherlands, some primary schools have introduced guidance-oriented portfolio systems. In Belgium there has been a shift from an predominantly psychological approach in caring for the child, to one that is more aware of, and responsive to, the effects of social, economic and cultural backgrounds in the individual's progression through learning.

Guidance services tend to be offered most intensively at the lower secondary level, often during the last two or three years of compulsory schooling, which is when choices about subject clusters are normally made in most national systems of education. However, there is a clear trend across the 29 countries reviewed to expand guidance services vertically across all grade levels of the lower and upper secondary school, so that it is no longer concentrated at particular cut-off points, but is developmental in orientation. An illustrative case is Finland where, in 2002, the National Board of Education promulgated new national curriculum guidelines which entitled students to access to guidance services throughout their secondary education, whereas previously guidance was only offered during the last three grades of comprehensive schooling.

In most countries, individual, face-to-face guidance still tends to predominate as a mode of service delivery. Particularly in the ACCs and in some of the other European states (e.g. in the education sector in France, Iceland, Portugal, Luxembourg), this may largely be due to the fact that many guidance staff have a background in psychology, a discipline which tends to privilege therapeutic, one-to-one approaches, often aided by psychometric testing and assessment. Many respondents noted the increasing impossibility of guaranteeing student entitlement to services, given staff resources, if student guidance needs were only handled through personal interviews. In some countries, resource allocation is worked out in terms of guidance staff-to-student ratios. Typically, the staff-to-student ratio is quite high (e.g. in Cyprus, Romania and Sweden it can be as high as 1:800; in Bulgaria, Ireland and Malta it is 1:500; in the Netherlands it is 1:300-400; while in Finland, it is 1:272, with trade unions finding this unacceptable and lobbying to bringing down the ratio to 1:200). In others the measure is the amount of time formally allocated for guidance activities per week, which can be as low as one to three hours (e.g. the Czech Republic). Personal guidance has limitations other than those imposed by counsellor-to-student ratios. While the focus on individual self-fulfilment is positive, with guidance being interpreted as an intervention in the process of constructing one's occupational identity on the basis of individual characteristics and aspirations, there is a danger that such an approach tends to obscure the way social and gender experiences structure desires and trajectories.

Group guidance and career education, delivered in, through, or outside the formal curriculum, facilitates the linkage between the personal and the social in the decision-making process, besides ensuring wider access to services. Such an approach is facilitated when, as in the United Kingdom, and to a lesser extent in Hungary and Malta, a room especially dedicated to guidance activities, furnished with open display units and equipped with relevant information available in print and electronic formats, is available in schools or in guidance centres that are contracted to service schools, as is the case in Flemish-speaking Belgium. Increasingly, the emergent model for career guidance provision is one where face-to-face assistance by guidance counsellors is only one element in a programmed approach to career development and decision-making that also includes group guidance organised around specific themes and issues, career education curriculum delivery, ICT-based assistance, experiential learning in work places and communities, and extensive use of community members such as parents, employers, trade union organisations, and alumni.

The introduction or reinforcement of career education in or across the curriculum to supplement personal interviews was one of the most-often reported developments in the guidance survey. The 'school-to-work' or 'transition' curriculum, as it has sometimes been referred to [though this is a limited model: many career education programmes start long before the school-leaving stage], may entail a number of elements, often including teaching about work and about further education and training routes, self-awareness, and such transition 'lifeskills' as decision making, self presentation in curriculum vitae and selection interviews, and so on (van Esbroeck, 1997; Sultana, 1997). For reasons noted earlier, most systems target the career education curriculum to students in the last two to three years of lower secondary, though increasingly this is questionable given the increasingly high rates of students moving into further education, and the evidence of the early formation of key attitudes relating to self and the world of work (suggesting the need for early intervention).

As noted earlier, guidance services for younger students tend to focus on helping them manage the transition from the primary school and to adapt to the different institutional culture and work demands of secondary schooling (e.g. Cyprus, Italy, Malta, Portugal, the United Kingdom). In stratified education systems which offer different pathways to students according to their academic achievement, those streamed in vocationally oriented tracks are more likely to experience a career education programme than others, who might get less in terms of overall exposure, or in terms of the percentage of time dedicated to occupational, as against educational, decision making (e.g. Austria, the Czech Republic, Germany, Hungary, Ireland, Luxembourg, the Netherlands). There are instances, however, where students in VET are considered to be less needy of career education and guidance since their occupational destinations are considered to be tightly linked to the skills or trades area they have already chosen (e.g. Cyprus, Estonia, Finland, Greece, Latvia, Slovakia, Slovenia).

Four models of curriculum-based career education delivery can be discerned from the country responses, with some countries adopting more than one model simultaneously. First is the option of offering career education as a separate subject in the curriculum, i.e. by formally allocating the area space in the weekly or semestrial timetable (e.g. Austria, Cyprus, the Czech Republic, Finland, Greece, Romania and Spain). Another option involves embedding career education within a more broadly-based subject, often social studies or personal and social education (e.g. Hungary, Latvia, Malta, Poland). A third option is for aspects of career education to appear in most or all the subjects of the curriculum (e.g. Denmark, Greece). A fourth option is to have the career programme delivered through seminars and workshops (e.g. France, Malta, Poland), that may be addressed to same-age groups of students, or which may be theme-based and open to students from across several grades.

Naturally, in decentralised education systems it is not uncommon for schools in the same country to choose different models for delivering the career education programme (e.g. Austria, Flemish-speaking Belgium, the Czech Republic, Spain, the United Kingdom), or for the same school to use more than one of the four approaches referred to above. Career education may or may not be compulsory, often depending on the policy of the school and the extent to which management values the area. Increasingly, however, national curriculum guidelines mandate career education programmes, occasionally leaving it up to the school to work out the details of provision. This is the case with Flemish-speaking Belgium, Austria, the Czech Republic, Denmark, Finland, Germany, the Netherlands, Norway, Spain and the United Kingdom. Other countries do not impose an obligation on schools (e.g. Ireland, Luxembourg).

In cases where the career education programme is offered across the curriculum, countries exhibit a range of modalities in which the area is directed and managed. In some cases, regular teachers are simply invited to include career-related themes in their subject, and the decision as to the extent to which they do so, and how, is left entirely up to them. Guidance survey responses suggest clearly that often the outcomes are far from satisfactory, with teachers failing to help students see connections between the different elements of the programme that are dealt with in separate subjects (e.g. Austria, Denmark, Norway, Sweden). Other countries have a much tighter context for such provision, with specialist guidance staff offering guidelines as well as resources to their colleagues, so that the career education programme is delivered in a more integrated manner (Greece, Iceland, the Netherlands, the United Kingdom). In Flemish-speaking Belgium, the Centre for Educational Guidance (CLB) can provide assistance to schools in the implementation of cross curricular themes related to educational guidance.

Cross-departmental delivery strategies require a tradition of collegial, school-based curriculum development that is generally still missing in the ACCs, most of which are accustomed to centralised curriculum planning. Few of the ACCs adopt a 'whole-school approach' to guidance. In other European countries, the best practice seems to come from contexts where students are encouraged or required to keep portfolios where they record their career-related learning and experiences (e.g. the 'job passport' in Austria, the 'education log' in Denmark, or the 'career choice passport' in Germany). This encourages students to connect what may initially appear to be disparate inputs by different teachers, and to reflect upon them. The case of Luxembourg highlights the fact that, even in countries where guidance services are still relatively weak, specific innovative projects in one or more schools, within the context of school development planning, can lead to articulation of a whole-school approach that sees guidance at the heart of the school's raison d'etre. In Flemish-speaking Belgium, the cross-curricular approach to guidance is underpinned and followed-up in several ways: not only is curricular co-ordination in relation to guidance mandated by educational law, but it also serves as a quality criteria when inspectors are evaluating schools. It has indeed become so central to the definition of guidance that schools strive to ensure that it is operationalised and in some cases it has become the focus of school-based curriculum development projects and research.

The Malta Cooperatives in Schools (Scoops) initiative sets out to teach secondary school students about the world of work in an experiential manner, complementing other aspects of work education provided across the curriculum in such subjects as social studies, religion, home economics, and personal and social education. It provides students with an opportunity to organise themselves into cooperative units to run, manage and market their own creative projects, and to develop the knowledge, skills and attitudes which will help them to identify their occupational strengths and their potential contribution to the local labour market, and to create for themselves a viable self-employment option. They are supported by a team of mentors, specially trained in the setting up and running of cooperatives. The curricular goals for the Scoops project are the following:

Knowledge: about the meaning and value of work; about the duties and the rights of the worker; about safety regulations; on the global economy and its effect on the local economy; on social and political history concerning the Maltese worker; about workers unions and movements; on the Maltese Cooperative Movement; on social benefits of different categories of employees; about the taxation system; about the range of job vacancies available and their requirements; about finding a vacancy; on subsidies and financial schemes; and on work ethics.

Skills: Working in groups and self control in critical times; planning and organisation; developing one's own potential; discussing issues and negotiating deadlocks; time management; project management; evaluation of one's activities; presenting of projects or business plans; finding solutions to problems encountered during work; concentration; detecting dangers and concern for safety at work; interpreting regulations, instructions, orders and directives; choice of one's career; handling an interview; writing of a curriculum vitae and presenting one's portfolio; financial management of one's earnings; keeping up to date with one's field of work; preparation for temporary unemployment; awareness and experience of information technology; literacy, numeracy and operacy.

Attitudes: appreciate that business requires long-term planning; appreciate that motivation in education is important for one's future career; generate respect for all trades and professions; appreciate the need of workers to join groups; appreciate the importance of accountability and initiative; appreciate lifelong education.

Many countries provide 'work shadowing', 'work experience', 'work visits' and forms of work simulation in order to connect their career education programmes more directly and experientially to the world of work. Of course, many secondary level students are already involved in the 'twilight economy' of after-school, weekend and holiday labour, but the jobs they hold, while helping to develop various skills, serve more the purpose of 'earning' than of 'learning'. Structured experiences provided by the school, when well planned and followed up, hold great potential in helping young people understand some of the occupational implications of the educational choices they make, and aspects of working life more generally (Miller, Watts and Jamieson, 1991). Several countries reported that students have between one to two week supervised work placements or 'work tasters' prior to making their choice of subjects. This is the case in Cyprus, Denmark, Estonia, Finland, Germany, Latvia, Lithuania, Norway, Sweden and the United

Kingdom. Other countries, notably Austria, French-speaking Belgium, Bulgaria, France, Iceland, Ireland, the Netherlands and Slovakia have similar, though perhaps less extensive, provision. While in many cases the organisation of such activities is not mandatory, and depends on the initiatives taken by individual guidance staff or schools, there are instances where there are strong central policy leads in this direction. Estonia and Latvia, for instance, organise a 'work shadowing day' at a national level on an annual basis.

There is some evidence that these kinds of activities are on the increase, and not only in vocational school settings. Cyprus, for instance, has introduced a one week placement in work contexts for Grade 11 students, and is planning to introduce summer work placements as well. Lithuania has introduced 15 hours of work experience at Grade 11 and another 15 hours at Grade 12. The Moratti draft law is proposing the introduction of work experience in Italian schools. Other countries have developed school programmes that encourage students to set up businesses, helping them learn entrepreneurial skills experientially under the guidance or mentorship of established members of the business community. Latvia, Estonia and Ireland, for instance, participate in Junior Achievement. Ireland and the United Kingdom have the Young Enterprise scheme, while Malta has also developed the Scoops (Coops in Schools) initiative. Sweden and the United Kingdom use mentoring schemes to match adults with young people for various purposes, including coaching in relation to career plans.

Work place visits and work experience in Germany: Exploratory visits in enterprises are an integral part of vocational orientation in all Lander, and generally involve an element of work experience. Companies are increasingly appreciating the value of this form of contact between schools and industry, and there is a growing number of partnerships between schools and enterprises. Preparation for workplace visits and work experience generally takes placed during the key vocational lessons, but they also increasingly feature in other subjects, such as chemistry, physics, German or geography. As a rule, practical placements last between one and three weeks, and several Lander have published comprehensive teaching guides and didactic support material on practical placements. There are extensive health and safety provisions for legal and insurance-related reasons. In some cases, practical placements can also be spent in other European countries, with the aim of making pupils familiar with the practical side of vocational training and work in other Member States of the European Union.

Guidance services and career education programmes are delivered in schools in one of three ways. They can be wholly school-based, with one or more guidance counsellors working on their own or with a team of professionals that could include psychologists, social workers, and other professionals. Alternatively, they can be provided by an agency based outside the school, which can either be public or private. Finally, there can be a partnership in service provision, which includes both school-based and external input. It appears that the third model is the one that is proving to be most attractive in several European countries.

Those systems which are closer to the wholly school-based models (e.g. Malta) run the risk of having tenuous links with the labour market, and tend to privilege personal and educational rather than career guidance. On the other hand, there were several examples of school guidance systems that call on external agencies to provide the career guidance element. Latvia, for instance, refers students to Professional Career Counselling Centres; in Lithuania, guidance is delivered to students by Labour Market Training and Counselling personnel; students in the Czech Republic, Germany and Luxembourg tend to get guidance service support from the public employment service; in the United Kingdom, strong external support is provided by the Careers Service (or in England by Connexions), a service that helps students in the transition to work process. Such external support from providers who tend to be more knowledgeable about the labour market may help students develop a truer picture of the opportunities and constraints in the world of work. They are also more likely to focus on the provision of occupational guidance. But there may be shortcomings with this model. Providers may tend to emphasise realism at the expense of encouraging aspirations. They may also inadvertently give the message that career guidance is a 'frill', a mere addendum to the more serious business of schooling, and unconnected to core curricular concerns. These risks are reduced if the external agencies are seen as a complement to, rather than a substitute for, school-based provision.

Practically all country reports noted the trend to reinforce school-based guidance provision by involving external partners. In-house partners include form/class teachers and regular subject teachers who teach aspects of the embedded career education curriculum. In some cases (e.g. Latvia) the deputy director in charge of extra-curricular activities has responsibilities for guidance as well. External stakeholder input generally involves employers and representatives of employer organisations, and (less often) of trade unions. They provide information - which they may present in person, or through materials that are print-based or accessible by electronic means and on the web - about different aspects of the world of work during seminars, career fairs, and other curricular and extracurricular activities. Fairs, in particular, have, across most European countries, become an especially important manifestation of such partnerships, and are events that give high visibility to guidance in the community. Employers are also involved in offering students work experience/shadowing placements. Other forms of input are made by the community, including parents, alumni, and members of non-governmental organisations, all of whom may be asked to speak about their own occupational experiences, as well as to focus on specific aspects they have knowledge of in the world of work. Some countries have been particularly successful in forging such partnerships (e.g. Austria, French-speaking Belgium, Finland, Ireland, Latvia, Lithuania, Luxembourg, the United Kingdom). In many others, however, the involvement of external partners tends to be sporadic and dependent on the personal initiatives of individuals, rather than part of any institutionalised mechanism for coordination, delivery and policy-making.

Different Methods for Different Groups

While guidance services at the school level are generally offered comprehensively to all, there is also targeted provision for those students who are considered to be 'at risk'. These typically include those who leave school early without any qualifications, and who thus find themselves constantly on the brink between unemployment and unskilled, low paid work, if not petty criminal activity. While several education ministries across Europe have striven to cater for such students - many, for instance, have set up second chance schools - guidance services have not been particularly successful in developing effective strategies to respond to the needs of such young people. As the case of Slovenia suggests, this may be partly due to the fact that guidance services tend to be associated by such youths with the very system they resist or have abandoned - which is why the innovative use in Flemish-speaking Belgium of peer guidance counsellors, particularly when these themselves are ex-school dropouts, may be particularly promising.

The various country responses suggest that the aim of reintegrating such young people within education and/or training programmes as quickly as possible is more likely to be attained if the service is offered outside of the school, but in collaboration with it, either by public employment services, or by community associations with which young people are more likely to identify and feel at home. Public employment services in several of the countries involved in the survey (e.g. France, Germany, Italy, Luxembourg, Malta, Norway, Portugal, Romania, Sweden), many of them acting under a common understanding of the problem as articulated within the European Employment Strategy, have tended to adopt a broadly similar approach based on early intervention. At-risk youth are offered a range of individualised approaches where personal, educational and occupational guidance are woven together, and where pre-vocational programmes - including courses in basic literacy, in self-confidence building, and in job seeking - help the insertion of clients into training, and eventually into jobs. Often such interventions are supported by the European Social Fund.

Young people are encouraged to take responsibility for their own futures by drawing up an individual action plan, and in many cases are obliged to work through this with a guidance officer as part of a mutual obligation arrangement. Such early intervention is mandatory in some countries (e.g. Denmark, Italy, Sweden), where the relevant municipal authorities are obliged by law to make contact with, and offer guidance to, young people who have dropped out of schooling and lack any formal qualifications. In the best cases, public employment services as well as community associations work hand-in-hand with guidance staff from schools in order to ensure that resources are pooled in the interests of young people at risk.

Staffing

The career guidance labour force in Europe is marked by great diversity in the extent and nature of professional training required prior to entry, in the range of competences its members have to master and use on-the-job, in the overlap there is between their role and other roles, in the progression pathways offered, in the salaries it is able to command relative to other professions, and in the status it enjoys among the community it serves. Much of this diversity is evident not only between European countries, but within them as well, indicating that what we have here is a truncated and not fully realised process of professionalisation.

While career guidance can trace its origins to the early 20th century, it has not yet become professionalised in Europe largely because its ranks draw on other, often more strongly established professions, with which guidance staff might identify more strongly.

Typically, career guidance workers have a background in, or spend part or even much of their time as teachers, psychologists, counsellors, information mediators, and human resource specialists. The fact that access to the profession is not strongly regulated also contributes to weak professional framing, as does the lack of collaboration between those who work in education and labour market sectors, which further fragments the field.

The fragmentation and undefined boundaries of the profession partly explain why respondents to the survey of policies for career guidance found it difficult to provide anything but very approximate figures when asked to state the number of guidance-related workers in their respective countries. The overall picture is even more difficult to grasp because several are involved in guidance only on a part-time basis. Keeping in mind these limitations, and the fact that no relevant information was provided by some countries, while others gave only partial information, the total number of staff involved, to a greater or lesser extent, with guidance in the 29 European countries reviewed, is estimated at around 126 000.

Most respondents could not assemble reliable information about the age composition of the career guidance labour force, but all signalled the fact that the profession attracted women in the main - indeed, the percentage is between 80 and 95 in Hungary, Iceland, Poland and Romania - though there is a tendency in all countries for women to be less strongly represented in the labour market sector than in the education sector. Such gender clustering in the field could be explained by the fact that the work may be associated with nurturing, and in any case many of the recruits are from psychology, a discipline which also tends to attract women in the main (UNECE and UNDP, 2002). The feminisation of the profession has implications for occupational identity, for the way the field is defined (e.g. a focus on the personal counselling rather than on the labour market analysis aspects of practice), for the degree of unionisation among the practitioners, for the status accorded to the activity by society, and consequently for the salaries and resources it is able to command.

Established professions generally have a clear framework regulating entry and qualification routes leading into clearly defined occupational roles. They are also generally supported by a network of professional associations and training and research organisations. While such boundaries are often used to ensure occupational closure, thus controlling supply in order to ensure competitive wage structures, they nevertheless tend to have a positive effect in enhancing quality service. Many associations are presently involved in harmonising regulatory and qualification equivalence frameworks for their respective professions in order to better exploit the opportunities presented by open EU borders. In contrast, guidance workers who, ironically, are increasingly called upon to facilitate such Europe-wide mobility and 'boundaryless careers', have a most disparate background in terms of training and qualifications (Watts, 1992), which has serious implications for the quality of service that is offered - a point also made in the Commission's report on Quality Indicators for Lifelong Learning (European Commission, 2002a).

An attempt to overcome such disparity has been made by Austria, Germany, Hungary and Poland, which are working together on a Leonardo da Vinci programme that will lead to equivalence in certification for their career guidance staff. Concern about standards of professional qualifications is particularly justified in the case of several European countries where a person can, in some sectors, offer formal career guidance without having any specific training in the field at all, or where a few hours of in-service training, often offered in-house, are deemed to suffice (e.g. France, Greece, Italy, Luxembourg).

Other countries - including many CEE countries - are much more demanding, either requiring or encouraging guidance workers to have a masters degree (e.g. Bulgaria, Czech Republic, Finland, Poland, Romania), although this may be in psychology rather than in career guidance as such. Specialised masters-level degrees are offered by a number of countries (e.g. Finland, Poland, Portugal, Romania, the United Kingdom), but across the whole range of expectations, it is often the case that employers of career guidance staff - and therefore most frequently the state - demand qualifications from what are considered to be fields related to guidance rather than in guidance itself. Often these include psychology, education, sociology, economics and social work. While disciplinary overlaps with career guidance may be evident, there is often no sustained attempt to analyse whether the competences offered during the study period coincide with those required in employment. In most of these cases, the expectation is that career guidance workers learn their skills on the job.

Staff-Training Guidance in France

There are three main types of training in guidance counselling occupations in France:a higher university-level course, which is full-time and specific to a professional body: guidance counsellor/ psychologists of the public education service; higher education by alternance specific to a professional body, namely ANPE (Agence National pour l'Emploi) counsellors; university courses opening up prospects of employment in the area of guidance, labour and human resources such as Inetop's (Institut National d'Etude du Travail et d'Orientation Professionnelle) specialist higher education diploma (DESS) in psychology and career guidance. Research is also included in the higher education diploma (DEA) course in industrial psychology and transitions offered by CNAM (Conservatoire National des Arts et Metiers)/Inetop as part of the multipartner doctoral school 'enterprise, labour, employment' (CNAM-University of Marne-la-Vallee). This DEA leads to a doctorate in psychology.

These three types of training are supplemented by continuing training schemes based on mentored practice offered by public organisations such as AFPA (Association pour la Formation Professionnelle des Adultes) or CAFOC (Centre Academique de Formation Continue) or private agencies.

There is variation in entry requirements and in training both within the education and labour market sectors, and especially between them. As a general rule, it appears that career guidance staff in education have more opportunities for specialist initial training than their PES counterparts. There are some examples across the European countries surveyed where applicants to school guidance posts are encouraged to have a relevant degree, together with appropriate experience (e.g. French-speaking Belgium, Malta), a specialist diploma or certificate in guidance (e.g. Cyprus, Iceland, Ireland, Latvia, the Netherlands, the United Kingdom), but this does not mean that all guidance staff in school will have followed that training, and many countries indicate that they have substantial numbers of staff without such qualifications - up to a third or a half in some cases - despite the courses available (e.g. Germany, Malta, the Netherlands, Norway). Many education systems are happy to employ guidance staff if they have some years of teaching experience. In most cases, a teaching qualification is a prerequisite, though in Iceland the Association of Guidance Counsellors is lobbying for the removal of such a requirement, and in the Netherlands some schools are employing trained staff who are not teachers. In other countries (e.g. Latvia), psychology degrees may have special modules in guidance.

Poland, Romania and the United Kingdom seem to be among the most advanced in the range and level of initial training they offer, providing a host of specialised short and long courses in career counselling, some of which lead to masters level qualifications. Little information was provided in the guidance survey about how much the in-service training available to teachers focused on the specific needs of guidance staff, or indeed about the training offered to class teachers and others involved in delivering aspects of the career education curriculum.

Most career guidance staff in schools are required to combine their duties with other activities. They often teach a regular curriculum area for at least half or more of their time (e.g. Flemish-speaking Belgium, the Czech Republic, Denmark, Ireland, Malta, Spain). In Germany, staff employed in teaching full-time are given an extra allowance to provide career guidance over and above their regular duties. Many staff also find themselves bogged down by administrative duties, such as managing the exercise of choice of subject clusters, or helping students fill in further education application forms. Occupational roles are generally not well defined, with staff having to shoulder a broad range of responsibilities. Some countries are attempting to deal with this situation of indeterminacy in both job requirements and job role by establishing service manuals or competence frameworks, with good examples coming from Estonia, Greece, Malta, and particularly Poland.

Role indeterminacy also leads to difficulties in carving out clear progression paths in the profession from the less expert to the more expert worker, and from the para-professional to the full professional. Lithuania and Romania are exceptions in this regard, while Estonia, Ireland and the United Kingdom are among the few countries that report para-professional categories (e.g. information officers) to support the work of qualified guidance staff. As with most other linked professionals (e.g. social workers) and non-professionals (e.g. alumni, stakeholders, significant adults and peers who often work with the 'hard to reach') these attached staff require some training if they are to consolidate the mainstream work done by guidance staff. None of the countries involved in the survey - other than the United Kingdom in terms of the staff employed in the 'learndirect' initiative - made any reference to training provision of this sort.

The tertiary education sector displays many of the same characteristics described for schools, except that it tends to be even more weakly professionalised, and more fragmented in terms of provision. It is not unusual for guidance functions to be distributed among staff in different administrative units, with some being department or faculty-based, others operating from a counselling and student advice centre, others from an international office catering for foreign students, and yet others from a student union office. These different categories of staff may have little or no formal specialised training (e.g. Denmark, Germany); even where they do, there is usually no central regulation determining the qualifications required to practise, or indeed any monitoring.

Generally speaking, guidance staff in PESs tend to have still less initial specialised training to prepare them for their roles. Some have a psychology degree behind them, but their backgrounds are even more disparate than in the case of guidance workers in the education sector, with some having qualifications in law, business management, economics, and even engineering (e.g. Romania, Spain). Much of their guidance-related training comes through in-service provision, with staff in the ACCs in particular benefiting from professional development opportunities offered via such EU programmes as Phare and Leonardo. Some staff from Member States have also had access to training programmes through the European Social Fund (e.g. Finland, Greece, Ireland, Italy, Portugal, Spain).

Delivery Settings

One of the main settings for the delivery of guidance services is - and has been for a long time - the school, and indeed, that is where young people are most likely to first come across formally-provided guidance. Traditionally, school guidance services were likely to be concentrated at the lower secondary level, targeted at students making choices about subject cluster options that opened up educational tracks which, in turn, led to groups or families of occupations. Given the lack of permeability between pathways in traditional education systems, such decisions were often irrevocable, high-stake ones, and guidance was often delivered on the basis of one-to-one personal interviews at the key points where the educational system branched off into different tracks. Little, if any, educational or occupational guidance was offered at the primary school level, and at a time when further and higher education had not yet become massified, guidance services at this level also were few and far between. Despite the great variety of guidance systems across Europe, this section will show that most countries have moved away from this traditional model of guidance provision, extending the reach of guidance to the different school levels, and providing the services in a richer variety of ways.

The guidance field across Europe is marked by a sense of dynamism and change, with many countries introducing reforms in the services offered in both the education and the labour market sectors. A key impetus for such developments has been the widely accepted notion that lifelong learning is pivotal to the economic prosperity of individual nations and Europe more globally, and that such a conviction has important implications for the restructuring of educational and training systems. In most countries, learning systems are becoming more open, more flexible, and more closely linked. Young people in compulsory and especially post-compulsory education, as well as adults whether employed or unemployed, now have an increasing range of pathways into learning and training.

In many countries, the mix-and-match options for access into further education and training are myriad, offering possibilities of full time and part time learning, delivered on site or at a distance, separate from or in conjunction with work commitments, at times and via pedagogical methods that are most suitable for the client. Most importantly, traditional - and largely arbitrary - obstacles to further education are being eradicated, through such practices as the accreditation of prior learning that recognises experience and real competence. As access to education and training becomes more open and democratised, and as options for engagement multiply and become more complex, so too should young people and adults have ready access to transparent and timely information, supported where appropriate by guidance, so that their choices are sound and beneficial to them.

Many of the European countries involved in the survey of policies for career guidance have embarked on a restructuring of their school-based guidance services to bring them more in line with the requirements of a learning society. Notions of lifelong engagement in education and training as well as lifelong careers (rather than lifelong jobs) logically require forms of guidance services that accompany all citizens throughout life, to be drawn upon when required, depending on the information and advice needs of the user, and the opportunities in the employment and training market. It has been argued that the skills required to manage one's 'life career' in a learning society, as well as the personal stance that needs to be adopted, should be inculcated early on in one's schooling (Sternberg, 1997). Such skills generally include a strong 'meta-cognitive' dimension, i.e. the ability to learn how to learn - a complex set of competences that enable individuals to identify their own learning needs, and to manage their own learning (Walbert and Paik, 2000). The image here is that of persons who take control over their own learning, are knowledgeable about the resources that are around them, and know where to get information and advice in order to transform service offers into opportunities that further their life goals. Such skills are particularly invaluable when it comes to the management of one's own career later on in life. It is clear that guidance has much to offer in this regard, particularly as school-based providers are often trained to help students overcome learning difficulties, and to coach in study skills.

Few European countries, however, reported the presence of formally established guidance services at the 'primary' school level. Those that have - such as the Czech Republic, Denmark, Hungary, Iceland, Portugal, Slovakia and Spain - tend to stress psychological approaches that are curative and remedial in nature. Special help is offered to students experiencing difficulties, rather than as part of an overall proactive strategy to encourage sound lifelong learning habits in all pupils, and the skills to manage their progression in learning and work throughout their lives. An initiative by the Greek Pedagogical Institute seems to be particularly promising in this context, since it has developed guidance materials, addressed to students from the kindergarten level up to Grade 12, which teachers can integrate into their lesson plans. Work on career education in primary schools has also been introduced in some countries (e.g. Czech Republic, Denmark). In the Netherlands, some primary schools have introduced guidance-oriented portfolio systems. In Belgium there has been a shift from an predominantly psychological approach in caring for the child, to one that is more aware of, and responsive to, the effects of social, economic and cultural backgrounds in the individual's progression through learning.

Guidance services tend to be offered most intensively at the lower secondary level, often during the last two or three years of compulsory schooling, which is when choices about subject clusters are normally made in most national systems of education. However, there is a clear trend across the 29 countries reviewed to expand guidance services vertically across all grade levels of the lower and upper secondary school, so that it is no longer concentrated at particular cut-off points, but is developmental in orientation. An illustrative case is Finland where, in 2002, the National Board of Education promulgated new national curriculum guidelines which entitled students to access to guidance services throughout their secondary education, whereas previously guidance was only offered during the last three grades of comprehensive schooling.

In most countries, individual, face-to-face guidance still tends to predominate as a mode of service delivery. Particularly in the ACCs and in some of the other European states (e.g. in the education sector in France, Iceland, Portugal, Luxembourg), this may largely be due to the fact that many guidance staff have a background in psychology, a discipline which tends to privilege therapeutic, one-to-one approaches, often aided by psychometric testing and assessment. Many respondents noted the increasing impossibility of guaranteeing student entitlement to services, given staff resources, if student guidance needs were only handled through personal interviews.

In some countries, resource allocation is worked out in terms of guidance staff-to-student ratios. Typically, the staff-to-student ratio is quite high (e.g. in Cyprus, Romania and Sweden it can be as high as 1:800; in Bulgaria, Ireland and Malta it is 1:500; in the Netherlands it is 1:300-400; while in Finland, it is 1:272, with trade unions finding this unacceptable and lobbying to bringing down the ratio to 1:200). In others the measure is the amount of time formally allocated for guidance activities per week, which can be as low as one to three hours (e.g. the Czech Republic). Personal guidance has limitations other than those imposed by counsellor-to-student ratios. While the focus on individual self-fulfilment is positive, with guidance being interpreted as an intervention in the process of constructing one's occupational identity on the basis of individual characteristics and aspirations, there is a danger that such an approach tends to obscure the way social and gender experiences structure desires and trajectories.

Group guidance and career education, delivered in, through, or outside the formal curriculum, facilitates the linkage between the personal and the social in the decision-making process, besides ensuring wider access to services. Such an approach is facilitated when, as in the United Kingdom, and to a lesser extent in Hungary and Malta, a room especially dedicated to guidance activities, furnished with open display units and equipped with relevant information available in print and electronic formats, is available in schools or in guidance centres that are contracted to service schools, as is the case in Flemish-speaking Belgium. Increasingly, the emergent model for career guidance provision is one where face-to-face assistance by guidance counsellors is only one element in a programmed approach to career development and decision-making that also includes group guidance organised around specific themes and issues, career education curriculum delivery, ICT-based assistance, experiential learning in work places and communities, and extensive use of community members such as parents, employers, trade union organisations, and alumni.

Guidance services and career education programmes are delivered in schools in one of three ways. They can be wholly school-based, with one or more guidance counsellors working on their own or with a team of professionals that could include psychologists, social workers, and other professionals. Alternatively, they can be provided by an agency based outside the school, which can either be public or private. Finally, there can be a partnership in service provision, which includes both school-based and external input. It appears that the third model is the one that is proving to be most attractive in several European countries.

Those systems which are closer to the wholly school-based models (e.g. Malta) run the risk of having tenuous links with the labour market, and tend to privilege personal and educational rather than career guidance. On the other hand, there were several examples of school guidance systems that call on external agencies to provide the career guidance element. Latvia, for instance, refers students to Professional Career Counselling Centres; in Lithuania, guidance is delivered to students by Labour Market Training and Counselling personnel; students in the Czech Republic, Germany and Luxembourg tend to get guidance service support from the public employment service; in the United Kingdom, strong external support is provided by the Careers Service (or in England by Connexions), a service that helps students in the transition to work process. Such external support from providers who tend to be more knowledgeable about the labour market may help students develop a truer picture of the opportunities and constraints in the world of work. They are also more likely to focus on the provision of occupational guidance. But there may be shortcomings with this model. Providers may tend to emphasise realism at the expense of encouraging aspirations. They may also inadvertently give the message that career guidance is a 'frill', a mere addendum to the more serious business of schooling, and unconnected to core curricular concerns. These risks are reduced if the external agencies are seen as a complement to, rather than a substitute for, school-based provision.

Practically all country reports noted the trend to reinforce school-based guidance provision by involving external partners. In-house partners include form/class teachers and regular subject teachers who teach aspects of the embedded career education curriculum. In some cases (e.g. Latvia) the deputy director in charge of extra-curricular activities has responsibilities for guidance as well. External stakeholder input generally involves employers and representatives of employer organisations, and (less often) of trade unions. They provide information - which they may present in person, or through materials that are print-based or accessible by electronic means and on the web - about different aspects of the world of work during seminars, career fairs, and other curricular and extracurricular activities. Fairs, in particular, have, across most European countries, become an especially important manifestation of such partnerships, and are events that give high visibility to guidance in the community. Employers are also involved in offering students work experience/shadowing placements.

Other forms of input are made by the community, including parents, alumni, and members of non-governmental organisations, all of whom may be asked to speak about their own occupational experiences, as well as to focus on specific aspects they have knowledge of in the world of work. Some countries have been particularly successful in forging such partnerships (e.g. Austria, French-speaking Belgium, Finland, Ireland, Latvia, Lithuania, Luxembourg, the United Kingdom). In many others, however, the involvement of external partners tends to be sporadic and dependent on the personal initiatives of individuals, rather than part of any institutionalised mechanism for coordination, delivery and policy-making.

Integration into Other Subjects

The introduction or reinforcement of career education in or across the curriculum to supplement personal interviews was one of the most-often reported developments in the guidance survey. The 'school-to-work' or 'transition' curriculum, as it has sometimes been referred to [though this is a limited model: many career education programmes start long before the school-leaving stage], may entail a number of elements, often including teaching about work and about further education and training routes, self-awareness, and such transition 'lifeskills' as decision making, self presentation in curriculum vitae and selection interviews, and so on (van Esbroeck, 1997; Sultana, 1997).

For reasons noted earlier, most systems target the career education curriculum to students in the last two to three years of lower secondary, though increasingly this is questionable given the increasingly high rates of students moving into further education, and the evidence of the early formation of key attitudes relating to self and the world of work (suggesting the need for early intervention). As noted earlier, guidance services for younger students tend to focus on helping them manage the transition from the primary school and to adapt to the different institutional culture and work demands of secondary schooling (e.g. Cyprus, Italy, Malta, Portugal, the United Kingdom). In stratified education systems which offer different pathways to students according to their academic achievement, those streamed in vocationally oriented tracks are more likely to experience a career education programme than others, who might get less in terms of overall exposure, or in terms of the percentage of time dedicated to occupational, as against educational, decision making (e.g. Austria, the Czech Republic, Germany, Hungary, Ireland, Luxembourg, the Netherlands). There are instances, however, where students in VET are considered to be less needy of career education and guidance since their occupational destinations are considered to be tightly linked to the skills or trades area they have already chosen (e.g. Cyprus, Estonia, Finland, Greece, Latvia, Slovakia, Slovenia).

Four models of curriculum-based career education delivery can be discerned from the country responses, with some countries adopting more than one model simultaneously. First is the option of offering career education as a separate subject in the curriculum, i.e. by formally allocating the area space in the weekly or semestrial timetable (e.g. Austria, Cyprus, the Czech Republic, Finland, Greece, Romania and Spain). Another option involves embedding career education within a more broadly-based subject, often social studies or personal and social education (e.g. Hungary, Latvia, Malta, Poland). A third option is for aspects of career education to appear in most or all the subjects of the curriculum (e.g. Denmark, Greece). A fourth option is to have the career programme delivered through seminars and workshops (e.g. France, Malta, Poland), that may be addressed to same-age groups of students, or which may be theme-based and open to students from across several grades. Naturally, in decentralised education systems it is not uncommon for schools in the same country to choose different models for delivering the career education programme (e.g. Austria, Flemish-speaking Belgium, the Czech Republic, Spain, the United Kingdom), or for the same school to use more than one of the four approaches referred to above. Career education may or may not be compulsory, often depending on the policy of the school and the extent to which management values the area. Increasingly, however, national curriculum guidelines mandate career education programmes, occasionally leaving it up to the school to work out the details of provision. This is the case with Flemish-speaking Belgium, Austria, the Czech Republic, Denmark, Finland, Germany, the Netherlands, Norway, Spain and the United Kingdom. Other countries do not impose an obligation on schools (e.g. Ireland, Luxembourg).

In cases where the career education programme is offered across the curriculum, countries exhibit a range of modalities in which the area is directed and managed. In some cases, regular teachers are simply invited to include career-related themes in their subject, and the decision as to the extent to which they do so, and how, is left entirely up to them. Guidance survey responses suggest clearly that often the outcomes are far from satisfactory, with teachers failing to help students see connections between the different elements of the programme that are dealt with in separate subjects (e.g. Austria, Denmark, Norway, Sweden).

Other countries have a much tighter context for such provision, with specialist guidance staff offering guidelines as well as resources to their colleagues, so that the career education programme is delivered in a more integrated manner (Greece, Iceland, the Netherlands, the United Kingdom). In Flemish-speaking Belgium, the Centre for Educational Guidance (CLB) can provide assistance to schools in the implementation of cross curricular themes related to educational guidance.

Cross-departmental delivery strategies require a tradition of collegial, school-based curriculum development that is generally still missing in the ACCs, most of which are accustomed to centralised curriculum planning. Few of the ACCs adopt a 'whole-school approach' to guidance. In other European countries, the best practice seems to come from contexts where students are encouraged or required to keep portfolios where they record their career-related learning and experiences (e.g. the 'job passport' in Austria, the 'education log' in Denmark, or the 'career choice passport' in Germany). This encourages students to connect what may initially appear to be disparate inputs by different teachers, and to reflect upon them. The case of Luxembourg highlights the fact that, even in countries where guidance services are still relatively weak, specific innovative projects in one or more schools, within the context of school development planning, can lead to articulation of a whole-school approach that sees guidance at the heart of the school's raison d'etre. In Flemish-speaking Belgium, the cross-curricular approach to guidance is underpinned and followed-up in several ways: not only is curricular co-ordination in relation to guidance mandated by educational law, but it also serves as a quality criteria when inspectors are evaluating schools. It has indeed become so central to the definition of guidance that schools strive to ensure that it is operationalised and in some cases it has become the focus of school-based curriculum development projects and research.

Work-place Experience

Teaching for Entrepreneurship in Malta

The Malta Cooperatives in Schools (Scoops) initiative sets out to teach secondary school students about the world of work in an experiential manner, complementing other aspects of work education provided across the curriculum in such subjects as social studies, religion, home economics, and personal and social education. It provides students with an opportunity to organise themselves into cooperative units to run, manage and market their own creative projects, and to develop the knowledge, skills and attitudes which will help them to identify their occupational strengths and their potential contribution to the local labour market, and to create for themselves a viable self-employment option. They are supported by a team of mentors, specially trained in the setting up and running of cooperatives. The curricular goals for the Scoops project are the following:

Knowledge: about the meaning and value of work; about the duties and the rights of the worker; about safety regulations; on the global economy and its effect on the local economy; on social and political history concerning the Maltese worker; about workers unions and movements; on the Maltese Cooperative Movement; on social benefits of different categories of employees; about the taxation system; about the range of job vacancies available and their requirements; about finding a vacancy; on subsidies and financial schemes; and on work ethics.

Skills: Working in groups and self control in critical times; planning and organisation; developing one's own potential; discussing issues and negotiating deadlocks; time management; project management; evaluation of one's activities; presenting of projects or business plans; finding solutions to problems encountered during work; concentration; detecting dangers and concern for safety at work; interpreting regulations, instructions, orders and directives; choice of one's career; handling an interview; writing of a curriculum vitae and presenting one's portfolio; financial management of one's earnings; keeping up to date with one's field of work; preparation for temporary unemployment; awareness and experience of information technology; literacy, numeracy and operacy.

Attitudes: appreciate that business requires long-term planning; appreciate that motivation in education is important for one's future career; generate respect for all trades and professions; appreciate the need of workers to join groups; appreciate the importance of accountability and initiative; appreciate lifelong education.

Many countries provide 'work shadowing', 'work experience', 'work visits' and forms of work simulation in order to connect their career education programmes more directly and experientially to the world of work. Of course, many secondary level students are already involved in the 'twilight economy' of after-school, weekend and holiday labour, but the jobs they hold, while helping to develop various skills, serve more the purpose of 'earning' than of 'learning'. Structured experiences provided by the school, when well planned and followed up, hold great potential in helping young people understand some of the occupational implications of the educational choices they make, and aspects of working life more generally (Miller, Watts and Jamieson, 1991). Several countries reported that students have between one to two week supervised work placements or 'work tasters' prior to making their choice of subjects.

This is the case in Cyprus, Denmark, Estonia, Finland, Germany, Latvia, Lithuania, Norway, Sweden and the United Kingdom. Other countries, notably Austria, French-speaking Belgium, Bulgaria, France, Iceland, Ireland, the Netherlands and Slovakia have similar, though perhaps less extensive, provision. While in many cases the organisation of such activities is not mandatory, and depends on the initiatives taken by individual guidance staff or schools, there are instances where there are strong central policy leads in this direction. Estonia and Latvia, for instance, organise a 'work shadowing day' at a national level on an annual basis.

There is some evidence that these kinds of activities are on the increase, and not only in vocational school settings. Cyprus, for instance, has introduced a one week placement in work contexts for Grade 11 students, and is planning to introduce summer work placements as well. Lithuania has introduced 15 hours of work experience at Grade 11 and another 15 hours at Grade 12. The Moratti draft law is proposing the introduction of work experience in Italian schools. Other countries have developed school programmes that encourage students to set up businesses, helping them learn entrepreneurial skills experientially under the guidance or mentorship of established members of the business community. Latvia, Estonia and Ireland, for instance, participate in Junior Achievement. Ireland and the United Kingdom have the Young Enterprise scheme, while Malta has also developed the Scoops (Coops in Schools) initiative. Sweden and the

United Kingdom use mentoring schemes to match adults with young people for various purposes, including coaching in relation to career plans.

Work Place Visits and Work Experience in Germany

Exploratory visits in enterprises are an integral part of vocational orientation in all Lander, and generally involve an element of work experience. Companies are increasingly appreciating the value of this form of contact between schools and industry, and there is a growing number of partnerships between schools and enterprises. Preparation for workplace visits and work experience generally takes placed during the key vocational lessons, but they also increasingly feature in other subjects, such as chemistry, physics, German or geography. As a rule, practical placements last between one and three weeks, and several Lander have published comprehensive teaching guides and didactic support material on practical placements. There are extensive health and safety provisions for legal and insurance-related reasons. In some cases, practical placements can also be spent in other European countries, with the aim of making pupils familiar with the practical side of vocational training and work in other Member States of the European Union.

Information Provided by Public Employment Service

Unemployed adults are the main recipients of career guidance across Europe. Often, the providers are Public Employment Services (PES). While European PES offices share much the same goals and methodologies of similar services worldwide, those in EU member and accession states have tended to adopt common policies in dealing with unemployment, in relation to the targets and priorities established by the European Employment Strategy. Such concerted strategy building is facilitated by the Network of European Public Employment Services. The latter's joint statement on their role in the labour market (2002) promotes guidance as an effective tool for assisting jobseekers. Increasingly the aim following the Luxembourg Summit has been to 'activate' clients who are required to develop a personal action plan with the support of PES staff. Indeed, the European Employment Strategy and the European Employment Guidelines not only have had a major impact on the customer orientation of the PES, but enjoin the latter to provide in-depth guidance to clients. European countries involved in the guidance survey target a whole range of unemployed persons who are considered to need special support, including the long term unemployed, women returnees, persons with disabilities, ethnic minorities, young people with no formal qualifications and work experience, and (less often) asylum seekers and ex-convicts.

Despite the fact that the overall framework driving PESs in Europe highlights the role that guidance can play in routing clients through training and into jobs, and that clear cultural change is underway in many PES towards a more supportive and facilitative role, with the service becoming a gateway to guidance rather than a gatekeeper, the survey nevertheless suggests that this guidance role is often underdeveloped, and subordinated to other tasks which tend to take precedence in the broad remit of responsibilities that PES staff have to shoulder. Thus, several European countries, and particular those in the process of accession to the EU, report that their PES focus tends to be on training for employability, on information giving, and on job brokerage. They also report that the guidance function in their work often ends up being muted. PES staff are typically overburdened with multiple roles (e.g. Cyprus, Czech Republic, Denmark, Germany, Latvia, Malta, Netherlands, Slovakia), and the fact that the criterion for evaluation of provision tends to be the rate of successful job placements of clients skews services towards brokerage and networking with potential employers. Staff are also involved in channelling the unemployed towards training and re-training tracks, and in many cases they administer income support schemes for clients.

This multiplicity of roles tends to be exacerbated by the trend of establishing 'one-stop shops' (e.g. Flemish-speaking Belgium, Cyprus, Denmark, Finland, Germany, Greece, Iceland, the Netherlands, Spain, the United Kingdom), where clients can more readily have access to the whole range of PES services at the same site. While clients might find this convenient and practical, the multitasking implications for staff lead to potential role conflict, since they have to both encourage clients to take them in their confidence, while at the same time policing the provision of unemployment benefits. It becomes very difficult for guidance staff to find a resolution between the norms of professionalism and of administrative demands.

While some countries are keeping the roles and tasks of PES staff integrated (e.g. Denmark, Iceland, Norway, Spain), others are reforming their services in such a way that different categories of unemployed are better served by specialised provision. The most notable case in point here is Greece, which is privatising its PES (the OAED - the Manpower Employment Organisation) and distributing its different roles to four different companies. One of these companies will focus specifically on information and guidance services. Another country that has retained a separate and highly professionalized career guidance service within its PES is Finland. In the accession countries, Poland (through its Poviat Labour Offices and its 51 Centres for Career Information and Planning in Voivodship Labour Offices), Lithuania (through its Labour Exchanges and its Labour Market Training Authorities) and Slovenia stand out in the extent to which they offer employment counselling over and above the range of information-based services that are common to many PESs.

One of the options that exists for public employment offices that have not separated out the different roles and functions is to organise their service in tiered levels. This can help them to cope with the diverse needs of clients, and to free up time and resources for guidance. There are typically three levels or tiers of service. At the first level, PES users have access to information in a self-service mode, through the use of dedicated materials or on-line.

A second tier of service provides group-based help, which can include job clubs, sessions that help clients recover self-confidence and motivation, or that teach them basic literacy skills, how to write curriculum vitae, how to sit for interviews, and a range of other employability skills. A third tier of service provides personal guidance to those who are perceived to need it, and/or who feel they can benefit from it. The management of the service in this way not only contributes to more efficient use of resources through screening, but also enables some role differentiation, with semi or para-professional categories catering for basic information and advice needs, while others with more professional training in guidance provide the third-tier services.

Linked to the development of tiered services is the shift to a self-service mode which frees up staff from dealing with information requests that can be more or less easily handled by clients themselves. A key exemplar of this is Sweden, which has set up several 'Infotheques' to enable open and unaided access to information. Other reports that highlighted this shift to self-help strategies include Flemish-speaking Belgium, Denmark, Finland, France, the Netherlands, Norway, Romania, Slovenia and the United Kingdom. Most countries report a major investment in the development of websites that not only provide information on job vacancies, labour market trends, and occupations more generally, but also include diagnostic instruments such as interest inventories and self-assessments of work values and skills.

Open Access and Self-service Guidance in Flemish-speaking Belgium

In 2001, the PES in Flemish-speaking Belgium, the VDAB, introduced a system of universal services with the aim of (a) increasing the use of self-assessment and self-direction instruments by people looking for work or interested in changing their employment, and also (b) to increase the independent use of information on the part of employers. MY VDAB is the next step in the evolution of a generation of tools that support client independence and the use of an electronic portfolio. In fact, MY VDAB integrates existing instruments, such as the file manager, information on vacancies, curriculum vitae, training possibilities, and so on, and brings them on line so that people can manage their own profile, and can analyse and compare the information they have about themselves with other data sets. VDAB also has a clientvolgsysteem, which allows the follow-up of clients in the different stages across the pathways they embark on. For others to have access to the files the client must first give their permission to the VDAB. A manual supports the user in the exploitation of the clientvolgsysteem.

Reference has been made to the EU's commitment to LLL as a key strategy in maintaining competitiveness in a global economy. That commitment filters through several areas of public policy within member and accession states. The Joint Statements of the European Public Employment Services on their Role in the Labour Market (European Commission, 2002e for instance, underscores the responsibility of national PESs to support LLL by assisting individuals throughout their working lives in order to promote occupational mobility and flexibility). This survey however shows that career guidance for adults, within the EU and across Europe more generally, tends to remain narrowly focused on the unemployed. Few countries have developed strategies to help working adults to sustain employability by regularly reviewing new opportunities for enhancing their skills. As the Danish survey report notes, PES offices tend to be associated with unemployment queues and the doling out of welfare benefits, serving little to attract employed adults who feel the need for occupational guidance. Some countries (e.g. the Netherlands, Norway) have redesigned their PES offices so as to structure the flow of unemployed away from the main entry, and resourced them in such a way as to also prove inviting to the employed. There are also some signs that a shift towards the career information and guidance needs of employed adults might be happening in some countries, with a growing awareness of the need to ensure that adults who are not job seekers and not students, but who wish to re-engage in learning or to develop their careers, do not fall through the cracks. The potential demand for such services is amply illustrated by Austria, where in 2001 the number of adults accessing services in the 56 regional Career information centres ('BIZ' centres) grew by 15% compared to the previous year, bringing up the percentage of adult 'BIZ' users to 47% of all clients.

Guidance at Tertiary Level

Several countries note that higher education students have, over the past decade or so, greatly increased in number, and have consequently become a much more heterogeneous group than before. They are no longer all the same age, with the same basic abilities and the same orientation to learning, as they tended to be when universities were elite institutions, catering for about 2 % of the population (Halsey, 1991). Increasingly, their age, experience and background vary, and it has become more necessary to provide a much broader range of guidance services to meet the growing diversity of student needs. In a Europe which actively promotes and facilitates student mobility - through such programmes as Socrates and Leonardo, through the European Credit Transfer System (ECTS), and through the harmonisation of the degree structure as part of the Bologna process - foreign/exchange students are increasingly present on campuses, and have special guidance needs which also have to be attended to.

In addition, the number of higher education establishments has increased, both in quantity and in type of institution, in order to cater for larger numbers of students who have different expectations from higher learning programmes. Many institutions have also adopted modular structures of course delivery, giving students a great deal of flexibility in designing their own programme of studies, in relation to their own learning needs and occupational goals. Such individualised pathways make the links between courses and the graduate labour market more complex. All this diversity and extended opportunity both create challenges for career guidance, and make it all the more necessary and relevant.

Country responses from across Europe show that guidance services at the tertiary education level have either already been stepped up (e.g. the French SCUIOs - the Joint University Information and Guidance Services), or are in the process of being developed. Germany, for instance, has passed a Framework Act for Higher Education which requires institutions of higher education, including universities and

Fachhochschulen, to inform students and applicants on the opportunities and conditions of study and on the content, structure and requirements of study courses, and to assist students by providing subject-oriented advice. Many German institutions of higher learning have established Central Student Counselling Services, while 50 out of about 350 universities have set up their own careers services in order to facilitate the transition between study and the field of graduate employment. Guidance staff in the Nordic countries have established the Nordic Forum for Higher Education Career Services to facilitate their own professional development, while the United Kingdom has an Association of Graduate Careers Advisory Services, which, among other activities, is supporting the development of certificate and diploma courses in higher education career guidance. Others still have underdeveloped services in this sector, but are in the process of establishing or strengthening them. Austria is a case in point here, as are Cyprus, Finland, Greece, Italy, Lithuania and Norway. In Finland and Ireland, recent evidence showing that there is a link between guidance provision in higher education and student retention has proved to be a particularly motivating factor in stimulating investment in guidance services at this level.

Many of these developments are spurred on by client demands. Where the state or the university administration fail to provide services for which there is a felt need, students themselves have sometimes mobilised in order to find alternative ways of accessing guidance. In Finland, for instance, higher student associations train peer tutors both nationally and locally, organise career information fairs with stakeholders, and are represented in key national working groups involved in guidance. The National Union of Students in Austria has set up an advisory voluntary service providing information about university life, housing, finance and other practical issues, as have their Slovene counterparts.

Sometimes, tertiary education institutions develop their guidance and information services because they have to compete with other establishments for students. In their attempt at boosting recruitment, often in contexts where funding follows students (e.g. Denmark, the Netherlands, the United Kingdom), institutions of higher learning have become increasingly aware that they have to provide such information as details of courses on offer, learning pathways that can be followed, resources that are available, and career opportunities at the end of a programme of study. This may put guidance staff in an awkward situation, as they may be expected to attract and retain students in their own establishment, even if this is not in the best interests of their clients.

Increasingly, information is provided to prospective students in handbooks and guides that are made available in a range of formats, including print, CD-ROM, and online. Much of the material is produced either by the state (centrally or by the regional administration, as in Spain, to mention just one example), or by the institutions themselves, though increasingly the private sector is playing an active role, either under contract (as in Austria, the Netherlands) or on a commercial basis (as in the United Kingdom). It is uncommon, however, for such material to feature information about student satisfaction with the quality of teaching, and rates of successful placement of graduates, which might render the guidebooks and handbooks more helpful in making choices between different institutions. The only example reported in this regard concerned a government-funded publication in the Netherlands. Some universities do, though, organise and publish the results of tracer studies of graduates in order to be in a better position to guide students regarding likely employment trajectories after finishing a course (e.g. Estonia, Malta); in some cases such studies are carried out on a nationwide basis (the United Kingdom, Ireland).

There is a great deal of disparity in the guidance services offered in institutions of higher learning, both between and within countries. In the first place, their location varies. They are sometimes to be found outside the institution, offered by an external agency that caters for the guidance needs of students, as in the case of Austria's network of Psychological Student Counselling Service. More frequently, guidance is offered inhouse, as with the 'Laboratoire d'Ergologie at the Universite Libre de Bruxelles'. In some cases, services are based in faculties or departments (e.g. Denmark, Greece, Italy, Norway, Sweden), while in others they are constituted as a separate service offered centrally (e.g. France, Poland, Romania, the United Kingdom). Sometimes both modalities are available (e.g. Ireland, Sweden). In this case central services fulfil a broad guidance remit, often including different aspects of student welfare. On their part, faculty-based services - often offered by an untrained member of the academic staff - take on responsibilities which can include induction, study support, and the provision of information about graduate employment opportunities. Sometimes, faculties also develop strong networks with potential employers which facilitate placements for work experience or graduate employment purposes.

Whatever the modality of provision, the guidance survey confirms findings of an earlier study by Watts and van Esbroeck (1998) which indicated that much of the focus in European universities is on educational rather than occupational guidance, largely as a result of the very broad remit they may have to fulfil. Assistance and advice regarding course choices are often integrated with personal counselling, that typically includes guidance on stress management. Increasingly, however, higher education institutions are under pressure to develop a range of career management and student employability skills. This occasionally produces forms of work experience or internship (e.g. Spain, the United Kingdom), and the keeping of portfolios recording learning of work-related competences (e.g. the United Kingdom). Increasingly too we find the development of job brokerage and graduate placement services designed to help students facing tight and competitive graduate labour markets.

Services Provided by Private sector

The private sector has a limited but expanding role in offering career guidance services. Increasingly the private sector publishes further education and training guidebooks and handbooks, often on contracts outsourced by government. Apart from this, however, in most European countries the private sector's role tends to be limited to finding, selecting and placing personnel in highly qualified and specialised labour niches. In the CEE countries, such private employment services have started appearing in the last decade (e.g. Bulgaria, Hungary, Latvia, Lithuania, Romania, Slovakia), and it is really only in Poland that they are established in any significant number. Typically, private-sector services have a job brokerage and head hunting function, and the guidance function is underdeveloped. The private-sector career guidance market is small in Denmark and Ireland, for instance, though it is more extensive in French-speaking Belgium, the Netherlands and the United Kingdom. In general, there does not seem to be much enthusiasm for individuals to pay for career guidance services, and the main way a market or quasi-market has developed has been through the purchase of services by large companies or through the transfer of public funds via outsourcing. This survey clearly shows that there is an information gap on the extent, nature and costs of private sector guidance.

Public Encouragement to Private Organizations

Several respondents to the survey noted that their governments were increasingly attracted by outsourcing, particularly in relation to the provision of guidance within public employment services (e.g. Austria, the Czech Republic, Estonia, Finland, France, Germany, Iceland, Italy, the Netherlands, Romania, Spain, the United Kingdom). Subcontracting can be an attractive policy measure for a number of reasons: it can be a way of recruiting staff at lower costs, without having to extend the usual benefits that have to be given to civil servants; the subcontracted services may not be as bureaucratically tied up by complex civil service regulations, and hence may be more nimble and flexible in their response to new challenges; and community and not-for-profit organisations in particular may be closer to the target clients than government institutions, and hence more likely to be knowledgeable about - and responsive to - their needs.

For these and other reasons, several countries across Europe have adopted quasi-market models in their approach to funding career and information services, outsourcing functions that traditionally had been carried by the PES. Examples from the guidance reports abound, particularly for the older EU Member States. Thus, the Austrian PES (the AMS - i.e. the Federal Employment Office) contracts out some guidance services to a range of for-profit and not-for-profit organisations, which normally cater for six-week orientation courses to improve the employability of 14 to 20 year old youths. It also contracts out the production of career information material, as do its Czech, Finnish, German and Spanish counterparts. In the case of Germany, the Federal Employment Service has outsourced some of the profiling work with unemployed and disadvantaged individuals, plus their training in job-seeking skills. Iceland's Ministry of Social Affairs has subcontracted trade unions to manage projects for enhancing the services for unemployed people. Spain gives great importance to funding community-based organisations to cater for the guidance needs of disadvantaged groups.

In some cases, outsourcing is done indirectly, with the state giving a voucher to clients, who can then buy a service from a provider of their choice. Such schemes have been tried out in Flemish-speaking Belgium, France, Germany and Italy, for instance. A variation on the voucher model is the contract model that has been trialled in the United Kingdom, and more recently in Estonia and the Netherlands. This involves giving the choice of provider not to the client, but to the official authorities concerned, who are deemed to be more knowledgeable about what will offer best value for money. As in the case of devolution, outsourcing - in all its guises - poses important questions about the role of the state in monitoring the quality of the services it funds, and in ensuring equity in access. A good example of this is provided by the United Kingdom, where all guidance services in receipt of public funding have to meet the 'matrix' quality standards. Estonia too is planning to develop regulations governing service standards that external providers will have to follow.

Learning and Guidance Cheques (Vouchers) in Flemish-speaking Belgium

While Learning cheques or vouchers have been in circulation in Flemish-speaking Belgium for some time, the whole system has recently been reformed, following an agreement between the Flemish government and the social partners, signed in March 2003. Under the new system, all funding for training and learning facilities are brought together and will be used for (a) the development of career guidance and the recognition of prior learning, and (b) financing the learning cheques scheme.

The scope of the existing system is being broadened, mainly by (a) adding the possibility of its use in the private sector, (b) targeting the at-risk groups by increasing the number of vouchers they receive, or the value of their cheques, and (c) by setting up a voucher system for employees as well. While previously cheques were delivered to employers, there is now a system that issues cheques to employees, who have complete autonomy in making use of them be it to fund training and learning, to pay for guidance services, or to gain certification for prior learning. Every employee is entitled to a cheque of Euro 250 annually, which an individual is required to supplement according to his or her financial standing.

Several countries also noted that there is a growing private market offering different aspects of guidance, though, this sector is still small. It is also less likely to be found in the new Member States, and tends to be confined largely to the production of career information materials (such as handbooks, guidebooks, CD-ROMS, and websites), to employment agencies (with an overwhelming focus on job brokerage and head hunting), and to outplacement agencies (that offer career counselling). In some cases, a limited market for career guidance services paid for by individuals has also appeared (e.g. in French-speaking Belgium, Germany, the Netherlands, Norway, the United Kingdom - and to a lesser extent in Denmark, Ireland and Sweden). In many cases, these services have found it difficult to survive, largely because individuals do not seem to be willing to pay for guidance at full-cost rates.

Three factors can help explain the growth of the private market in the career guidance field:

1. first is the fact that government outsourcing and subcontracting has tended to stimulate the market, providing a reliable source of funding which makes investment on the part of private entrepreneurs a feasible option. Governments have also stimulated competition in the provision of employment services by doing away with the monopoly that their PES often used to enjoy - until the legality of such a monopoly was challenged in at the European Court of Justice on the grounds that it was impeding real competition. Private employment services have been legalised in Denmark (in 1990), Sweden (1993), Germany (in 1998), and Norway (in 2000). Greece has gone one step further and has actually recently privatised its PES, with Cyprus soon to follow suit.
2. a second factor that has contributed to the growth of a private market in the guidance and information field is the increasing readiness of employers to pay private, external providers to meet the careers guidance and development needs of their employees (e.g. French-speaking Belgium, Denmark, the Netherlands). Employers may do this for a number of reasons: guidance may be part of a service they offer to their management, in order to ensure continued development of their skills and motivation. It may also be offered to employees who are about to be laid off due to recession or restructuring. In this case, the obligation of paying for such career guidance may have been agreed by employers as part of a collective agreement with unions, and sometimes the state may partially subsidise the costs of the guidance service offered.>
3. a third stimulus for private provision of guidance is the increasing demand for services, and the inability of the state to satisfy such demand.

A key factor here is that, despite the increase in private provision, most European countries seem to know little about its extent, and have made few attempts to regulate it. This has serious implications, especially if the premise is that guidance is a public as well as a private good. If this is the case, the state has a responsibility to ensure that services offered through the market are sound, and also to compensate for any market failure as a result of which client entitlement to guidance services may be jeopardised.

Roles of Other Organizations

Unemployed adults may have access to career information and guidance in other settings than those provided by the PES. Most often, community-based organisations provide services to specific groups, especially if they are the target of national equity policies. Few of these initiatives were reported for ACCs, where the key provider remains the state. Other European countries (e.g. Belgium, Luxembourg, Portugal, Spain, Sweden), however, reported an increasing number of projects which community-based associations organised on their own (either as self-financed initiatives, or more often through outsourcing by the PES), or in collaboration with a public agency (e.g. Luxembourg's Femmes en Detresse project; the Adult Educational Guidance Initiative in Ireland, which targets unemployed adults who wish to take up education and training). Typically, such initiatives cater for unemployed adults who suffer from social or physical disadvantages: community-based organisations that work with them are considered to be closer to the realities of these target groups, and therefore potentially more effective in responding to their needs. Clients might also feel more comfortable with such forms of provision, which tend to be built around personal rather than bureaucratic service cultures.

Adults, whether unemployed or in part-time employment, can also access career guidance services if they are enrolled in higher education institutions or in other forms of adult education and training. Here, some institutions have developed guidance services targeted specifically at mature students, including women who are hoping to return to the labour market after a period of time out for child rearing. Increasingly falling within the remit of guidance services are 'second chance' schemes which try to facilitate the entry of under-educated but highly motivated adults into higher education and training tracks, through the accreditation of prior and experiential learning. In some cases, such accreditation is based on a guidance-oriented dialogue, where individuals are helped to identify and value the knowledge they have acquired informally. Some countries have taken this kind of strategy on board at a national level - England, for instance, has established regional adult, information, advice and guidance partnerships with the intention of encouraging poorly qualified and low-skilled adults to return to education. France, Norway, Portugal, Flemish-speaking Belgium and Greece have also made strides towards the development of systems of assessment of prior learning, or bilan des competences.

Some large enterprises provide career information and guidance services in-house, either through their own personnel in HRD departments or by buying services from specialised external agencies and consultants (e.g. Germany, the Netherlands, Spain, the United Kingdom). This they may do for one of three reasons: (a) to facilitate career development within the company, (b) to guide employees towards training in skills areas that management envisages will become necessary for the company's growth - this may entail training needs assessments, and (c) to support workers who will be made redundant or outplaced, by offering them access to re-training routes and alternative employment. Few of the guidance reports from ACCs and the small nation states in Europe made any reference to such services. Larger countries were more likely to indicate the incidence of such practices, especially where the state supports such initiatives through including career guidance provision within expenditure allowable against training levies (e.g. the Netherlands), through awarding a Quality Mark to enterprises that invest in the development of their own employees (e.g. the Netherlands, the United Kingdom), and through making Public Employment Service guidance staff available to companies, particularly small and medium-sized ones that do not have the capacity to develop guidance services in-house (e.g. Germany).

Delivery Methods

Responses obtained from the survey of policies for career guidance clearly indicate that several countries are trying to broaden access to career information and guidance to a wider range of client groups, using diverse and often innovative strategies. Responses also indicate some of the gaps in provision across several European countries, though there are examples of good practice which signal ways in which these gaps can be addressed. The issue of access has been highlighted by the Commission's deliberations on the role of guidance in supporting LLL and the Objectives for Education and Training. The Commission's LLL Communication (2001a) emphasises the need for guidance to be organised as an open service that is continuously and locally accessible for all; as a client-centred service which reaches out to citizens and follows up on their needs rather than waiting for them to come; and as a diversified service offered through such non-formal and informal channels as NGOs and community-based associations so that disadvantaged groups are more effectively reached. Reporting on young people's views on guidance services in the White Paper A New Impetus for European Youth (European Commission, 2002b), the Commission also notes the emphasis young people placed on having access to user-friendly guidance systems that were easily accessible in places where they spent their time.

Access has been improved in several ways. Guidance, for instance, is increasingly acknowledged to be a right to which all citizens are entitled throughout their lives, and not just an ancillary service aimed at those who are in crisis or unemployed. There has been a diversification in terms of the sites in which guidance is offered (not restricted to institutional sites, but also available at leisure sites, in the community, and in the home), in terms of the providers (not just the state, but also community-based and private services), and in terms of modality of provision (not based solely on one-to-one input, but also on group-based, curricular and self-service modes of delivery; not homogeneous but differentiated according to specific client needs).

Underlying all these trends is a change in the way guidance staff perform their work, largely - though not solely - as a consequence of the use of new information and communication technologies. ICT has become increasingly harnessed across most European countries in order to support and complement traditional forms of guidance, such as face-to-face interviews, assessment tools, and printed career information materials. It is used to more widely disseminate information about occupations, and also to support a number of guidance functions via CD-Rom software, career navigation systems, or the Internet.

Typically, ICT applications help clients increase their self-awareness (i.e. by developing knowledge about themselves, which can then be related to learning and work opportunities); to increase their opportunity awareness (i.e. by providing access to databases about learning, training and working); to facilitate decision-making (i.e. by helping clients narrow options by balancing opportunities and feasibility); and to support transition learning (i.e. by assisting clients to implement decisions, on the basis of skills needed to apply for jobs, to sit for interviews, to secure education and training grants, and so on). In the more sophisticated systems, several of these different functions are available to the user, with the software more fully and comprehensively reflecting and supporting the complex nature of career decision-making. At a more basic level, CD-ROMs and especially the Internet are used to make a great deal of information about educational programmes and institutions, as well as about labour markets, available at the touch of a button. Again, the more sophisticated websites have the capacity of linking different databases together to support a multidimensional approach to decision-making.

Most frequently, however, ICT tools reproduce the traditional matching model of guidance, with the main difference being that it is the client who is responsible for the matching.

ICT can help widen access to guidance in two important and related ways. First of all, it encourages a different approach to service provision, where self-help takes precedence over direct delivery by professionals. Clients can carry out a great deal of initial self and opportunity-related exploration and assessment thanks to ICT, prior to asking for a face-to-face interview if necessary. Many employment services (e.g. in Flemish-speaking Belgium, the Netherlands, Norway, Slovenia, Sweden), as well as guidance offices and career information libraries in schools and tertiary education where these exist, are good examples of this highly significant shift.

Private-sector ICT-based Guidance in Finland

In 1999 Helsingin Sanomat, the newspaper with the widest circulation in Finland, made career services available to all citizens on the Internet. The newspaper's website offers those who access it a multitude of career planning and job search tools and services. All services, including online self-assessment exercises, e-mail guidance counselling, a Curriculum Vitae Wizard, and an option to forward applications to employers online, are free of charge.

Secondly, ICT brings information and guidance services to the client. Increasingly, computer terminals - often linked to the Internet - are available in non-institutional sites. As Kress (2000) has noted, the boundaries between spaces dedicated to learning, to working, and to leisure are becoming blurred. Young people and adults can access many guidance-related services in bars and cafes, in youth and community centres, and at home.

Several countries (e.g. Belgium, Cyprus, Finland, Iceland, Sweden, the United Kingdom) have set up Internet points in leisure and public spaces in the community, with links to sites that offer assistance in discovering aptitudes and interests, and in matching profiles with opportunities for further education and employment. E-mail queries can be quickly sent to a central information bureau, or to the communication offices of educational institutions and enterprises. This has important implications for mainstreaming guidance in the seamless flow of life, helping remove the stigma that it has occasionally had, particularly when it was seen as a peripheral service to be used by those who either could not manage their lives effectively or had become marginalised through unemployment. It also has important implications for overcoming barriers of service delivery to the remoter regions in countries that have scattered populations, particularly when the software used permits several of the functions referred to earlier, including interactive sessions with counsellors, and where Internet connections provide a portal into a broad and flexible network of inter-linked services. Distance career guidance is therefore increasingly on the agenda (e.g. Flemish-speaking Belgium, Austria, the Czech Republic, Estonia, Germany, Greece, Iceland, Latvia, Poland, Romania, Spain, Sweden).

Despite the opportunities that ICT offers, there are nevertheless important issues to consider in attempting a cross-European survey of guidance provision. The first and most obvious one concerns differential access to hardware, to software, and to Internet connection. The digital deficit is particularly serious when one considers the situation in many CEE countries. But the digital divide is present across Europe in other ways as well, affecting poorer groups, older people (who may feel uncomfortable with new technology), and those living in remote areas (where penetration of telecommunication services is lagging behind the more urbanised zones). In addition, skills in the use of ICT, as well as costs and bandwidth access, differ greatly between, and sometimes even within, countries in Europe, all of which affect the extent to which the opportunities made available by the new technology can be exploited. In some ways too, certain cultural contexts within Europe predispose people to shun the rather impersonal approach to guidance. Others might still prefer to consult information in traditional print format, even though the information is available electronically. This is reported to be the case with Romanian students, and Tricot (2002) reports the same pattern in the case of French students, though there is an assumption that it is a transitory phenomenon.

Differential Access to ICTs Across Europe

Other technologies that have opened up new opportunities for guidance service delivery are call-centres. While several countries report that call-in services tend to be associated rather more with help-lines and hot-lines providing crisis support (in relation to a range of problems such as domestic violence, child abuse, attempted suicides, rape, substance abuse), they are nevertheless being used to good effect in some career guidance contexts, with clients being able to telephone in queries. Other countries - including Germany, the Netherlands, and Norway - are planning to develop call-centres, suggesting that this might very well become one of the ways through which guidance services are increasingly delivered at national and local levels.

Providing Guidance Through Call-centre Technology in the United Kingdom

The 'learndirect' service in the United Kingdom was launched in 1998, and its core is built around call-centre technology. There are two call-centres in England (in Manchester and Leicester), one for Northern Ireland, and smaller centres in Scotland and Wales. The 'learndirect' initiative is funded through the University for Industry, and aspires to offer free and impartial advice that can assist adults to access further education and training opportunities. Such information could include, for instance, availability of funding for learning, and of childcare facilities to support parents with young children. Call-centre help lines are open all year round till ten in the evening in order to ensure as much accessibility as possible. Over five million people have called 'learndirect' since it was opened. There are three tiers of staff: information advisers handle basic information enquiries; learning advisers handle the enquiries of those who need more than basic information; lifelong learning advisers deal with more complex enquiries and requests for help. All staff levels receive special training, and all have access to an online database of information on some 600 000 education and training courses, at all levels, as well as a wide variety of other printed information.

Other forms of communication have increasingly made guidance services more accessible to a wider range of people. Some of these modes of communication are not innovative in themselves - rather, it is their marshalling in the service of guidance that should be highlighted in this context. Many countries make use of television, mass media, road billboards, and other advertising strategies and outlets, in order to ensure that information related to further education, training and employment opportunities reach the community. This may be part of a regular, on-going strategy, or may be targeted in time and focus with the intention of promoting specific action. A case in point would be the annual initiative in Flemish-speaking Belgium called De grote leerweek (Adults' Learning Week). Here, the mass media networks with a number of partners active at the community level in order to reach specific target groups. In many countries too, several newspapers feature supplements on careers, as well as on education and training courses, besides advertising job vacancies and labour market trends. Particularly interesting is the innovative use of mobile, peripatetic counselling teams to cover communities that are hard to reach, or because there are not enough resources to cover demand (e.g. Austria, Bulgaria, Estonia, France, Hungary, Latvia, the United Kingdom). The case of Latvia is particularly instructive as an example of a creative way of still providing a service, despite resource limitations. Thus far, the country has managed to establish Professional Career Counselling Centres in only 19 out of its 26 regions. But its mobile teams cater for the needs of the other seven.

Career Information

Much of educational and career guidance involves assisting clients in making informed choices. It is the soundness of this information - in terms of the usual criteria of validity and reliability - that should, in principle, distinguish professional guidance services from the information provided to individuals by other, more informal sources, such as family and peer networks. However, the fact that professionally-provided information is more valid, objective, reliable and comprehensive, or to put it more simply, that it corresponds more closely to reality, does not necessarily mean that it is of use to clients. Indeed, research presents us with quite a different picture, alerting us to the fact that informal sources tend to be more influential than formal ones, with young people and adults alike (Arnold, Budd and Miller, 1988; ——NICEC, 1996). Theories that focus on the ways human beings process data (inter alia Chapman and Mahlck, 1993) remind us that, like all pedagogical events, the reception and use of information depends on several factors, including

(a) the extent to which it connects to the recipient's prior experiences and frameworks of relevance, and

(b) the extent to which such information is perceived to be useful in solving or at least addressing present problems or queries, in context.

This is particularly true in the information age - or rather, information dump, as Grubb (2002a) refers to it - where people are constantly bombarded by a surfeit of data, much of which is not even requested. Not only that, but, as Tricot (2002) has noted, much of this information is largely provider-driven - i.e. it highlights information that the provider wants to present - rather than consumer-driven - i.e. working from questions which individuals want to ask. The Education and Training Council in French-speaking Belgium is perhaps exemplary in the attention it has given to such matters, carefully defining the nature of information suitable in guidance, distinguishing objective information from information that aims to advertise, pointing out the difference between information and guidance, and promoting the education of citizens so that they have a critical approach to information (Avis 78, 21st June 2002, Guidance and Information on Education, Training and Work).

These and related issues about the nature, quality and intelligent and critical use of information are particularly pertinent when it comes to consider information provided through ICT, which differs from print-based data in one essential manner, namely, that it invites the user to shift from a linear reading of text, to one that is hyper-linked to related data. At the click of a button, readers are deviated from one focus to another, gaining access to associated worlds of facts, images and sounds. Only the most steadfast and those with sharp information management skills are capable of re-routing themselves back on track, making use of unexpected insights that have been vicariously developed in order to make wise decisions. This is an important issue, not only because it reminds us that self-service approaches to information require the back-up of skilled personal support, but also because ICT tends to be rather uncritically touted as the panacea to plug information gaps. There is indeed much that commends the use of ICT in the career information field. Not only does it help widen access, but it also dramatically reduces the production costs associated with print-based alternatives; it permits quick, cheap and regular updating of information; it facilitates linkage to personal assessment tools and other relevant resources; and it has features which permit searching and trawling through a great deal of diverse material, which would be much less accessible in print form. Despite such advantages, it remains a tool that requires both basic skills (e.g. in reading), and more sophisticated ones (e.g. confidence in manipulating the technology, ability to access information in a systematic manner), and therefore raises serious equity issues, particularly if provision is not complemented by skilled support, as well as by alternative sources and channels of information (Offer and Sampson, 1999; Grubb, 2002a).

Other issues come into play in providing information that is valid, reliable, timely, contextual, relevant and useful. Several countries involved in this survey acknowledge the fact that the provision of adequate career and labour market information is a public good, which should be freely available to all for reasons of equity and efficiency. This echoes the European Commission's concern - expressed in its Action Plan for Skills and Mobility (European Commission,

2002c) - about the need for education, training and labour market data to overcome their tendency to be (a) fragmented, and (b) lacking in transparency. As pathways into education, training and work become more diversified and complex, so clients need to have access to clear road maps that help them navigate systems of provision, with full knowledge about which options they open and which they close when embarking on a particular track.

This kind of transparency and complexity cannot be handled by one-dimensional tools, which would be akin to trying to find new destinations with old maps. In contrast are multidimensional, matrix-based management information systems which privilege synergy between different databases, connecting educational and career information with labour market data such as vulnerability to unemployment, current and projected supply and demand, and average earnings compared to minimum salary. Some systems, for instance, those used in Greece, Finland, Hungary, Iceland and Lithuania, also have an experiential component, enabling users to get a feel for the occupation they are investigating, through the possibility of downloading short films and interviews with workers.

Such systems are, however, not very common in the guidance field. In many cases, CD-ROMs and websites end up being nothing more than a replica of print-based materials, giving more importance to cramming information in rather than designing it in ways that render it useful to specific groups of users. This is especially true for the ACCs, although some advanced systems are being developed in Hungary, Poland and Romania, thanks to World Bank aid. Bulgaria, Cyprus and Slovakia too are making progress, benefiting from EU funding.

Multidimensional Career Information Systems in Poland

Poland has developed a multidimensional career information system - 'Counsellor 2000' - integrating the most recent developments in Artificial Intelligence, stimulating the client's efforts by linking information management with decision-making strategies. Information about educational and training pathways, and the relevant occupations they lead to, is linked to the personal profile of the client using the system, itself developed after accessing self-assessment tools available on the same software. In addition, the system has been adapted so that it can be targeted at particular groups of users, such as persons with disabilities.

Another reason to explain the fragmentation of education and career information provided by guidance-oriented services, other than the technical one referred to above, is the lack of cross-sectoral collaboration. In most countries, much of the formal responsibility for the provision of career and labour market information lies with the state: government agencies collect the information, organise it, and disseminate it. Often, however, different ministries collect different information, creating data sets that cannot always be consolidated in a way that helps users make better sense of options and opportunities. It is not unusual for governments to produce a number of overlapping databases, which together provide only partial coverage of what is available - this is the case with French-speaking Belgium, Finland, Norway, and Sweden, to mention just a few cases. Even more striking is the situation in Germany, where the Federal Employment Service has separate databases on occupations (BerufeNET), on training opportunities (KURS), on apprenticeship and training vacancies (ASIS), and on job vacancies (SIS) - all of them unconnected to available career selection programmes (such as Machs Richtig) and other self-exploration programmes, although they are presently being integrated within a web portal.

The problem is compounded in countries with decentralised federal governments like Belgium, Germany and Spain, where each region might develop its own systems which, while possibly being more relevant to users since they reflect local labour market realities, do not facilitate either student or worker mobility across the whole territory. The challenge for the EU is still greater, in view of the goal of creating a common space for a more efficient and equitable human resource deployment, with the Euroguidance network and ESTIA and the Ploteus portal being steps in this direction.

Some countries have started taking measures to combat fragmentation. Different initiatives have involved:

- The establishment of a platform of common standards and specifications agreed to by different ministries responsible for data collection (e.g. Estonia);
- The formalisation of agreements, or the promulgation of laws, specifying the nature of the coordination that must exist between different ministries in the delivery of guidance services, and encouraging cooperation between and among institutions at national, regional, district and local levels (e.g. Bulgaria, Slovakia);

- The setting up of agencies which have the task of comprehensively managing career information systems (e.g. Onisep in France; Formabanque in French-speaking Belgium; the Careers and Occupational Information Centre in the United Kingdom; the Foundation for VET Reform in Estonia; the Open Society Fund in Bulgaria). In many cases, such agencies are external and government-funded. Sometimes such agencies are privatised (e.g. the National Career Service Centre in the Netherlands), or their activities are partially or fully outsourced to the private sector (e.g. the Czech Republic, Finland, Germany, Iceland, Ireland, Spain).

Financing

While the overview report has indicated several areas of deficit in guidance provision, it has also shown that the tendency has been for the field to expand in extent, reach, and variety of provision, both in the education and the labour market sectors. Such developments require extensive funding, and it is important to see where such resourcing is coming from in the European states under review, and the different models that are most commonly used in providing such resources. Each of these will be examined in turn.

A caveat must however be made from the outset. This is that, in most cases, respondents to this survey found it difficult, if not impossible, to provide even approximate estimates concerning national expenditure on guidance. If the focus is on outlay by the state, then most countries note that the costs of delivering guidance services are included in broader budgets that cannot be readily broken down and are therefore difficult to compute. Often too there is no differentiation in central records between how much is spent on guidance-related activities (e.g. personal counselling), and on career and educational guidance as such.

The picture becomes more complex in contexts where central funds are allocated to regions or institutions that have a degree of autonomy in the way they allocate budgets. Where some statistics were provided in the country responses, they tend to show an increase in government investment in guidance services, even if the general comment made by most was that overall aspirations, in terms of providing more comprehensive guidance services, were hampered by lack of sufficient funding. France's Centres d'information et d'orientation (CIO), for instance, saw an increase in funding of 6.2% between 1998 and 1999, and another 5% in the following year. Similarly, the budget for the Agence National pour l'Emploi (ANPE) was boosted by 9.2% between 1998 and 1999. Of the 29 countries, only Bulgaria, the Czech Republic, Poland and Sweden signalled significant state cut-backs in funding support for aspects of the guidance services provided. Given the commitment of European governments to LLL, and consequently to lifelong guidance, guidance services need to expand to cover the life-long and life-wide range of needs. Needless to say, the funding of such intensified investment represents a policy challenge for all European governments.

Information about the extent of private investment in guidance is even harder to come by in the country reports. Private companies are offering services for which individuals pay, either directly or indirectly. Other individuals will be paying for guidance as part of a fee which purchases a package of services - as in the case of students attending non-state educational institutions. In very rare cases (e.g. Finland, Iceland, Romania) certain state guidance services (e.g. processing of occupational inventory tests) are provided at a cost to the client, but often such fees are largely symbolic. It is not possible, however, to calculate any of these private investments in guidance on the basis of data provided in the country responses.

While most often, national expenditure on guidance services draws directly on government budgets deriving from tax contributions, this is not the case with all the countries reviewed. In Germany, for instance, the Federal Employment Service is funded through social insurance contributions from individuals and their employers; the role of the Federal Ministry of Labour and Social Affairs is to ensure that the service complies with statutes and legal requirements. A somewhat similar model has been put into place in Greece, where employees and businesses indirectly finance guidance services through national insurance contributions, a percentage of which is earmarked for the Manpower Planning Organisation (OAED). Elsewhere, such contributions play a more limited role. In Cyprus and Poland, some of the state authorities or bodies involved in delivering aspects of the guidance services fund their activities by imposing a levy on the payroll of private and semi-public entities, and some sectors in the Netherlands have developed a number of services based on training levy funds from employers and employees. Austrian employers fund aspects of guidance services through membership fees to the Economic Chamber, to which they are obliged to belong.

Other funding for aspects of guidance services comes through international programmes. EU Member States access such support through participation in the European Social Fund. In addition, and together with the ACCs, they also benefit from a whole platform of Community funding programmes such as Socrates and Leonardo da Vinci. Over and above this, Hungary, Poland and Romania have been able to develop their guidance systems and resources thanks to targeted funding and technical expertise made available by the World Bank. Once again, however, when compared to the investment made by the state, these and other forms of external funding, while often having a substantial impact on service development, represent a tiny fraction of the overall outlay. Also there is a problem of sustainability when the project money dries up.

An analysis of the 29 countries involved in this review suggests that government funds can be directed at a package of services, of which guidance represents only one facet, or alternatively, they can be targeted at guidance activities specifically. In addition, government funds can be channelled to the client via national, regional, or local governing bodies. Irrespective of the way the funding is packaged, and the governing apparatus used to channel it, state funding reaches the guidance service user in one of four main ways. It can: (a) be managed directly by the national, regional, or local government itself; (b) be delegated to a government-controlled agency; (c) be devolved to a range of institutions; or (d) be outsourced or sub-contracted to, for instance, community and other not-for-profit organisations, or private companies. Examples of all four modalities can be identified across Europe. Here, they are discussed in terms of the policy mechanisms which seem to have the most impact on the way funds flow through the system and become converted into services for the user, namely devolution (to regional or local governing apparatuses, and to institutions) and outsourcing.

The current policy climate across Europe tends to encourage devolution to local levels, in the belief that this encourages ownership of challenges and of initiatives to meet them. In the CEE countries, decentralisation tends to be particularly attractive as an antidote to a heritage of tight central control, and as a mechanism to diffuse power that had previously tended to be concentrated in the hands of a few. Moves towards devolution are evident in most of the 29 European countries surveyed - only Finland and Iceland reported a reverse trend.

Several countries that have decentralised their systems also noted, however, that the shift of responsibilities has generated new problems, and that devolution offers no guarantee for the efficient and effective use of resources (e.g. Czech Republic, Denmark, Italy, Finland, France,

Latvia, Poland, Spain, Sweden). Indeed, devolution of responsibilities within a policy vacuum can lead to costly overlap, lack of coordination within and across sectors, a deficit in comparable standards between regions leading to inequitable access to services, and an overall degeneration in standards (Grubb, 2002b). The case of Poland is instructive in this regard. Here, the winding down of the national network of labour offices in favour of local government provision has led to a serious deterioration in the quality of provision. In Latvia, decentralisation became a convenient mechanism to devolve responsibilities to local government without passing on the necessary funding; while in the Czech Republic, the transfer of authority for managing the consulting centres which offered career information and guidance to the regions has led to a dramatic reduction in services. In the absence of central policy leads, the career guidance services in Luxembourg have ended up manifesting a number of gaps. Such central steering is difficult to achieve when, as in France and the United Kingdom, decentralisation leads to too much diversity in service provision on the ground.

These and other experiences across Europe support the view that the best way forward may very well be a judicious mix of centralised and decentralised models, where municipalities develop their own policy in the context of central guidelines reached after wide consultation with stakeholders. Estonia, Finland, Portugal and Sweden, among others, seem to have adopted such a model, stipulating contracts between central and regional government, with the centre prescribing the minimum level of guidance services that should be available, thus avoiding undue variability between regions.

Organisation of a Guidance Programme

Guidance is regarded as a core element of the school's overall programme. The guidance programme seeks to respond to the needs of the students at all stages of their education in the school. The objectives of the guidance programme are not only framed by reference to the legislative requirements, but are also referenced by the good practices. A programme is a temporary organisation either within an organisation or across several organisations.

The organisation structure and governance arrangements will vary depending on the nature of the programme. It is important to consider how the governance of the programme will fit with already established governance arrangements e.g. in a local authority existing governance arrangements may include:

- Cabinet arrangements and decision-making
- Executive Management Team
- Overview and Scrutiny
- Local Strategic Partnership
- Departmental Management Teams

Partnership programmes will usually necessitate a more complex governance structure than an internal programme. For example, in a Shared Services Partnership programme rhere may be complex integration issues (across organisations), which need to be factored into how the programme is governed and managed.

Meshing programme governance with the standard local and regional authority governance can be complicated. It is essential at the outset of a programme to set out a framework for decision making within the programme. Early consideration of who makes which decisions ensures they are are taken in a timely manner and that they are made by the appropriate people.

Possible decision makers are: Project Manager, Project Executive, Programme Manager, Business Change Managers, Senior Responsible Owner, Programme Board, Sponsoring Group, Chief Officers/Directors, and Council Members (either collectively or individually). Tolerances should be designed to pass down some decision-making. Each programme will need its own type of decision points.

Creating a framework for decision-making at the outset not only stops things grinding to a halt in a flurry of indecision but allows for Chief Officer and Member decisions to be scheduled well in advance. Creating a programme organisation structure is not an exact science. It is useful to seek the advice and experience of others who have worked in a similar programme environment.

Programme Organisation

Every programme needs to define the leadership and staffing structure needed to run the programme effectively. Careful consideration should be given at the outset to what is expected in terms of skills, time and experience from the people who take on role typically include:

- Sponsoring Group
- Senior Responsible Owner
- Programme Board
- Programme Manager

- Business Change Manager
- Benefit Owner
- Project Executive
- Project Manager
- Programme Support
- And other established roles from within the organisation, such as Finance Officer, Risk Manager, ICT Officer, Procurement Officer, Senior Supplier and Senior User

The Guidance Programme, like any other educational programme, requires careful and consistent development. This ensures that the programme responds to the unique needs of its clients. It provides benefits to students by addressing their intellectual, emotional, social and psychological needs. For any guidance programme to meet successfully the needs of all students, it must be developmental, preventive and remedial rather than crisis-oriented. Further, a comprehensive and developmental guidance and counselling programme is not only preventive but also pro-active in preventive orientation. Consequently it must be well planned, goal-oriented and accountable. It is an integral part of the school programme, and complements other school activities. It is important for today's guidance and counselling programme to be developmental, so that it assists students who are growing up in a complex world. It should help them to develop into full human beings, capable of maximizing their potential in all personal, educational, social or career-related respects.

A comprehensive guidance programme should be balanced, and encompass all the four fundamental areas of guidance, viz.: personal, educational, social and vocational. It should provide students with the assistance necessary for their maximum development. The programme should also decide what services to offer, such as information, consultation, referral, counselling, placement, career follow-up and evaluation services. The programme should use all staff members and determine their roles in it. It, therefore, demands consultation, co-operation and co-ordination. A programme should define the role of the guidance personnel, who should be fully informed about the programme. It should create a teamwork approach, in which every member of staff is considered responsible for contributing to the success of the programme.

For a guidance programme to be comprehensive, it should also be relevant for the clients, and not merely maintain a status quo. It must be purposeful, and designed to meet the priority needs of the clients. These needs should be met in an efficient and effective manner. It should be stable and unaffected by the loss of personnel, as this determines the extent to which it meets the desired goals and objectives. Each programme must be specifically designed for the clients it serves. There is, therefore, a possibility for both similarities and differences in programmes. Effective programmes are flexible, since this allows for adaptation to future growth and effectiveness. Programme development not only calls for needs assessment but reflects other characteristics of the clients, such as age, location or environment, cultural background, sex and economic status.

Any service as comprehensive as guidance must be carefully planned if it is to meet the desired goal. When the programme is well organized, there is no doubt that all involved will participate to the fullest extent. The teachers should see it as their own, rather than the headmaster's or the guidance teacher's programme. Their involvement is crucial right from the start.

Benefits of the Guidance and Counselling Programme Programme development is a systematic process that requires following a series of steps. A developmental and comprehensive school guidance and counselling programme not only benefits the students, but also the parents, teachers, administrators and the business community. The benefits to the various groups are as follows:

Students

- Increases self-knowledge and how to relate effectively to others.
- Broadens knowledge about the changing environment.
- Helps them reach their fullest academic potential.
- Provides opportunities for career exploration, planning and decision-making.
- Provides an opportunity for networking with services and thus establishes an effective support system.
- Teaches responsible behaviour.

Parents

- Provides parents with support for their child's educational and personal development.
- Increases opportunities for parental involvement in the education of the child.
- Equips parents with skills necessary to support their child.

Teachers

- Enables students to master effectively their subjects with an understanding of the importance of each one.
- Provides an opportunity to work in collaboration with other teachers and parents.

Administrators

- Enhances the image of the school in the community, reduces strikes, and improves thegeneral appearance of the school.
- Allows for systematic evaluation.
- Provides a structure which can be monitored easily.

Business, Industry, the Labour Market

- Provides the potential for a well-informed workforce, with positive attitudes and thenecessary skills.
- Provides an opportunity for collaboration with teachers in preparing students for theworld of work, through participation in career fairs, and other career guidance activities.

Reasons for Planning

Planning and Programme Leadership: Guidance and Counselling is a continuous and on-going process. For it to meet students'needs, it must be formalized. The initial stage of programme development planning is of vital importance. The following reasons are advanced to emphasize the importance of planning, viz.:

1. It forms the basis for action.
2. It forms the basis for organization.
3. It provides the basis for involvement and assignments.
4. It forms the basis for programme evaluation.
5. It provides the basis for decision-making.
6. It provides the basis for commitment.

Planning provides an opportunity to convert ideas into action. It is at this stage that the relevant personnel in the provision of the Guidance and Counselling service are identified and their roles described. For instance, in a school, the principal, teachers, ancillary staff, students, parents and community members should have their roles in the provision of services clearly defined. An organization must identify co-ordinators of the programme who will play a leading role in its development. Personnel should include everyone who has direct, or indirect, contact with those for whom the programme is developed, which in a school, are the students. It is at this stage that the programme co-ordinator informs the Guidance personnel of their roles. In identifying the leaders of a programme, there is a need to consider leadership qualities. A true leader should possess some of the following characteristics:

A record of success: It is important to identify a leader with good experience, and who is a competent professional who has had the relevant training. Such leaders can direct a programme competently, and adhere to the ethical and legal issues related to it.

Inspires confidence: A realistic and supportive programme leader inspires confidence and trust among subordinates, and acknowledges the accomplishments of the support staff and gains their confidence. This provides the organization with a group of dedicated and confident staff.

Promotes partnership: A good programme leader ensures teamwork. The success of the organization is shared between him and his subordinates, and this creates a feeling among them of belonging. This partnership is important, since it builds a solid and well-founded programme in which everyone feels responsible for its success. No one looks only to the leader for success but considers it instead a shared responsibility.

Motivates: A good leader should be able to motivate subordinates to realize their full potential. Motivated staff members are always willing to take initiative and promote a lot of activities. This is of vital importance. As the one who understands what the programme is about, it is important that the leader is ready to clarify and explain the approach. The leader should always identify the tasks to be performed and explain them to the staff.

Creates a positive atmosphere: The creation of a professional atmosphere is the responsibility of the programme leader. A positive and conducive atmosphere is dependent on the organization, management and administration of the programme. Planning, for instance, is important to ensure that all those affected are part of the programme from the start.

Possesses visibility and vision: A good leader is readily available to support staff. This is because frequent interaction with staff members allows for informal exchanges of ideas which are vital for success. A leader should have vision. There is a need to plan for the future or anticipate the direction of a programme. This allows for any necessary adjustments.

Has good decision-making skills: An effective programme leader should be able to make appropriate decisions. This rests on the understanding that he/she should consider various alternatives before making a final decision.

The above may assist in the identification of suitable programme leaders. Many programmes have collapsed because of poor leadership, and it is important to choose leaders who possess the right qualities rather than just fill a position. A good leader should be able to use supervisory skills to set up and consolidate the programme. By appraising, motivating and consulting with all the staff, the programme can be sustained. It is the leader who sets the mood and the means of operation. Competence is of the utmost importance. It is important to lead and not to direct, as behaving like a director may result in resentment among subordinates.

Planning is crucial to the survival of a programme, because poor planning adversely affects the programme. Planning formalizes it, creates an atmosphere of team work and commitment, and allows consultations and shared responsibilities. An effective plan of action should be developmental, with a logical, sequential pattern, be flexible, provide a basis for resource employment, and give priority to communication, co-ordination and cooperation.

Needs Assessment

Needs assessment finds out what is needed. It is the basis for accountability, and ensures a greater degree of programme relevance. Any practical programme should address the needs of those it is designed to serve. An accurate and continuous assessment of the needs of the beneficiaries is vital for the success of a programme. It is the needs that determine the programme goals and objectives. For the programme to serve its beneficiaries, it should address their intellectual, emotional, social and psychological needs. Apart from accountability, needs assessment allows for programme evaluation. When conducting a needs assessment survey, both the beneficiaries and the environment should be taken into account, as they have an influence upon, or directly affect, each other. For example a programme designed for a school in Gaborone, Botswana, must consider the needs of the students and the school. When identifying needs, it is important to focus on the personal, social, educational and vocational needs of the clients, in order to provide a balanced and comprehensive guidance programme which is concerned with their well-being. The programme should also address the varying needs of boys and girls. Needs assessment should allow the service to compare the current status with future outcomes.

Steps to Follow in Conducting a Needs Assessment Survey

Step 1: Identify and list all those to be served, e.g.:

- students;
- teachers;
- patients;
- school administrators; and
- ancillary staff.

At this stage, several classifications such as ethnic, socio-economic, political, grade level and educational, may be used. A survey of the people who have direct contact with the programme's beneficiaries is also important. Their opinions or contributions are of value for the quality of the programme.

Step 2: Collect data using any one of the following systematic approaches. These are useful in the identification of guidance-related needs. The methods include:

- questionnaires;
- interviews;
- brainstorming;
- school and community records;
- follow-up studies; and
- stratified random sampling.

Step 3: It is important that after the data has been collected, it is compiled, classified and analysed. Accumulated data help programme developers to determine priorities. Classification should be according to the areas of Guidance, namely: personal, educational, social and vocational.

Programme Goals and Objectives

In order to determine the goals and objectives of the programme, it is important to assess the current situation with regard to Guidance and Counselling. The programme developer must clearly indicate the position of the organization in terms of clients and their problems (gathered through a needs assessment). The general needs of the country, which existing programmes have not met, should also be taken into account. After the identification of students' needs and the environment, the aim of a Guidance programme should be to provide beneficiaries with the skills and attitudes necessary to function fully in society. It emphasizes decision-making skills and the development of a positive self-image. The goal of the programme also emphasizes the need to assist young people to become responsible citizens, who develop realistic and fulfilling plans for their lives based on self-knowledge, their own needs and those of the environment.

The goal of all programmes should be the development of a complete person, capable of surviving in a complex world, and to provide all individuals, despite their socio-economic status, sex and cultural background, the information to fall back on when needs arise. It is after the identification and the prioritization of clients' needs that goals and objectives are formulated. These must be clear since they will determine the programme in terms of the resources required. The objectives should be specific to each topic.

Selection of a Programme Structure

After the needs of clients have been determined the programme structure should be described. A decision is then made on which content needs are to be addressed first. As the content is structured, the delivery methods are also considered. It is during the programme development that the standard one contents are separated from the standard two contents and put in order. That is, the lower and upper class contents are determined. The content is in accordance with the fact that Guidance is developmental and systematic. Since school guidance and counselling programmes consist of structured development experiences, they must be presented systematically through classroom and group activities. This then takes care of the school Guidance and Counselling curriculum, as topics are dealt with in a systematic way, and provide students with what they need to know for normal growth and development, and promote their mental health and acquisition of life skills. It is important to sequence the content appropriately, since students' guidance is continuous from the time of an individual's initial entry into the educational system, and throughout the period of formal education. The structuring of the content offers time to think about the most suitable implementation strategies, and the resources needed to implement the programme. Various strategies can be used to assist clients to meet their objectives. It is important to select specific and appropriate strategies for implementation.

The school Guidance Committee is part of the selection of the programme structure, and the established leadership is responsible for the design of the programme. The structure has to take into account the following: Individual Planning, Guidance Curriculum,

Responsive Services and Systems Support. When activities are devised, they should provide a comprehensive programme and follow a particular structure, and not be a haphazard collection of topics. These structural components are very important when developing a

Guidance and Counselling Programme

Individual Planning

This includes the counselling activities meant to assist all students to plan, monitor and manage their own personal development. Activities of this component of the programme are offered to all students, and are meant to assist them in the development and implementation of their personal, educational, social and career components, in accordance with the skills and information they gather. This component generally offers students the opportunity for self-appraisal, and to plan for the world of work. One way would be to help students to understand themselves through individual or group activities.

School Guidance and Counselling Curriculum

This refers to a curriculum which is systematically organized according to grade level. It is designed to serve all students at the classroom or group level. The curriculum emphasizes decision-making, self-knowledge, career exploration and career development. The curriculum is organized around three major areas:

a) Learning to Live
   - Understanding and appreciating the self
   - Understanding and appreciating others
   - Understanding and appreciating home and family
   - Developing a sense of community
   - Making decisions and setting goals
   - Understanding safety and survival

b) Learning to Learn
   - Making decisions, setting goals, and taking action
   - Understanding interaction between home, family, school and community
   - Understanding factors which affect school achievement

c) Learning to Work
   - Learning the relationship between personal qualities and work
   - Exploring careers

- Learning how to use leisure time
- Learning the relationship between education and work
- Learning to work together
- Learning how the community relates to work

This curriculum should state the goals for guidance instruction as well as student outcomes. Here, collaboration with, and the education of, parents and the community are essential. The purpose of the curriculum is to provide students with knowledge and life skills. The curriculum is delivered through the following:

a) Classroom activities - classroom teaching of Guidance and Counselling.
b) Group activities – offering structured group activities in Guidance and Counselling, i.e., career fairs, plays, etc.
c) Parent education - this is done outside the classroom and establishes a link with the parents through seminars and meeting.

Services

Responsive Services: This includes services that are responsive to students' concerns regarding their healthy personal, social, educational and career development. This includes preventive, developmental and remedial counselling. Other than the counselling service, consultation and referral services will also be utilized. Counselling is either individual or in groups. Consultation would be with parents, teachers and other professionals, while referrals would be to other specialists or programmes. Support groups such as Alcoholics Anonymous, people living with AIDS, diabetics, etc., form part of the support services. It is important for the programme leader to understand the role of each service as stipulated in Shertzer and Stone (1981). These services offer opportunities for students as follows:

Counselling Service: It is a social service based on the recognition of an individual's uniqueness, dignity, value and respect, and of the fact that every individual has a right to personal assistance when needed. This service recognizes the need to offer individuals an opportunity for self-knowledge and self-development through individual or small group interventions. The counselling service's main purpose is to nurture a relationship leading to personal development and decision-making, based on an understanding and knowledge of oneself and the environment. The service provides an opportunity for verbal interaction between the counsellor and the client, with the sole aim of assisting the client to deal with a specific problem which could be physical, academic, emotional/personal, and/or social.Basically, this service offers clients the chance to make decisions and solve problems. This service has a direct link with other services, especially the referral service because, when the need arises, a counsellor may have to refer a client to other specialists. The provision of such a service acknowledges the fact that students need assistance to cope with the complexities of life, since classroom teaching alone may not meet the needs of the client effectively.

Referral Service: Since some problems and concerns are beyond the capability of the school counsellor or guidance teacher, it is important to establish a referral network. This should consist of a team of well-trained and skilled professionals who have expertise in assisting referred individuals. Referral does not imply the helper might have failed, but signifies strength on the part of the helper, who recognizes his/her limitations, and explores opportunities to maximize the help he/she can offer. A programme leader should, therefore, be well informed about referral services, which include social workers, doctors, psychiatrists, psychologists, priests, police and others.

Consultation Service: This service underscores the fact that other people's opinions and decisions may have a positive impact on the programme. It also emphasizes that clients are not only students but children, sportsmen and women, boys and girls, who work with a number of people who can contribute to, and have an interest in, the students' welfare. It is, therefore, important for the counsellor or guidance teacher to the students to consult parents, boarding personnel, and other teachers who might be subject teachers and coaches. This will give the counsellor or guidance teacher an opportunity to ascertain various changes in behaviour that might have occurred. Such consultations may also demand referral.

The consulting service supports the fact that collective decision-making and problem exploration allow for more objectivity. The programme leader has to promote relations with community agencies, which helps to establish contacts and effective communication channels. Once channels of communication are open, it is easy to exchange information and ideas with other beneficiaries. Consultation with teachers is an important means of increasing teacher awareness of issues their students face.

Appraisal: This service provides essential facts about the learner, giving the counsellor, or guidance teacher, a basis for decision-making. It gathers personal information about the learner, and assists the individual to understand himself/herself better. Once an individual is aware of himself/herself, he or she is able to make informed decisions.

Placement and Follow-up: This service is designed to enhance student development by assisting them to select, and use, opportunities inside and outside the school. It is oriented to the preparation of an individual for admission to other educational, vocational or work-related programmes. Its main purpose is to assist students to achieve their career goals, e.g. by assisting them with subject selection, or placement, in a class or school, based on the subjects offered. It takes into account the interests, aspirations and abilities of the learner. Where educational placement is concerned, a student should be allowed to choose the subjects he/she would like to pursue. Their subject choices should be determined by their self-image, career preference, and the availability of the subject option. It is the role of the counsellor or guidance teacher to ensure that the curriculum addresses the needs of the client.

Career placement should also be seen as an integral part of a student's career development and, as such, the counsellor or guidance teacher has to identify appropriate vocational or career placement centres, in accordance with the career aspirations of their pupils. This exploration is crucial for career decision-making, since it gives students an opportunity to gain an insight into a career which interests them. All students should be thoroughly prepared before career placement occurs, so that they can make the most of it.

As a service, it strengthens the career guidance aspect of the school guidance and counselling programme. It helps the students to know their strengths and limitations and, through this, achieve self-direction. This service offers the counsellor/guidance teacher an opportunity to collect, analyse, and use, a variety of personal, psychological and social data about the students. Not only does it offer the counsellor an opportunity to understand the pupils, but it also provides them with a guideline for the type of help required. Further, the counsellor/guidance teacher will be able to assist students/pupils to understand themselves better.

The learner may contribute to the effectiveness of this service by providing information through self-evaluation activities, such as writing an autobiography or completing self-rating forms. Peers or classmates may also be used to collect information about a learner. In order to avoid character destruction, peer evaluation must be properly co-ordinated by the counsellor or guidance teacher. The information collected helps the students, teachers, parents, and school administrators, to create and maintain an environment conducive to the healthy growth and development of an individual. It allows the counsellor, or guidanceteacher, an opportunity to establish a structure which helps the client. Several activities can be used to appraise students; for instance, naming the 'person of the week', writing about the kind of person one is, naming one's favourite food, naming favourite personalities, naming leisure activities, etc. Psychological tests may be issued when they are available. These go a long way towards helping students to understand themselves.

Research and Evaluation Service: Research and evaluation are designed to determine the effectiveness of a guidance programme. Further, they provide the counsellors or guidance teachers with the opportunity to be resourceful and independent. Evaluation and research encourage programme leaders to continue to find solutions to the problems of their clients. It is through active research that counsellors or guidance teachers can upgrade their programmes, to ensure that they address the needs of the clients.

Systems Support: This includes the direct guidance management activities that maintain and enhance the guidance programme. A fully fledged Guidance programme needs systems support. This ensures that the programme is sustained. Such support includes staff development so that the implementors are well equipped for the job, and the necessary resources and facilities for programme implementation, finance, and policy support, are available. The above support is crucial and needs to be considered when designing the Guidance programme to guarantee its implementation. The guidance programme should also identify other programmes that need its support, such as special education, vocational education, etc.

It is important that the committee discusses all the topics so that the final agreement will have been considered by all the implementors. It is through programme design that developers will define a programme, state its rationale and decide principles that shape and guide the programme. It is at this stage that documentation is prepared on what should be done to ensure programme sustainability, and to describe the relationship between guidance and other school activities. It is indicated in the design stage how, through direct and indirect activities, the guidance teachers will work with students, parents, other teachers, the school administration and the general community. A balanced programme with varied activities needs to be directed and designed to meet the needs of all the students. The necessary referral agencies are identified and documented. Consultations and team work are very important at this stage.

The Identification of Resources

The programme design and desired student outcomes have a bearing on the allocation of available resources, and may dictate programme design. These go a long way towards providing a comprehensive programme. Resources should be commensurate with needs. When they are not, programme leaders must ensure maximum utilization of limited resources, which is particularly the case in African countries. Guidance teachers must keep the available resources in mind, and take into account school realities and priorities. Collaboration with other programme leaders is important, and several ideas should be explored on possible alternatives. Since there are four components of a guidance programme, there might be a need to emphasize some rather than others, when resources are limited. It is, therefore, obvious that resources affect the scope of a programme, and call for serious consideration of priorities lest resources are wasted. This confirms the need to determine priorities. Resources are both human and material. These need to be identified and documented, so that they are readily available. For instance, if a guidance lesson needs clay, it should be readily available on demand. If a class has to make a trip, transport should be available. The lack of the necessary resources will adversely affect the programme.

The Guidance Calendar

The Guidance Calendar is part of a school guidance programme. It takes care of the needs that cannot be met in a classroom, such as tours, career fairs, talent shows, seminars, visits, drama, etc. This Calendar shows all guidance activities that are planned in the school. It helps to allocate time to school activities, and avoid clashes. It is for an organization to develop a monthly, quarterly, termly or yearly calendar. Like the Guidance Programme, a school Guidance Calendar is governed by the needs of the clients. It is meant to complement classroom activities. The Calendar ensures that particular needs are addressed at appropriate times and places, and accomplishes certain activities in a sequence. For instance, after a career talk, a visit to a work place might be the most appropriate complementary activity, or after a lesson on cleanliness, a nurse or health worker could be invited to address the pupils. This is an indication that a calendar is in line with identified needs.

A Guidance Calendar promotes good management, and developers will take into account the time of the year most suitable for certain activities. It also ensures the appropriate use of resources. The programme leadership should involve staff, parents and community members in drawing up the calendar, as not to do so might adversely affect the programme. For instance, a nurse might not be able to address students if he/she was not told the date when needed to support the programme. In drawing up the calendar, there is a need to indicate the date, time, target group, guidance service activity, and human and material resources.

Factors Affecting Implementation

Programme implementation refers to the execution of programme strategies. The tasks required to follow the strategy are detailed and carried out. In addition, programme development considers the skills and knowledge needed by the implementors. Staff development opportunities are looked at to ensure that the implementors are well equipped to play their roles. It is when the programme strategies are implemented, and monitored. Formative evaluation techniques are important here. Staff competence is taken into account, and enables the leadership to decide whether team teaching will be used or not. It is important to consider the human, financial and political resources at the implementation stage. Human resources include the counsellor/student ratio, and the number of committee members and teachers who actually offer their services. Financial resources include the school budget for Guidance and Counselling, other sources of finance, and the adequacy of Guidance facilities. Finally, political resources are related to policies and procedures, resistant staff members, implementation guidelines and administrative support. It is important to consider all these aspects at the implementation stage as they determine the direction of the programme. Although good programmes may exist on paper they may not yield the desired results. The implementation stage determines the effectiveness of a programme.

Human Resources: It is important to have a good counsellor/student ratio. This will depend on the organization of guidance services in a given school. It will depend on whether there is a part- time or full-time guidance teacher/school counsellor. Despite the large numbers that guidance teachers/school counsellors work with, they are expected to implement the programme, and ensure that its goals are achieved. It is important that thought be given to the provision of a suitable ratio, as too many students can prevent the counsellor/guidance teacher from giving good service. For someone to carry out duties efficiently, he needs to have a clear job description. The roles and functions of guidance personnel must be clearly outlined as this allows them to use their education and talents to good purpose. (N.B: Policy Guidelines for the Implementation of Guidance and Counselling in Botswana's

Education System). All implementors should have clearly defined roles, as this enables administrators to understand the skills required when recruiting staff. Professionals, para-professionals and support staff should have the competence to run well-balanced and comprehensive guidance programmes. For any programme to achieve success its implementors should be helped to reach their full professional potential. The programme leader should be personally suitable, and educationally prepared, to assume the leadership role, and should have a professional and productive relationship with students.

Financial Resources: For a programme to be sustainable, financial resources are needed. It is, therefore important to determine the cost so that a feasible budget can be drawn up. This avoids unnecessary over-expenditure and disappointment. A budget enables the programme leader to operate within defined funding limits. It is important to explore other possible funding opportunities or sources. Non-governmental organizations and donor agencies such as SIDA, USAID and UNESCO, may be willing to fund certain activities. Such organizations may want to fund activities such as career resource centres, video production, life skills programmes, research, and many others. There is a need to explore such opportunities. Although such organizations may not fund an entire programme, they often provide the necessary support, which goes a long way towards supplementing state funds. The provision of such funds requires a detailed project proposal and a plan of action. When writing the proposal and plan, the programme leader must only emphasize the areas of interest to the sponsor. There is a risk of including other areas since there might be a fear that the funds may be diverted. A report is required on the use of donated funds.

Programme activities determine the materials and equipment required. It is important for the programme leader to ensure that all these are readily available. The materials chosen will help the students/ pupils to attain the outcomes identified at the planning stage. Apart from materials, it is also necessary to ensure that there are adequate facilities and equipment. Such facilities include counselling rooms, and resource rooms. For example, students will use the counselling service when an adequate, comfortable and private room is available for counselling. The availability of the necessary facilities also has a positive impact on teachers and parents. They attach value to the programme when financial support and recognition are given.

The four components of guidance demand proper facilities for effective implementation. Functional physical facilities are necessary, and they should provide adequate space, privacy and accessibility, which are the corner stones of a good quality guidance programme. A guidance centre would be an appropriate location for services. Such a centre can be used for individual activities which enable students to work on their own, or with teachers and/or parents. The identification of the resources helps determine the financial implications of programme implementation. Adequate financial support is crucial, since the services provided are related to the costs available. Programme outcomes should match costs.

Political Resources

The policies and procedures governing the implementation of a programme should be well known to the implementors. An understanding policy will enable the programme leader to deal with resistance and matters of shared responsibility. For instance, in the case of Botswana, the Guidance teacher works with the Teaching Service Management Department, the Secondary Education Department, and the Department of Curriculum Development and Evaluation. It is, therefore, necessary for these departments to work together when redeploying Guidance Teachers. The understanding of policy ensures shared responsibility when the need arises. It also gives implementors the ability to distinguish between issues. When guidance teachers involve other beneficiaries, it is important that they know and understand their responsibilities, to avoid any clash of interest. Guidance teachers should know the appropriate links and channels of communication on various issues affecting their clients. Inability to connect, and to refer issues to relevant beneficiaries, may retard progress.

Guidance teachers must understand their role, as a lack of understanding may adversely affect the programme. Open communication in programme implementation is essential, and goes a long way towards ensuring that their concerns and fears about the implementation of Research and Evaluation Service the programme are addressed. Implementation calls for the programme leader to commend those who make a conscious effort to give support, and ensure that the programme moves in the right direction. This is an effective strategy, as it motivates them to work towards the achievement of positive results.

Implementation Strategies

After a consideration of factors affecting the implementation of the programme, it is important to explore various strategies. It is at this point that the programme leader will have to prove himself/

herself able to run an effective programme. The leader has to have imagination and foresight. Different delivery mechanisms are employed with individuals and groups. They will vary from one school to another and are not definitive. Some implementation techniques, however, are common to most programmes. They include the following:

Extended Registration

This occurs when certain topics are addressed by class teachers during the registration period. Other teachers may alternate, or team-up with, the class teacher. These sessions allow the teachers and students to know each other, and for the students to consider the class-teacher to be a confidante. It is important that these sessions are planned so that they meet the needs of the students effectively.

General School Assembly

School assembly may be used to provide general guidance and information on various topics. Such topics may be thematically arranged. Teachers and students may alternate in providing this service. Such general talks complement what happens in class, and allow for the covering of a wider programme.

Time Tabling

It is important to provide time for the provision of guidance. This allows for continuity. It provides an opportunity for schools to address the needs of the students, and formalize the programme. It allows for the provision of information which makes programme evaluation easier. The time tabling of Guidance and Counselling in schools allows it to have a recognized place in the school, rather than be relegated to an extra- curricular activity. One period per week has been found effective when complemented by activities outside the classroom.

Community Involvement

The invitation of guest speakers to visit schools helps the community to understand its role in the implementation of the programme. This enables the programme leader to address those needs that cannot be dealt with in a classroom setting. External resource persons also add value to the programme, and help students to realize the link between education and the world outside. It offers an opportunity to network with community members from whom they may need more information. The invitation of external resource persons requires planning to guarantee the success of such activities. There is a need to plan with the beneficiaries so that clashes are avoided. This provides an opportunity to invite role models who will have a positive impact on students.

Educational Tours

Another implementation strategy includes visits and educational tours. Resource centres, work places and others places of interest, help to explore all opportunities that have an impact on students. Activities such as job shadowing may be used here. This is when a student is attached to a career or occupational mentor. The mentor allows the student to observe and ask questions, so that he/she can gain practical knowledge of the job. Shadowing can last from one day to about a week. It allows students to think and make realistic decisions. This has proved successful in career exploration and decision- making. This exposure to reality has a greater impact than the provision of information. It is important to prepare students adequately for such tours. That is, they should know the purpose, and know what information to obtain.

Research Projects

Guidance teachers/school counsellors should encourage students to carry out small research projects on their own. This will empower them to know how to gather data, and systematically arrange it in an understandable form. Students will also be trained to be more curious and able to gather information for themselves rather than wait to be spoon-fed. It prepares them adequately, and allows them to take pride in themselves. Preparing students to carry out their own research serves multiple purposes. The documentation of the research findings enables other students to benefit. If properly arranged and monitored, students may gain much from this exercise.

Career Fairs/Seminars

These are common activities in Guidance programmes. They enable external resource persons to provide career information, facilitate career planning, exploration and decision-making. The activity can be run at a school, or at the regional or national level. It helps students to develop a vision, and study for a purpose. Various ways of running such an activity can be explored depending on the resources available.

Curriculum Infusion

Guidance concepts are such an integral part of the general school curriculum that it is difficult to separate them. All subject teachers need to play a part in infusing guidance concepts in their subjects, and help augment the programme. Subject teachers who are not guidance- and counselling-oriented, need to change their attitude because this implies a lack of concern for students. Effective teaching cannot take place in a vacuum. Students should understand the relevance of each subject to life outside the school. This allows them to establish a link between education and employment. There is a purpose in studying the subjects in the school curriculum and this should be clearly understood by students. Infusion helps students understand, and develop, a more positive attitude towards the various subjects they are taught.

Workshops

These should be run for students, teachers, parents and community members. The need for support from other beneficiaries is important, and this is more likely if people are well informed, and educated to see how they fit into the structure. Such activities can be operated in the same programme. Unless people understand what the programme entails, they will not willingly support it. A successful workshop depends on good planning and organization.

Peer Counselling

Young people can be trained to offer guidance and counselling to their peers. This is based on the understanding that students tend to relate more to those peers with whom they are comfortable. The peer counsellor also assists in identifying and making referrals to the Guidance teacher. Days should be set aside for them to share experiences and information with their peers, through various means such as dramas, role-playing, talks, poetry, etc.

Bulletin Board and the School Library

These can be used to disseminate information. They can be made the responsibility of the students on a rota. The provision of such an opportunity will help to cover areas that the programme might not have planned. A wealth of information can be shared among students through such boards and libraries. It is at this point that a resource room for Guidance can be well equipped with up-to-date information including books, career manuals, videos and other resources. Providing access to such information will allow students to search for information of interest to them. It should be noted that implementation strategies, which vary from discussions, drama, composition writing, questionnaires, and those mentioned above, may be utilized. Variety helps students to avoid boredom. A more innovative leader can manage to make the programme interesting without reducing its strength.

Value and Purpose of Evaluation

Gibson and Mitchell (1995) define programme evaluation as a systematic set of data collection and analysis of activities, undertaken to determine the value of a programme in order to aid management, programme planning, staff development, public accountability and promotion. Evaluation activities make it possible to make reasonable judgements about efforts, effectiveness, adequacy, and provide a comparison of programme options. They determine the worth of a programme, and provide an opportunity to explore other alternative approaches or strategies to reach specific objectives. Evaluation seeks to provide objective evidence of whether the programme has met the desired objectives. It provides an opportunity for programme planning and decision-making. It is, therefore, important to evaluate programmes since this offers a chance for continued programme improvement.

Shertzer and Stone view evaluation as necessary to provide for the effectiveness of achieving programme goals, in relation to specific standards. Concrete data, indicating the benefits and limitations of the programme, can be accumulated through programme evaluation. The effectiveness of any programme can be sustained through continuous evaluation, and practitioners need to carry it out rather than pay lip service to it. It should, therefore, be noted that the main purpose of evaluation is to improve the implementation of a programme. It also provides a means of communication among school counsellors, guidance teachers, school administrators, parents and the community in general. It defines expectations for counsellors, and provides a systematic means of measuring the counsellor's or guidance teacher's performance in relation to programme expectations. The most compelling reason for evaluation is to improve the effectiveness of every counsellor or guidance teacher, as well as the programme itself.

The evaluation process consists of a series of interdependent steps by which a judgement is reached. The success of any programme in achieving its goals depends upon the monitoring and evaluation process used. This improves the quality of the service, and the support given to staff employed in the guidance and counselling services. The future of any guidance programme depends on providing concrete data, and helping school personnel to judge how well they are doing, and to determine the improvements needed. Evaluation should be an on-going process. It provides an opportunity to modify the programme when necessary.

Evaluation helps to check:

- programme effectiveness;
- programme response to changing needs;
- strengths and limitations of the programme;

- staff development; and
- reporting and follow-up.

Evaluation determines what the programme achieves. It also provides a basis for identifying critical gaps in service delivery, and for planning programme changes. In evaluating the programme's effectiveness, the following can be measured:

- student awareness of the services;
- satisfaction of students involved in individual counselling; and
- satisfaction of students involved in classroom, and out-of-class, guidance activities.

The following steps can be taken to assess the current/existing programme:

1. Identify current resource availability and use.
2. Identify current guidance and counselling activities.
3. Determine students' outcomes.
4. Identify who is served.
5. Gather perceptions.
6. Determine involvement of personnel in a region or school.

Evaluation offers a programme leader an opportunity to evaluate himself/herself and guidance personnel. It also gives him/her a basis for assessing the attainment of goals. The evaluation of individuals assesses their performance skills and proficiency, while the assessment of goal attainment focuses on the individual's programme and improvement efforts. It checks the quality of the programme, and its attempts to address the needs of students. It is, therefore, important to evaluate ourselves in terms of skill application and programme leadership. This helps to determine professional competence, though it should not be considered judgemental. Proper supervision and programme monitoring provide an opportunity for checking if the structure and implementation of the programme are appropriate. Programme standards in terms of the guidance curriculum, individual planning, responsive services and systems support, can be set through systematic evaluation, and programme leaders can collect data which enable them to amend their programmes. It is, therefore, important to decide on an appropriate evaluation design, which will provide feedback on the programme, and the competence and efficiency of the programme leaders.

The value of evaluation must be recognized by all programme implementors. It performs several functions which benefit the programme and its consumers. For instance, it:

1. verifies or rejects practices by indicating what works and what does not, and shows the extent to which an activity is effective. It helps the implementors to do away with unproductive innovations.
2. provides a basis for improvement in terms of operation and implementation strategies.
3. suggests a continuous search for better ways of doing things, and a willingness to look at performance, and increases the search for improvement.
4. provides an insight into the programme, and helps implementors to understand their functions and the consequences of what they do.
5. places responsibility on individuals, and increases the participation of beneficiaries. It helps in the allocation of roles and responsibilities. For the guidance programme to be accepted and valued, there is a need to produce documentation of benefit to the clients. Evidence that guidance services produce designed, demonstrable, behaviour changes in students are demanded by the public, and such information can only be secured through research and evaluation.

Periodic and formalized evaluation yields data in which confidence can be placed. It enables schools to judge how well they are doing, and provides a basis for decision-making on programme improvements. Through it, school personnel can interpret the effectiveness of the programme for the community. Also, if parents are well informed about the programme, they can help in supporting and defining the direction of the programme. Each school should determine its own evaluation procedure.

The programme leader has to determine the methods of evaluation to be used, the appropriate time for evaluation, the purpose of the evaluation, the rationale, the sample to be used, and appoint the evaluator. This preparation enables the programme leader to carry out the evaluation systematically. The evaluation procedure should explore several methods of evaluation, so that they complement each other in providing the necessary feedback.

Bibliography

Aggarwal, Santosh: *Three Language Formula: An Educational Problem*, Sian, New Delhi, 1991.

Allen, G.: *Pre-Primary Education: American Opinion*, May issue, 1971.

Altbach, Philip G. and Gail Kelly: *New Approaches to Comparative Education*, The University of Chicago Press, Chicago, 1986.

Barnes, D.: *From Communication to Curriculum*, Pelican, London, 1990.

Bentley, T. : *Learning beyond the Classroom: Education for a Changing World*, Routledge, London, 1998.

Carl R. Rogers: *Client-Centered Therapy: Its Current Practice, Implications and Theory*, Houghton Mifflin, Boston, 1965.

Carr, W. & Kemmis, S.: *Becoming Critical: Education, Knowledge and Counselling*, Falmer, London, 1986.

Chumbow, B.S.: *The Place of Mother Tongue in the National Policy of Educational Guidance*, Port Harcourt, Nigeria, 1990.

Diller, D.: *Literacy Work Stations: Making Centers Work*, Stenhouse, Portland, 2003.

Donaldson, Gordon A.: *Cultivating Leadership in Schools*, College Press, New York, 2001.

Elliott, J. : *Action Research for Educational Change*, Open University, Milton Keynes, 1991.

Evers, C. & Lakomski, G.: *Knowing Educational Administration*, Oxford, Pergamon, 1991.

Fogarty, Robin: *How to Integrate the Curricula*, Palatine, IRI/Skylight, 1991.

Galbraith, M.W.: *Education Through Community Organizations*, Jossey-Bass, San Francisco, 1990.

Gardner, H. : *The Unschooled Mind: How Children Think and How Schools Should Teach*, Basic Books, New York, 1991.

Gibson, R. : *Critical Theory and Education*, Hodder & Stoughton, London, 1986.

Hirsch, Bette: *Languages of Thought: Thinking, Reading, and Foreign Languages,* The College Board, New York, 1989.

Kakar, Sudhir : *The Inner World: A Psychoanalytic Study of Childhood and Society in India*, Oxford University Press, New Delhi, 1978.

Lovett, T. : *Adult Education, Community Development and the Working Class*, Ward Lock, London, 1975.

McConnell, C. : *Community Education: The Making of an Empowering Profession*, Edinburgh, Scottish Community Education Council, 1996.

McGivney, V. : *Informal Learning in the Community, A Trigger for Change and Development*, NIACE, Leicester, 1999.

Nadler, L.: *Designing Training Programs: The Critical Events Model*, Addison-Wesley, Reading, PA, 1982.

Poster, C. and Kruger, A. : *Community Education in the Western World*, Routledge, London, 1990.

Premi, M.K. : *Vocational Educational Planning in India*, Sterling, New Delhi, 2001.

Reimer, E. : *School is Dead, An Essay on Alternatives in Education*, Penguin, Harmondsworth, 1971.

Simkins, T. : *Non-formal Education and Development*, Manchester University, Manchester, 1977.

Stenhouse, L. : *Authority, Education and Emancipation*, Heinemann, London, 1983.

Taylor, C. : *Multiculturalism: Examining the Politics of Recognition*, Princeton University Press, NY, 1994.

Wiggins, Grant : *Educative Assessment: Designing Assessments to inform and Improve Student Performance*, Jossey-Bass, San Francisco, 1998.

Index

A

Ability Model, 175, 176, 182, 187, 188.
Accreditation, 12, 63, 64, 88, 101, 115, 123, 150, 250, 261, 263, 279, 301, 316.
Alexithymia, 179, 180, 181.
Apprenticeship, 6, 25, 51, 52, 54, 58, 59, 61, 62, 64, 66, 67, 68, 69, 86, 87, 105, 106, 117, 118, 123, 147, 232, 289.
Aptitude Testing, 201, 207, 209, 210, 211, 216.

B

Bar-On Model, 179, 180.
Blended Mentoring, 121.
Business Mentoring, 121.

C

Career Counseling, 8, 33, 34, 35, 36, 37, 195.
Central Route, 208, 212, 213, 215.
Cognitive Ability Tests, 200.
Counselling, 33, 34, 35, 121, 133, 142, 144, 146, 149, 150, 286, 290, 295, 296, 301, 302, 303, 305, 309, 312, 313, 314, 315.

D

Delivery Methods, 281, 301.
Delivery Settings, 259.
Dynamic Assessment, 173, 174.

E

Education Retrospect, 11.
Educational Quotient, 97, 146, 174.
Emotional Intelligence, 162, 170, 174, 175, 176, 177, 178, 179, 180, 181, 184, 185, 186.
Employment, 6, 26, 34, 40, 50, 51, 72, 74, 75, 76, 77, 81, 84, 85, 89, 90, 93, 94, 100, 101, 103, 106, 110, 113, 238, 239, 240, 243, 244, 249, 250, 252, 253, 254, 256, 257, 260, 263, 267, 280, 281, 283, 299, 313.
Employment Testing, 198, 199.

F

Flynn Effect, 151, 158, 160, 173.
Formal Mentoring, 117, 118, 119.

G

Goals, 1, 4, 9, 23, 37, 41, 45, 68, 70, 71, 73, 95, 96, 101, 104, 105, 117, 136, 141, 230, 231, 232, 236, 239, 242, 245, 249, 261, 267, 269, 273, 296, 299, 300, 301, 302, 303, 314, 315.
Group Differences, 158, 169, 170.
Guidance Programme, 2, 3, 5, 6, 11, 28, 30, 143, 145, 146, 147, 293, 295, 299, 306, 307, 309, 310, 314, 316.